Date Due

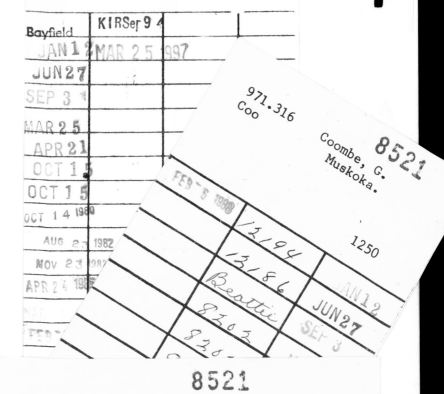

8521

MUSKOKA
past and present

MUSKOKA
past and present
Geraldine Coombe

McGraw–Hill Ryerson Limited
Toronto   Montreal   New York   London

MUSKOKA Past and Present

ACKNOWLEDGEMENTS

For their generosity in supplying family histories, documents and other historical information, I thank:

Hugh Anderson
John Bascom
Sarah McCulley Brady (1861–1958)
Dorothy Coate
J. Roy Cockburn (1879–1964)
Doris and Tom Cooper
Professor G. M. Craig
Enid and Sidney Cribb
Marjorie Demaine
District Municipality of Muskoka
   Administration staff members
Alberta Doan
Dorothy and A. H. Duke
Eanswyth Flynn
Margaret (Cooper) Harding
Mrs. Carl Harvey
Hugh T. Hill (1889–1974)
Verva and Frank Hull
W. B. Judd (1897–1975)
Philip LaForce (1891–1965)
Alberta Langford (1886–1974)
Mary Lean
Love family
Maurice Margesson
Thora McIlroy Mills
Museums in Huntsville and Port Carling

William Partridge
Alma Peacock
Elizabeth Penson (1884–1974)
Josephine Plaskett
Cecil Proudfoot
Robert Purves
Helen Ratcliffe
Florence Rebman
Dwight Ross
Joyce Schell, Wood Winds Museum
Catherine (Jenner) Scott
Gil Scott
Duncan Shay (1883–1974)
Lily Smith
Claude Snider
Art Sopher
Mrs. A. Spinney
Stanton family
Dennis Stone
Charles Thompson
Constance Sparrow Trusler
Bryan Vaughan
Frances Von Alma
Jack Walker
Olive and Duncan Whitsun
Donald Whitton

The Muskoka Tourist Association and the Ontario Ministry of Transportation and Communication for the use of parts of a 1973 road map of the District Municipality of Muskoka.

Many other Muskoka residents and cottagers, in addition to those listed above in that category, have given me the benefit of their knowledge, and I thank them.

For advice and support during the writing and production of this book, I am particularly grateful to:

Barbara C. Arnott
Marie Crookston
Dorothy and A. H. Duke
Murray D. Edwards

my husband, Alvin
and McGraw-Hill Ryerson editorial and art departments.

Author's Note: Some resorts have been included in the text because of their historical background or as examples of modern accommodation, but those intending to visit Muskoka should choose a resort by consulting all the advertising material available, including the booklet issued by the Muskoka Tourist Association.

Hardcover ISBN 0-07-082333-2

Softcover ISBN 0-07-082365-0

1 2 3 4 5 6 7 8 9 10   JD   5 4 3 2 1 0 9 8 7 6

Printed and bound in Canada

CONTENTS

Acknowledgements

I AN INTRODUCTION TO MUSKOKA   1

Geography   1
Maps   6
Muskoka Tourist Association   6
Historical Background to the Settlement of Muskoka   6
Free Land Grants, 1868   16
Emigration Societies   17
See maps on p. 2 and p. 4.

II SEVERN BRIDGE TO KAHSHE LAKE   19

Severn Bridge Today   19
Severn Bridge and Morrison Township History   19
Severn Bridge to Kahshe Lake   23
The Von Alma Family   26
See map on p. 30.

III SEVERN BRIDGE TO RYDE TOWNSHIP   29

Wasdell Falls   29
Cooper's Falls   29
Emma and Thomas Cooper   29
Ryde Township   34
William Lowe   36
See map on p. 30.

IV SEVERN BRIDGE TO PORT SEVERN   39

The Trent-Severn Waterway   39
Sparrow Lake   39
The Lehmanns from Germany   41
Other Sparrow Lake Pioneers   45
Port Stanton   45
Sparrow Lake to Georgian Bay   47
Port Severn   50
See map on p. 40.

V GRAVENHURST 51

To Muskoka Township with James McCabe 51
Thomas M. Robinson 51
A. P. Cockburn and Steam Navigation 54
Gravenhurst 57
Dr. Norman Bethune 65
See map on p. 59.

VI BRACEBRIDGE 67

The Reay Road 67
Muskoka Road 4 East (The Peterson Road) 69
Muskoka Falls 70
Thomas McMurray 71
Bracebridge 75
Recreation Areas 82
Bracebridge Boat Cruise 87
Fraserburg Road (Muskoka Road 14) 88
See maps on p. 68 and p. 77.

VII PORT CARLING 89

Bracebridge to Port Carling 89
Port Carling Today 92
Port Carling History 98
Penson, Adams, and Rogers 100
The Early Steamboats 103
Sarah McCulley Brady (1861–1958) 106
The Plaskett Family 108
Windermere 111
The Muskoka Lakes Association 114
See map on p. 90.

VIII THE PENINSULA ROAD TO ROSSEAU 116

Port Sandfield 116
The Cox Family and Prospect House 116
The Muskoka Express 121
Supply Boats 121
North from Port Sandfield 122
The Top of the Lakes 125
Icelanders 128
The Shadow River 128
Camp Hollyburn 130
Rosseau 131

Kawandag 131
The Coate Family 133
See map on p. 117.

IX BALA 136

Wood Winds Museum 136
Torrance 139
Bala Today 141
The Muskoka River 144
Cavalcade of Colour 145
Bala History 145
North of Bala 146
The Canadian National Institute for the Blind 148
Lake Joseph Adjustment Training and Holiday Centre
See map on p. 137.

X GIBSON INDIAN RESERVE 150

Gibson Reserve History 150
William and Mary Kendall 155
Gibson Reserve Today 155
See map on p. 157.

XI WEST MUSKOKA AND GEORGIAN BAY 160

Georgian Bay 160
Honey Harbour 165
Highway 103 166
MacTier 169
MacTier History 170
Freeman Township 172
See map on p. 157.

XII THE LAKE OF BAYS 174

Highway 117 174
Mark Langford and McLean Township 176
Baysville 179
Bigwin 181
The Lake of Bays 184
Leslie M. Frost Natural Resources Centre 185
Dorset 185
Algonquin Park 187
Dwight 187
See map on p. 175.

XIII SKELETON LAKE AND MARY LAKE   192

Skeleton Lake   194
Port Sydney and Mary Lake   194
Port Sydney History   198
Navigation   201
See map on p. 193.

XIV HUNTSVILLE   203

Madill Church   203
Huntsville Today   203
Huntsville History   208
Rev. Robert Norton Hill   212
Cruising the Lakes   215
Hidden Valley   218
Muskoka Road 8 (formerly Highway 514)   219
Dyer Memorial   223
See map on p. 221.

XV STISTED   225

F. M. Delafosse, an "English Blood"   225
Ilfracombe   230
Hoodstown   231
Stisted Township   231
The Demaine Family   233
St. Mary's Church, Aspdin   236
Yearley   237
See map on p. 221.

CONCISE BIBLIOGRAPHY   239

SELECTIVE INDEX OF NAMES AND PLACES   241

I AN INTRODUCTION TO MUSKOKA

Muskoka to me is a canoe in a quiet cove, the nearest thing to paradise. It's a view from a high rock cliff of a lake sparkling in the sun, a walk down a path canopied with swirls of green pine and carpeted with brown needles, the Aurora Borealis creeping up the vault of heaven at midnight, a golf game surrounded by a riot of autumn colour, and six-foot snowbanks bordering a ploughed country road. Sometimes it's a loon sweeping up and down the deserted lake at night making frenzied sounds. Sometimes it's an afternoon swimming party and people waiting for their turn on waterskis. It's artists and craftsmen, and it's country folk farming the land broken by pioneers of the 1860s.

GEOGRAPHY

Muskoka is a district measuring 60 miles at its widest and 42 miles at its longest, within Ontario, a Canadian province roughly 1,000 miles wide and 1,000 miles long. It is bounded by Georgian Bay on the west and the Severn River on the south. Bracebridge, the District Town, is 120 miles north of Metropolitan Toronto and adjoins the 45th Parallel of Latitude, half way between the equator and the north pole.

It owes its dramatic beauty to the rock formations of the Precambrian shield, shaped between one and two billion years ago and among the oldest we can observe today. Its multitudinous lakes were carved by the ice-sheets of the last glacial period. Pockets of good farming land are scattered throughout, but the soil is generally shallow, and massive rocks rise out of land and water. Much of the land is covered with natural new forest and reforestation plantings, the heavy virgin forest having been cut over by pioneer families and lumbermen.

A heat wave in the city almost always guarantees perfect Muskoka weather—hot days ranging between 24° and 32°C,* warm lakes and cool nights. In winter the temperature can drop down easily to −32°C,** but people who go outdoors often for work or recreation soon adjust to Muskoka's winter temperatures.

Severn Bridge, the southern entrance to Muskoka on Highway 11, is roughly 725 feet above sea level. The town of Huntsville, about forty miles north, is 931 feet above sea at Fairy Lake level; readings northeast of Fairy Lake go as high as 1296. In Muskoka's northwest, Lake Joseph is 739 feet above sea level and contains the district's recorded deepest water at 308 feet.

---

*75° and 90°F, respectively
**−25°F

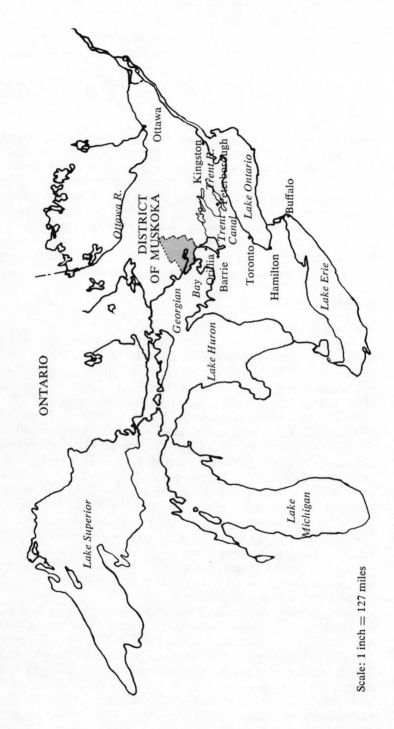

Map of Great Lakes area, showing location of Muskoka.

Scale: 1 inch = 127 miles

The headwaters of the main Muskoka rivers rise in Algonquin Provincial Park in the northeast. The Big East River comes down from McCraney Lake into Lake Vernon and through Huntsville to Fairy Lake, emerging as the Muskoka River, North Branch. Proceeding via Mary Lake and about fifteen miles of river, it drops over High Falls at Highway 11 (north of Bracebridge). This is the river that flows over the Bracebridge falls.

The Oxtongue River comes down from Algonquin's Canoe Lake into the Lake of Bays, emerging as the Muskoka River, South Branch. Winding down the watershed, it drops over Muskoka Falls at Highway 11 (south of Bracebridge) and joins the North Branch a short distance below Bracebridge. The merged rivers flow into Lake Muskoka on the east and out on the west at Bala on their way to Georgian Bay.

Lakes Muskoka, Rosseau and Joseph, the big three, have been joined by rivers since their existence was first recorded. To some people, these particular lakes are what come to mind when Muskoka is mentioned, but a quick glance at the district map will reveal that Muskoka is much more than these.

Muskoka was originally called a "District" to denote a new frontier at a time when the population was concentrated farther south in land divisions called "Counties". The change to "District Municipality" occurred on January 1st, 1971, with the official formation of a Regional Government, designed under the aegis of the provincial government to achieve a unit of municipal government large enough to deal with today's problems in land use, roads, education, ecology, industry and business.

Formerly the majority of the earlier 22 townships had their own councils. With the formation of Regional Government, three or four townships, or parts of them, were banded together into the following six Area Municipalities:

	Approx. Acreage	Approx. Water Acreage	Approx. 1971 Population
Town of Bracebridge	163,850	10,350	6,898
Town of Gravenhurst	131,850	11,400	6,572
Town of Huntsville	185,650	15,850	9,529
Township of Georgian Bay	161,250	25,450	1,914
Township of Lake of Bays	191,350	27,600	1,801
Township of Muskoka Lakes	241,300	41,600	4,381

The Crown holds 221,000 of the total 1,075,250 acres.

Each Area Municipality has a Council composed of a Mayor and a varying number of Councillors. Bracebridge, for instance, has eight Councillors.

The District Municipality Council, at the higher level, is composed of the Chairman, the six Area Municipality Mayors, and three Coun-

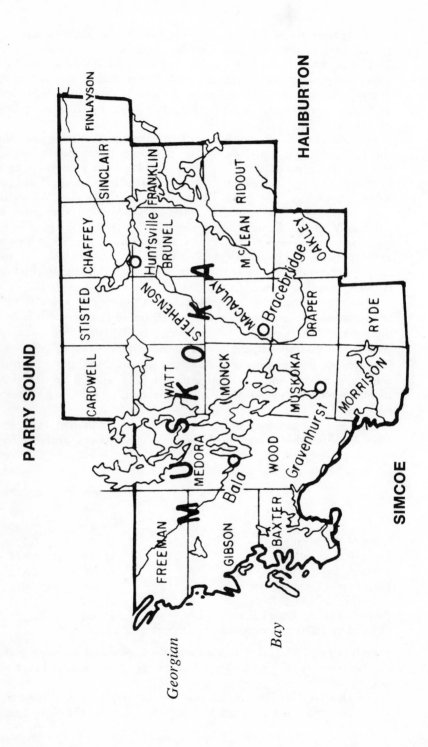

cillors from each Area Municipality, except the Townships of Georgian Bay and Lake of Bays which send only two because of their smaller populations. Milton Tibbet, previously Mayor of Huntsville, was appointed the first Chairman for a four-year term by the Provincial Government to get the new type of regional government rolling.

In addition to the 32,000 permanent population (the 1971 census figure that has been rising by about 5% per year), the non-permanent population occupying vacation homes in the summer was estimated at 72,000. The District contains roughly 9,800 permanent dwellings and 18,400 vacation homes. The term "vacation home" is used instead of "summer cottage" because many of these are suitable for occupancy in winter and are used on weekends and longer holidays throughout the year.

The three secondary schools at Gravenhurst, Bracebridge and Huntsville have a current total enrolment of 2,500. Today's 5,500 elementary school pupils generally attend the centrally-located schools which have replaced smaller schools. In all, 5,000 elementary and secondary students are transported daily by school bus.

A great deal of Muskoka's income is brought in by cottagers and tourists paying for supplies and services. Not all Muskoka resorts, however, are owned by Muskoka people. Resorts which operate only in the summer are often owned by people outside the District who give only part of their time to the resort.

Eighteen new industries located in the District between the years 1960 and 1971, some influenced by federal and provincial government incentive programs. Advantages of the District as an industrial location include water, hydro and natural gas power sources, attractive terrain with reasonable land purchase costs, and road and rail links with northern Ontario natural resources and southern Ontario markets. These important firms are among those presently in Muskoka: Alcan Canada Products, Brown's Beverages, Cumberland Packaging, Domtar, Fowler Construction, Kimberley-Clark, Parlett Transport, Planing Mills (Acme, Huntsville and Northern), Rubberset, and Swift.

"One of the best options open to Muskoka", say the planners, "would be to induce 'footloose' offices to locate in the region's healthy and pleasant living environment." (Operations which do not have to be located in any particular place, such as some research, computer, data bank or accounting enterprises of government and major companies are known as "footloose".)

The area devoted to agriculture in Muskoka has been declining for a long time, a trend particularly pronounced since 1966. Farms decreased from 73,320 acres in 1966 to 43,746 in 1971, or from 7.2% of Muskoka's total land area in 1966 to 4.3% in 1971. Farm population has also decreased from 11.9% of the local population to 2.7% in 20 years. General farming is typical, but most farms with yearly sales of at least $2,500 are dairy, cattle and hog farms.

Maps

District Municipality maps are available from the Administration Office in Bracebridge.

The Ontario Ministry of Highways, Toronto, sells a district road map, and the Muskoka Tourist Association reproduces it for distribution through its members.

The Ontario Ministry of Natural Resources (Map Distribution), Toronto, stocks the large-size map sections of the National Topographic System (1.25 inches to one mile) and nautical charts for the Muskoka Lakes, Trent-Severn Waterway, and Georgian Bay.

MUSKOKA TOURIST ASSOCIATION

The Muskoka Tourist Association has three information offices for Muskoka visitors at the following locations:

1. Highway 103 in West Muskoka north of Port Severn.
2. Highway 11 north of Severn Bridge.
3. Highway 35/60 at Dwight.

Founded in 1935 as the Muskoka Tourist Development Association for the purpose of attracting more tourists to Muskoka, its first president was Harmon E. Rice, owner of the *Forester*, Huntsville's weekly newspaper. ("Development" was dropped from the name in 1953.) Its funds come from resort and business members' annual fees, and grants from the District Council and Ontario Government. The Managing Director is Dennis Stone, Box 58, Gravenhurst, PoC 1Go.

HISTORICAL BACKGROUND
TO THE SETTLEMENT OF MUSKOKA

Algonquin Indians were the first recorded inhabitants of the territory that became Muskoka. Samuel de Champlain's description of Georgian Bay, Muskoka's western boundary, on his 1615 visit to the Hurons, is the first written record of the area. Following Champlain's visit, missionaries from Quebec began to establish themselves in Huron Indian country to the south of Muskoka and began to record contacts made with the Algonquins.

The Algonquins were nomadic, lived in wigwams, and subsisted by hunting, fishing and extensive trading with the Hurons to the south. The Hurons grew beans, squash, sunflowers for oil, Indian hemp for fishnet fibre, and great fields of corn. Unlike the Algonquins, the Hurons cleared the forest with stone axes and fire and built palisaded villages of communal houses covered with bark, shaped rather like Quonset huts. The Algonquins gave the Hurons furs, hides and meat in exchange for agricultural products.

The Algonquins, according to records made by the Jesuits who were in charge of the missions from 1626, were driven by the Iroquois from

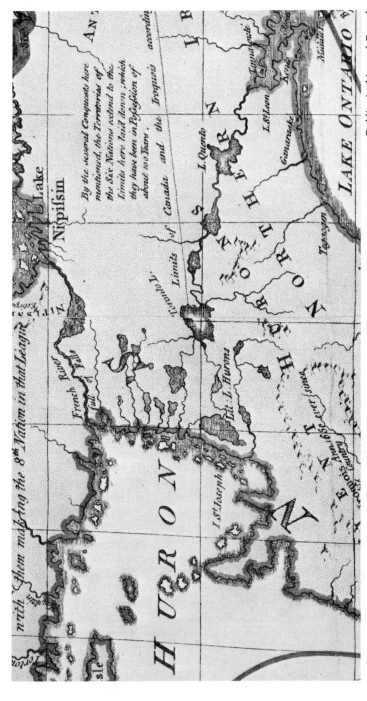

Huronia area of "A Map of the British and French Dominions in North America," by John Mitchell, 1755.

Public Archives of Canada

their territory along the St. Lawrence River and were hunted in the forests. The Jesuits recorded assisting the Algonquins in the winter of 1643–4, for instance, when they fled to the Huron territory (Huronia) to seek refuge.

In the meantime, the 1615 Huron population, estimated to have been 30,000, had been reduced to 10,000 by white men's diseases, particularly measles and smallpox. The final blow to the survival of the Algonquins, dependent as they were upon the Huron economy, was delivered in March 1649 by the Iroquois. About 1,000 Iroquois, mainly Mohawks and Senecas, encouraged by the Dutch at Albany with muskets and rum, had marched north and spent the winter in the woods. Before dawn on March 16, they attacked the Hurons for reasons of revenge, furs, trade, and long-standing enmity. The Hurons and missionaries, taken by surprise, were slaughtered and routed, the few survivors escaping to the Georgian Bay islands and beyond, many to die subsequently of famine and disease. The Algonquins did not escape completely. One record tells of a party of Algonquin men, women and children, who, surprised in their hiding place, were slaughtered by the Iroquois.

By destroying Huronia and by raiding up and down the St. Lawrence, the Iroquois had seriously curtailed supplies of fur to New France. Consequently, Louis XIV, the young French king, sent over a regiment of 1,000 officers and men to restore and protect its supplies. The regiment built forts on the Richelieu River from which to intercept raiding Iroquois, and, in 1666, it marched into the heart of the Mohawk country and destroyed villages and crops in the fields. This show of strength resulted in the signing of a peace treaty in 1667, after which the Iroquois concentrated on warring for furs with tribes in the Ohio and Mississippi valleys.

During the same period, individual traders from New France paddled farther into the interior, north of Georgian Bay and into Lake Superior territory, to make contact with the Hurons and other tribes driven there by the Iroquois. Few appear to have gone through Muskoka territory, particularly after discovering that beaver from farther north generally had finer, denser coats of fur.

Two early maps—the 1656 "Sanson" map and the 1657 *Novae Franciae Accurata Delineatio*—show lakes in the Muskoka region, presumably discovered by Jesuit missionaries to the Hurons and Algonquins. In 1669 Jean Peré, fur trader, is known to have crossed by Lake Simcoe and the Severn River to Georgian Bay. Knowledge of Muskoka territory was increased by René-Robert Cavelier, sieur de LaSalle, a man prominent in the history of North American exploration. He followed the Severn River to Georgian Bay in 1680, one of three (possibly four) times he navigated the Severn. In 1755, Dr. John Mitchell published in London *A map of the British and French Dominions in North America* which shows lakes and rivers in Muskoka.

Then British forces attacked French colonies in North America as part of the strategy of the Seven Years' War. The Battle of the Plains of Abraham between the forces of General James Wolfe and Louis Joseph, marquis de Montcalm, was one of the actions in this war in which the French were defeated, but it was the Treaty of Paris, signed in February 1763, that decisively ceded to Great Britain the territory that became Canada.

Explorations and surveys were undertaken to delineate the vast territory, then known as British North America, and the first detailed description of the Severn River, although somewhat inaccurate, came from a party under orders from General Haldimand on a 1780 trip. That party followed the Severn River downstream, turned north through Baxter Lake, entered Georgian Bay at Honey Harbour, turned south to the Severn, and returned upstream by it to Lake Simcoe.

By the time the British had taken over in 1763, the Ojibwa Indians, ("people whose moccasins have puckered seams", known also as Chippewas) of Algonquin stock, claimed much of the territory that became Ontario. They had started to move into Southern Ontario from the north and west after the power of the Iroquois had declined in the second half of the 17th century. An Ojibwa band under Yellowhead (followed by his son) were the Indians most closely connected with the Muskoka District, as they claimed the lands around Lake Simcoe and the Severn River. In 1785 an agreement was made with them which gave the British Crown the right to make roads and carry on trade through their country and, according to the interpreter, Jean-Baptiste Rousseau, included the purchase of land one mile on each side of the Severn River.

In 1791, the Constitutional Act established Lower Canada (now Quebec) and Upper Canada (now Ontario). John Graves Simcoe, the first Lieutenant-Governor of Upper Canada, had been a British Captain in the American War of Independence, and he believed the opening of a route from Lake Ontario to Georgian Bay by way of Lake Simcoe was a military necessity as a defence against American invasion. To assess the possibilities, he travelled through Lakes Simcoe and Couchiching, descended the Severn River and visited Beausoleil Island in September 1793. The War of 1812 justified Simcoe's fears, but the Severn Route was temporarily abandoned in favor of one to the south with a portage to the Nottawasaga River.

The 1813 white population in Upper Canada was 94,000, an estimated 80% of whom were of American origin. Probably one-quarter of these were people of Loyalist stock who had emigrated to Canada because of the War of Independence, which had ended in 1782.

In 1815, in conjunction with a survey of the Great Lakes for military purposes, Captain William Fitzwilliam Owen examined the Severn River and appointed Henry Wolsey Bayfield to begin an accurate survey of the Georgian Bay islands. (His survey was completed in 1822.)

On November 5th, 1818, Mississauga Indians associated with the territory that became Haliburton, surrendered a tract of 1,951,000 acres which included parts of Muskoka south of the 45th Parallel, the approximate latitude of Bracebridge.

Lieutenant Joseph E. Portlock re-examined the Severn and made recommendations for dams and canals to avoid the falls about 1819. By this time the possibility of completely by-passing Lake Ontario with a longer water route between the Ottawa River and Georgian Bay was being explored.

Lieutenant Henry Briscoe, Royal Engineers, was the first man who recorded venturing away from the outskirts of Muskoka and into the interior. He crossed the heart of Muskoka as a result of instructions received in 1826 to survey the Talbot and Black Rivers. It was hoped that the Black River, which runs through the eastern part of Muskoka, would provide communication between the Ottawa and Georgian Bay via Lake Simcoe. Unable to carry out his instructions to the letter because he could find no Indian guides familiar with that section, Briscoe elected to use guides who took him down the Severn River, up Morrison Creek to Morrison and Muldrew Lakes, over a portage to Lake Muskoka, across Lake Muskoka to the South Branch of the Muskoka River, ascending it to the Lake of Bays, and finally reached the Ottawa River by way of the Oxtongue and a series of lakes, rivers and portages. (The modern Muskoka names, of course, were not used at that time.)

Sir James Carmichael Smyth, president of the Commission which instructed Briscoe, was not displeased with these explorations, because he saw possibilities for future settlement in this vast territory between the Ottawa River and Lake Simcoe once communication could be established by water routes. Smyth's superior, the Duke of Wellington, however, was greatly disgruntled, and ordered that, in the future, army officers report on what they had been ordered to examine.

British North Americans found reasons for concern other than defence and security when newly-constructed U.S. canals started taking the trade of the western states to the Atlantic ocean, by-passing the St. Lawrence. The pressing need was for a water communication from Georgian Bay to the Ottawa, which would provide the shortest route to the sea from Lakes Superior and Huron and would regain some of the western trade for the St. Lawrence River.

Charles Shirreff, in January 1829, proposed a route from the Ottawa to the Moon River and Georgian Bay through a chain of lakes which turned out to be the Muskokas. His son, Alexander Shirreff, and a crew of five started out on August 30th of that year, from the Ottawa, and by portages, lakes, and rivers reached the South Branch of the Muskoka River, proceeding by way of Lake Muskoka to Georgian Bay. They started their return journey by the Severn River and Lakes Morrison, Muldrew and Muskoka.

In January 1834 the House of Assembly requested the Lieutenant-

Governor, Sir John Colborne, to send out an exploring party from different points on Georgian Bay, to survey lines for 50 or 60 miles in the heart of the country, and to make notes about soil, timber, water and minerals. They begged permission to suggest that the expenses of such an exploration be paid out of the "Territorial Revenue", pointing out that the results could not fail to be highly beneficial to the interests of Upper Canada as well as to the empire at large. Early action, however, was not taken on the survey lines requested by the House.

Between July and November, 1835, a party led by Lieutenant John Carthew, Royal Navy, with Lieutenant F. H. Baddeley, Royal Engineers, as geologist, ran the 77-mile line which eventually formed the eastern boundary of the townships of Morrison, Muskoka, Monck, Watt, Stephenson, Cardwell (crossing Skeleton Lake) and ended into Parry Sound territory. They explored the Black, Severn, Muskoka and other rivers in lateral surveys, making mention of some smaller Muskoka lakes for the first time. In his report, Carthew also mentioned an Indian band under Pamosagay who had cleared forty acres of land and were growing corn and potatoes on an island in Lake Rosseau.

David Thompson, the famed explorer of the Columbia River, was sent out in 1837 (when he was 67 years old) to examine the practicality of a water route between Lake Huron and the Ottawa through Muskoka and the Madawaska. Setting out from Penetanguishene, he succeeded in finding the mouth of the Muskoka River and proceeded up-river through Go Home Lake into Lake Muskoka. Between August 14th and 26th his party surveyed Lakes Muskoka, Rosseau and Joseph, proceeding then up the South Branch of the Muskoka River to the Lake of Bays, continuing on through many lakes to the Madawaska River and the route to the Ottawa. He overestimated the amount of land fit for cultivation along the Muskoka River as 1,024,000 acres: "Although the examination of the Muskako [sic] River for a canal was a failure, yet it brought us acquainted with a valuable tract of Country for settlement." He mentions Indian lodges on an island in Lake Muskoka in his report.

While these explorations in and around Muskoka were taking place, a considerable amount of turmoil and unrest was fermenting in the main Upper Canada settlements around Lakes Ontario and Erie. The population was increasing (reaching 150,000 by 1824) with the arrival of a large number of British, German and Dutch immigrants, and there was widespread discontent with the administration of the province. Among the number of grievances were inadequate roads, Crown grants of land to a favoured few, and Clergy Reserves. Under the authority of the 1791 Constitutional Act, one-seventh of the vacant lands had been reserved for the Crown and one-seventh "for the support and maintenance of a Protestant clergy" upon the survey of a township. The word "Protestant" had been interpreted by the administrators as meaning Anglican, but many Protestant settlers were of denominations other than Anglican, and wanted their churches to receive a share of this revenue.

This unrest culminated in the 1837 Rebellion in Upper Canada (led by William Lyon Mackenzie), coinciding with an uprising in Lower Canada. Queen Victoria and her government, thoroughly distressed by the two rebellions, sent Lord Durham to investigate the causes and recommend ways of dealing with them. Since we are principally concerned with early land policies and land distribution as they influenced the opening of Muskoka to settlers, we turn to the section entitled "Disposal of Public Lands" in Lord Durham's *Report on the Affairs of British North America,* and find his observations that "it is either very difficult or next to impossible for a person of no influence to obtain any of the public land," and that "gross favouritism has pervailed in the disposal of public lands".

On the subject of poor roads, Lord Durham used the example of a settler in the township of Warwick taking 13 bushels of wheat on a wagon pulled by a yoke of oxen and a horse to the grist mill forty-five miles away at Westminster. The return journey took him ten days. Supposing the services of the man and his team to be worth $2.00 per day, Lord Durham concluded that it would not cost more to send the same amount of wheat from Toronto to Liverpool, England, to be ground.

By 1838 the population of Upper Canada had risen to 400,000. 50,000 of these people had settled on 500,000 acres on the north shore of Lake Erie under the direction of Colonel Thomas Talbot. The Canada Company and John Galt had settled thousands more on the Huron Tract, 1,000,000 acres north of the Talbot Settlement, bordering the southeastern shore of Lake Huron.

Various pieces of legislation enacted during the ensuing years concerning the disposal of public lands provided the base for "An Act to Amend the Law for the Sale and the Settlement of the Public Lands" which was passed in 1853. This Act stressed that no free grants of public land were to be made except for a few specific purposes. Among those exceptions was one permitting land grants to "actual" settlers upon or in the vicinity of any public roads in any new settlement. The settlers occupying these free grants on public roads were expected to keep them in repair. Anyone holding an office connected with the sale of public lands was prohibited from purchasing any of them, directly or indirectly. For the information of the general public, lists of Crown, school and Clergy lots (secularization occurred in 1854) for sale were to be made out from time to time and advertised and exhibited by the Commissioner of Crown Lands. Some Muskoka land was later included in these lists.

Back in the Muskoka wilderness, Robert Bell in 1847 marked out an important line, the line running west from the Madawaska River to Muskoka (South) Falls (this line thus intersected Carthew and Baddeley's 1835 north–south line). Bell's line was to become the east–west boundary line between the Muskoka townships of Macaulay and McLean on the north and Draper and Oakley on the south. Robert Bell

James W. Bridgland.

Robert Bell.

Angus Morrison (1822–1882).

David Gibson.

offered the opinion that the chief part of the country, although uneven and hilly, was fit for settlement, the greatest objection being the abundance of rocks.

An 1850 treaty with Ojibwa Indians concerning a large, ill-defined area was interpreted to include lands previously unceded in Muskoka.

J. W. Bridgland, surveying from the east of Muskoka in Haliburton District, examined the land around Lake Muskoka and the south bank of the Muskoka River towards Georgian Bay in 1852 and submitted a discouraging report. He warned that the land was generally rocky and broken, and advised against "incurring future expenses in the sub-division of a country into Townships, and farm lots, which is entirely unfitted, as a whole, for agricultural purposes". Surveying of the three townships bordering on Georgian Bay did not proceed (Freeman, for instance, was not surveyed until 1895), but Bridgland's opinion was not sufficient to offset pressure from the Legislative Assembly to open the Ottawa–Huron tract for settlement.

Alexander Murray carried out an important survey in 1853. At the forks of the Muskoka River above Lake Muskoka, he entered the North Branch and followed it to the lakes which he named Mary, Fairy and Peninsula, crossing the portage to the Lake of Bays. He had started in Georgian Bay with a plan to follow one of the main rivers to its source, hoping to be able to cross its watershed and find his way to the Ottawa by a river falling in the opposite direction. He accomplished all this and made a valuable analysis of the rocks and soil, but for some reason he was unaware that David Thompson had made a similar exploration in 1837. Thompson, however, had followed the South Branch of the Mus-koka River to the Lake of Bays rather than the North Branch through Mary, Fairy, and Peninsula Lakes.

In 1856, the Indians of Lakes Couchiching, Simcoe and Huron surren-dered all the islands in Georgian Bay to which they claimed ownership (including Beausoleil) except the Christian Islands.

The Muskoka district had been annexed to Simcoe County in 1851. The Parliamentary Representation Act of 1853 divided Simcoe into two ridings. The North Riding, which included Muskoka, elected Angus Morrison to represent it in 1854, 1857 and 1861. Angus Morrison, barris-ter, a Scot who had been brought to Canada by his parents when he was 12 years old, is credited with hastening the opening of Muskoka for set-tlement in conjunction with ambitious plans for roads announced by the government in the 1850s. These roads were called colonization roads.

Accompanied by a party of friends, Morrison secured guides from the Rama Indians, a band numbering about 200 under Chief Yellowhead which had established itself on Lake Couchiching. From Yellowhead—Mesqua Ukie or Mesquakie—Muskoka probably derived its name. Mus-koka was the favorite hunting ground of the Rama Indians, different families using different sections—Yellowhead between Lake Muskoka and Lake of Bays and the Bigwin family around Lake of Bays. The Rama guides led Morrison's party by canoe down the Severn River and through the lakes now known as Sparrow, Morrison and Muldrew to the present location of Gravenhurst on Muskoka Bay. Angus Morrison's enthusiastic report of this journey to the government spurred on construction of roads and the bridge across the Severn necessary to open up Morrison Township, later named in his honour.

David Gibson, Inspector of Crown Lands Agencies and Superintendent of Colonization Roads, decided to commence work on the bridge over the Severn River and the Muskoka Road north of the Severn without awaiting construction of a road from Orillia up the Lake Couchiching shore, a distance of about twelve miles. Boats on Lake Couchiching could be used to transport people and goods from Orillia to Washago Mills on the north shore of Lake Couchiching. From Washago Mills to the Severn there was a winter road, approximately two miles in length, over land owned by the Washago Mills, which he could use temporarily pending the establishment of a right-of-way. Accordingly, he surveyed a road line north from Washago Mills to the Muskoka (South) Falls to meet Bell's east–west line, and work began in 1858.

David Gibson (1804–1864) had been born in Scotland and became a surveyor and engineer before emigrating. He qualified as a land surveyor in Upper Canada on December 27th, 1825. He occupied the position of Inspector of Crown Lands Agencies and Superintendent of Colonization Roads from his appointment in 1853 until his death, an appointment of more than passing interest when we consider that he had taken part in the 1837 Rebellion and fled to the United States, returning to Canada after the 1848 amnesty.[*]

Thus, by 1859, within the century since Britain had acquired Canada from France, explorations and surveys had been carried out in Muskoka, the land had been acquired from the Indians by treaty, and a bridge had been built across the Severn River. A Bureau of Immigration was sending agents abroad to make Canada known and promote immigration, often picturing Canada as a kind of earthly paradise.

In the summer of 1859, the Crown Lands Department in Toronto made three pertinent announcements:

1. Opening for sale the lands in the townships of Draper and Macaulay [then in the County of Victoria, Upper Canada] as of August 17th, through the Crown Land Agent at Lindsay
2. Opening for sale the lands in the township of Muskoka [County of Simcoe, Upper Canada] as of August 24th, through the Crown Land Agent at Barrie
3. Appointing R. J. Oliver [August 20th] for the settlement of the Muskoka Road, "upon which grants, limited to one hundred acres, will be made, subject to actual settlement"

---

[*]He built a new house on the ruins of the one that government troops had burned, and, restored and furnished in its original style, it was opened as a museum in 1971. It is on Yonge Street behind the Willowdale Post Office in Metropolitan Toronto.

On October 1st, 1859, Mr. Oliver met a group of intending settlers and issued the first location tickets (17, according to Thomas McMurray in *Muskoka and Parry Sound*, 1871) on the Muskoka road. Seekers for land on the road assumed that Mr. Oliver could also help them purchase Crown lands away from the road, but he had to refer them to the agents in Lindsay and Barrie, creating almost insurmountable trouble and expense for the land seekers. After he reported this to his superiors, he was appointed Crown Land Agent for the townships of Morrison, Muskoka, Draper and Macaulay. By the end of 1862, there was a total population of 287 along the road and a further 743 on the Crown lands.

During the next decade, more roads were built to give settlers access to Muskoka. These roads, cut through virgin forest where sunlight rarely reached the ground, and generally not exceeding $200 per mile in cost, were seldom better than quagmires, as a result of rain and melting snow. Settlers used the trees felled when clearing their land to "corduroy" the roads in low areas by laying logs crosswise side-by-side. If the logs were split in half and the flat side laid downwards, the road would be smoother, and more so if stone and earth were piled in the declivities between the logs. But when the spring freshet was at its height, the logs would come floating up.

Free Land Grants, 1868

By January 1865, the year U.S. President Abraham Lincoln was assassinated, and two years before the Confederation of Canada's provinces, there were more than 100 settlers in the combined area of Morrison township and its northerly neighbour, Muskoka township, and they were allowed to elect one representative to sit on the Council of Simcoe County. That Council then had the opportunity to learn at first hand of the difficulties which the Morrison and Muskoka settlers were experiencing. Simcoe County, which had itself suffered injury through speculators' holding of lands and not clearing or fencing them, or joining in road improvement, could envisage similar problems arising in Muskoka if present and future settlers were unable to pay the money owed on their land, especially when arrears were increased by interest charges.

In June 1865 Simcoe County Council submitted a Memorial to the government urging the giving of free grants of land, with proper conditions for actual settlement, to encourage immigration, rapid settlement and a resultant increase in the number of taxpayers.

Partially through this Simcoe pressure, the First Session of the First Parliament of Ontario (constituted by Canada's 1867 Confederation) assented to "An Act to Secure Free Grants and Homesteads to Actual Settlers on the Public Lands" on February 28th, 1868. It provided for the distribution of the lands in the Districts of Algoma and Nipissing and of certain lands lying between the Ottawa River and Georgian Bay, including the Districts of Parry Sound and Muskoka. This Act and subsequent amendments entitled any settler, eighteen years of age and over, to select 100 acres in a surveyed township; any head of a family could select 200 acres; extra allowance of land, if requested, would be made to compensate for rocky portions.

Any person applying for a location had to make affidavit that he or she believed the land "suited for settlement and cultivation", and that the location chosen was desired for his or her benefit only and *not* for "the purpose of obtaining, possessing or disposing of any of the pine trees growing or being on the said land, or any benefit or advantage therefrom, or any gold, silver, copper, lead, iron or other mines or minerals, or any quarry or bed of stone, marble or gypsum thereon".

Within the five years following selection, the locatee was required to have at least fifteen acres of cleared land under cultivation ("whereof at least two acres shall be cleared and cultivated annually"); to have built a house thereon fit for habitation at least sixteen feet by twenty feet; and to have actually and continuously resided upon and cultivated the land, not being absent for more than six months in any one year. On the fulfilment of these conditions, the patent would be issued, and the settler would hold his or her estate in fee simple (that is, inheritable without limitation). All this was very enticing to land-hungry people in Great Britain and Europe, to the younger sons of Ontario farmers, to those with adventurous spirits, and to many others economically displaced or deprived.

The Muskoka townships opened for location after the passing of the 1868 Act were: Cardwell, Macaulay, Watt, Brunel, Draper, McLean, Muskoka and Stephenson. Seven others in Parry Sound and Nipissing were opened.

The censuses showed a steady rise in the population of Muskoka: 5,360 in 1871; 12,973 in 1881; 15,666 in 1891; 20,971 in 1901; it then remained relatively stable for several decades. By 1880 the Canadian West was opening, and many Muskoka farmers and new immigrants were relocating in Manitoba.

Emigration Societies

Emigration societies in England were a factor in the settlement of Muskoka. In London alone a dozen such organizations were helping families emigrate in 1869, although not all of them had altruistic motives. The accusation was made, for instance, that the aim of one Emigrant and Relief Committee, founded by a few wealthy people, was to remove from their neighbourhood the people they considered poor and unworthy of aid and to throw them on the charity of the Canadians.

By contrast, St. Paul's Church Emigration Society, Clerkenwell, London, was performing an exemplary role in sending skilled and adaptable settlers to the new country while relieving the old country of overpopulation. Composed of artisans and labourers who subscribed weekly to a fund out of which members were helped to emigrate to Canada, the motto of the St. Paul's group was "Self-help and Mutual Help". Its founder and president was the Reverend A. S. Herring, Rector of St. Paul's Church. He visited Muskoka in 1870 to learn at first hand how those who had gone there through St. Paul's Society were faring. He was given the honour of christening the Port Sandfield cut in September 1870. Made greatly welcome by immigrants at Bracebridge, Herring declared, "I am more and more convinced of the blessings of emigration. . . . I shall carry home the happy feeling that many who in the old country were in poverty and misery are now by the blessing of God comparatively in a state of happiness, contentment and comfort."

The Reverend Herring was instrumental in assisting over 3,000 desirable persons to come to Canada (but not all to Muskoka) in the years 1868–72, and the St. Paul's Society was still reported active in 1888.

II SEVERN BRIDGE TO KAHSHE LAKE

The four-lane bridge on Highway 11 over the Severn River, 100 miles due north of Toronto, is the southern gateway to the District of Muskoka.

SEVERN BRIDGE TODAY

Cowbell Lane is on the east side of Highway 11 just north of the bridge. Past a marina, grocery store, and the Severn Inn brick building, turn right and drive along the river past villagers' bungalows and Cowbell Lane Antiques. The river is attractively lined with a timbered retaining wall, docks, a cottage resort, and dozens of cottages.

More Severn Bridge villagers live on Muskoka Road 13, which runs off the west side of Highway 11 at the end of the deep cut through the rock ridge on the north side of the river. This section of Muskoka Road 13 was formerly called the Graham Road after the owner of the first blacksmith shop. The Free Methodist Camp Ground, the Severn Bridge Women's Institute (since 1919), and Morrison Public School are on this road.

The Morrison Agricultural Society Fair Grounds are on Muskoka Road 13 after it turns north at the school. The Society's Exhibit Hall and sheds are in fine condition, and the grounds are bordered with beautifully maintained stands of pine trees. The Society celebrated its Fall Fair centennial in September 1973 with the dedication of centennial gates. A sign of the times in Muskoka, as elsewhere, is the increase of entries in horse classes at the Fair, the result of a resurgence of interest in riding and the breeding of different classes of horses as a hobby.

Muskoka Road 13 goes past Morrison and Muldrew Lakes and the Southwood community to Torrance.

SEVERN BRIDGE AND MORRISON TOWNSHIP HISTORY

The first bridge over the Severn was built in 1858 after the government had decided to open the Muskoka territory for settlement. In order to delay the expense of improving the intermittent cart track from the village of Orillia to the Severn, it was decided to use the Washago Mills-owned winter road, approximately two miles in length, from the top of Lake Couchiching to the Severn, which meant that settlers and other travellers from the south had to travel by boat on Lake Couchiching to reach Washago Mills.

A few people then settled at Severn Bridge, and the colonization road toward the present location of Gravenhurst was commenced. When the government locating agent, R. J. Oliver, met a group of intending settlers on October 1st, 1859, at Severn Bridge and issued about 17 locations on the colonization road in Morrison township, James H. Jackson had been appointed Postmaster and Hugh W. Dillan was operating an inn.

In the next year (1860) Morrison township was subdivided into farm lots by Public Land Surveyor J. O. Browne, The land on the east side of the Muskoka Road in Morrison proved to be totally unfit for pioneer settlement, with the exception of a strip along the south boundary and a small portion near Kahshe Lake. But on the west some fine farms developed around Sparrow Lake. About half of the township was settled very early.

The 1861 report of J. W. Bridgland, Superintendent of Colonization Roads, describes in detail the difficult travelling conditions of those early years:

> ... the Severn River is crossed by a Wooden bridge, supported by log crib piers and three sets of King posts—the Piers are weak and ill founded—the King posts and brace beams too ponderous for the foundation—the result is shown in the swerved and sunken condition of the Bridge. The Abuttments are likewise very poor—The approaches are not carried out far enough to admit of an easy ascent so that in its present condition a short abrupt hill with a mud hole at its base has to be overcome from each side in order to ascend the bridge—The road from the Severn bridge for about two miles or more is in a wretched state—Bad mud holes, bad roots, and bad stones abound—indeed nothing but positive ingenuity, or invention, —offspring of necessity, avails a traveller to conquer certain impediments of the above nature. ... Occasionally from the end of this defective part there are rough portions but the greater part of the remainder of the road to the Falls [the falls on the Muskoka River, South Branch] is in a very tolerable condition.

James Hankinson Jackson, Severn Bridge's first postmaster, was appointed Clerk-Treasurer of the Municipality of Morrison and Muskoka at its first council meeting on January 16th, 1865. Some of Mary and James Jackson's ten children remained in the general area and some went much farther afield.

Mary Jackson had been born a Symington, a family which came to Canada from Ireland in 1840. After the Jacksons came to Severn Bridge, one of the other Symingtons came to settle in Morrison township, bringing six sons. The locating agent, R. J. Oliver, mentioned this family specifically as being intelligent, industrious and desirable settlers. The Symingtons did not find the opportunities in Muskoka sufficient to hold them all, and the father and four sons moved on, one to the Canadian west and the others to Iowa and Montana in the United States, where they and their families flourished. U.S. Senator Stewart Symington of Missouri is a descendant of this family.

John Canning and his wife, both born in Ireland, brought ten children to Morrison to take up land between the Muskoka Road and Sparrow Lake, and these twelve people became the nucleus of the Canning's Corners community (at today's intersection of Sparrow Lake Route C and District Road 13). John Canning was a councillor on Morrison's first council after it separated from Muskoka on January 1st, 1869 (both townships then having sufficient residents to operate separately). The reeve of that council was Moses Davis, who had settled on 100 acres on the river just west of Severn Bridge.

Mayme Davis, a fifth generation descendant of Moses Davis, read a paper on Morrison's pioneers before the Severn Bridge Women's Institute in 1929 in which she recalled a militia company organized and drilled in 1866 by J. T. Bailey (he became Morrison's first Superintendent of Schools) because of the Fenian Raids, but "the war was concluded before they were needed". The designer of the monument in Queen's Park, Toronto, in memory of the men who fell in the 1866 Fenian Raid was Gus Frère, an early Severn Bridge settler.

The Bailey family started a Boys' Club, "made up of the more educated class, who met once a month to study science and other subjects," Mayme Davis wrote. In the early '70s there was a flourishing branch of the Independent Order of Good Templars which "had essays on scientific subjects, such as astronomy, geology and botany".

In 1871 a new bridge was built over the Severn, described as one of the best bridges north of Toronto (and the second of six to date), and the Muskoka Road was planked. The men used portable sawmills along the road while planking it, as it was handier for them to move the mills than it was to draw the lumber along. The plank road was about 16 feet wide, built higher on one side for drainage. During bush fires burning trees fell on it and ignited the planks. Before the railroad reached Gravenhurst in 1875, stagecoach firms had as many as 100 teams of horses hauling passengers and heavy loads of freight from Washago to Gravenhurst and cutting the planks to pieces with their sharp shoes. A team coming on the plank road could be heard when it was miles away. On one recorded occasion, 16 double teams were used to take a government party bound for Parry Sound to Gravenhurst, where the party would transfer to a steamer.

After the railway had reached Severn Bridge in September 1874, Thomas Stanton placed a small steamer on the Severn waters to ply between Severn Bridge and Sparrow Lake.

The 1879 *Guide Book and Atlas* says that Severn Bridge had two stores, a hotel, post office, telegraph office, Orange Hall, and other buildings, as well as another hotel at the Northern Railway station south of the bridge. More than 100 settlers are indicated on the Morrison

The Road to Gravenhurst (The Muskoka Road), 1873. Sketch by
George Harlow White.

The Road to Gravenhurst 100 years later (Highway 11).

township map. Today approximately 2700 property assessments are listed in Morrison, breaking down into 2300 vacation lots and 400 permanent lots.

SEVERN BRIDGE TO KAHSHE LAKE

Travelling north from Severn Bridge, stop at Pioneer Handcraft, one-half mile north of District Road 13 on Highway 11. Frank Preston, from North Bay, founded this business in 1948. The Ontario white pine furniture designs he created at that time, based on 150-year-old pieces, are still being used today. When he started, the lumber came from Muskoka; now it comes from farther north.

Pioneer Handcraft Limited was bought in January 1972 by John S. Bell, from Toronto, who soon erected the new 6,000 square foot building for showroom, workshop and storage after a fire in the firm's former quarters. Five men, generally local craftsmen, make the white pine chesterfields, easy chairs, foot-stools, bedroom and dining-room furniture with tables up to eight feet long and benches, chairs or stools. Each piece of furniture is branded with the company's insignia, a pine tree in a picture frame. Ninety per cent of their business is for Muskoka cottages.

The Artisan's Gallery, opened in December 1974 by Wayne and Pat Church and their three children, is 100 yards or so north of Pioneer Handcrafts on the same side of Highway 11. Wayne Church creates metal murals and floor sculptures which he describes as "theme studies sometimes based on mythology." He also paints in oil, acrylic or water-colour, and designs and forges wrought iron furniture, etc., to the customer's order, a skill he learned while working for eleven years with his father at the Glen Orchard "Smithy". (During this period, he also played professional hockey.)

Bauhaus Docks (named after the German Bauhaus school of functional design) on the east side of Highway 11 north of Sparrow Lake Route C, ships its prefabricated docks, "basic sections", far afield, as well as throughout Muskoka. The Little Red Schoolhouse Antiques is north of Bauhaus on the opposite side of the highway.

Camp grounds, trailer parks and cottage resorts line this section of the highway. A Muskoka Tourist Association information office is about two miles north of Severn Bridge on the east side of the highway.

Next comes a link with the past, Bethel Cemetery, the burying ground of the church reputed to be the first in Muskoka—Bethel Methodist Church, the local religious centre of the Wesleyan Methodists. A set of stone-pillared gates on the south end of the cemetery is joined to a matching set on the north by the fence along the highway. A granite monument matching the gates stands in the cemetery, a simple square column of Muskoka stone on stone with a pyramid-shaped dome, all fashioned by a local mason, Bill Schell. The metal plate on the monument simply states, "In Memory of Morrison Pioneers." There is now no trace of the church; only the cemetery remains.

The first man buried in the cemetery was James Hannah, killed when the horse, on which he was galloping wildly in a race along the plank road, tripped and fell. This happened such a considerable time after the cemetery was set aside that people said, "Muskoka is so healthy a man had to kill himself to start the burying."

Many of the early stones mark the graves of young children, reminding one of the high infant mortality rate in the days when Muskoka settlement was new. For instance, in one family Josephine died at two years and three months; a year later her younger brother, Richard, died at ten months of age. Markers for graves other than of the young are few in the old part of the cemetery. The graves of older people, however, were not always marked because of lack of funds to purchase a headstone or because there was no family in the vicinity; but parents made a special effort to mark the graves of their children.

Another spot of historic interest is half a mile north of the cemetery on the same side of the highway, where the McLellan family operates a cement and gravel business. At one time the location was owned by a Mr. Cuthbert whose frame house had "Gibraltar" inscribed over the gateway. Cuthbert had constructed a replica of a fort on top of a rock (the one just to the south of the present McLellan buildings) and four man-sized dummy soldiers carved from wood stood on guard; all this was obviously reminiscent of England's military establishment on Gibraltar in the Mediterranean Sea. A traveller going up the road by stagecoach in the summer of 1869 has left a report of his amazement when, at a turn in the road, what appeared to be a massive fortification with mounted guns burst into view. Blackened logs projecting through the parapet gave the appearance of a tier of heavy guns. He was warned by a fellow-traveller that he would not be allowed to pass Gibraltar unless he was a loyal British subject.

When Lord Dufferin, the Governor General of Canada, was travelling up this road in 1874 to visit the people of Muskoka, Cuthbert saluted the Governor General by setting off a loud explosion in his fort, making it look as if it had been fired by one of the make-believe guns. Lord Dufferin was so delighted that he sent a small brass cannon for the fort.*

Once the cannon was installed, Cuthbert fired a salute on public holidays and at other times when a government dignitary travelled up the road. The local newspaper was by this time referring to him as "Colonel Cuthbert, the man with the vigilant eye". These activities with the cannon were not popular with all the neighbours, and one Hallowe'en

---

*Another version of this story, written by Harry S. Linney in 1929, states that it was the Hon. John Carling, Minister of Public Works, who provided the cannon, and that the fort was an imitation of forts on Scottish estates, James Cuthbert having emigrated from Scotland.

local pranksters invaded the rock and rolled the cannon over the back edge into the muskeg below. And it hasn't been seen since.

"Malta" was the name given to another small community that developed early between the Muskoka Road and Sparrow Lake.

An attractive park in the pines on the shore of the Kahshe River is about four miles north of Severn Bridge on the west side of the highway. It is a good place to break a car trip or barbecue a meal, provided you are equipped with insecticide. When the weather here is right, you may feel some of the impact of the hordes of mosquitoes that descended on the early settler. Look for the plaque commemorating the "Muskoka Road 1858".

North of the park, a small cemetery occupies the northwest corner of the Kilworthy Road at the junction with Highway 11. The property was donated to the community in 1862 by the Symington family, according to the monument in the middle of the cemetery. James Grant, the miller, who died January 2nd, 1866, is buried here under a headstone which reads "James Grant—A Native of Scotland—Born Aug. 1815". The early farmers had their wheat converted into flour at his small grist mill on the Kahshe River (it is said his grinding stones are still back in the bush), and he also operated a lumber mill capable of cutting 1,000 feet a day. The Township of Gravenhurst Firehall No. 2 is west of the cemetery.

Two roads on the east lead to Kahshe Lake, short for Kah-she-she-bog-a-mog, the Indian name meaning "Lake of Many Islands". The land around Kahshe Lake was not suitable for farming, but lumbering operations that started out in 1856 on the Severn and Black Rivers began to move into the interior of Morrison and Ryde townships about 1861. Logs floated down from Gartersnake Lake, Buck Lake and Bass Lake were collected in Kahshe and sent down the Kahshe River to Sparrow Lake. In the early days, the logs were then floated down the Severn River to Georgian Bay. (They could also be transported on winter roads by horses and sleighs.) Later, mills were built for local processing. The lumbering industry provided the great majority of jobs available to such early families as Boyd, Christie, Jackson, Locker, McClelland, Schell, Shier, Ruttan and Von Alma. Lumbering on Kahshe was carried on until about 1914.

The first settler registered on the Kahshe Lake shoreline in Morrison township was David McClelland (lot 6, Concession 8, 130 acres), April 13th, 1873. McClelland had been in the District for some time, as evidenced by his appointment as Tavern Inspector for the township of Muskoka on January 16th, 1865, when the council of the Municipality of Morrison and Muskoka met for the first time. The 1879 *Guide Book and Atlas* indicates that David Boyd and Joseph Locker were the only additional owners on the Kahshe shoreline.

The South Kahshe Lake Road leads to the bay known locally as Sopher's Bay. Albert Sopher and his wife, Jane Fitchett Sopher, came to Muskoka in 1900 when Albert Sopher was aged 34. He had been born in Stayner, Ontario; his wife nearby at New Lowell. In 1910 the Sophers opened a grocery and boat business on Kahshe Lake in a boarding house that had previously been used for men engaged in lumbering, and members of the family operated the business until 1967. Their location is now known as "Kahshe Lake Resort".

The North Kahshe Lake Road leads to Kluey's Bay, where, around 1910, the Kluey family took over the hotel originally operated by Gillie Anderson. The Kluey's Bay Hotel was a long two-storey building, typical of the early style of boarding house, facing the lake next to the government dock. Mrs. Kluey operated a store in the hotel; the living room with its piano was open to the cottagers, and anybody could pump drinking water from her well. After World War II a new owner modernized the hotel (renaming it Rockhaven), discontinued the store, built a motel unit and understandably restricted the use of the grounds to guests.

Kahshe Lake was not in the same fashionable, newsworthy class as the three large lakes to the north—Muskoka, Rosseau and Joseph—but many cottagers over the years have cherished its sylvan beauties.

Mary Lean, a long-term summer resident on Kahshe Lake, told me that her mother saw an advertisement in a Toronto newspaper about 1915 announcing that the railroad was disposing of land on Kahshe. Mrs. Lean bought two lots for $3.00 each, close to Nagaya Beach, although not on the water. As she didn't want the members of her family telling her how foolish she was, she kept her purchase a secret until a few years later when one of her sons was about to leave for Muskoka on a canoe trip with some university friends. The boys went to see the lots and ported back, "For $6.00 you can't complain." Various members of the family started taking campers up, some of whom eventually bought land and built cottages to form the nucleus of a summer colony.

When Mary Lean was on the Council for the Girl Guides, she had some buildings erected to accommodate Guides on Kahshe Lake. The present Wigwam Lodge, which she operated for its first eight years, grew out of this enterprise.

The Von Alma Family

The Von Alma family built more than 100 cottages around the lake, and the first main lodge and nine log cabins at Wigwam Lodge. The Von Alma story in Muskoka begins with Joseph, who came from Switzerland to Rosseau, then to Gravenhurst. While working in a Gravenhurst mill, Joseph Van Alma was severely injured and later died of his injuries. After his injury he had moved his family to a lot on the South Kahshe Lake Road. There were two lumber mills on the Kahshe south shore, one at Rocky Point and one in the bay that became Sopher's Bay.

An expert and artistic woodcarver, Joseph Von Alma fashioned a pair of life-size beavers to decorate the entrance of an Orillia building.

Joseph's son, John, who had been about thirteen years old when they moved to Kahshe, married Bertha Sopher, a sister of Albert Sopher. They lived in a small log cabin at Kluey's Bay until their first two children, William and Clara, were ready for school; then they bought lakeshore property on the South Kahshe Lake road with acreage extending back to the Muskoka Road, today's Highway 11.

John, when young, worked on river drives down from Gartersnake Lake. He farmed a little, growing potatoes mainly, and began building cottages. When an early would-be cottager named O'Brien was told by his architect that it would be outrageously difficult, if not impossible, to build a stable cottage on Kahshe Lake rock, John Von Alma persuaded O'Brien to let him do it and built the cottage named Crow's Nest, a permanently stable building. In 1936 he also worked on a Moon River dam project, building shelters for workmen and doing carpentry.

Bertha Sopher Von Alma died quite young. It is said that she never recovered from a terrifying night spent in a boat out on the lake during a dreadful bush fire, alone with the children as John was away, while she was in the late stage of pregnancy with her last child.

The marriage of William Von Alma (born 1896 to John and Bertha Von Alma) and Frances Nagy, who had emigrated to Canada from Austria, produced two sons who still live on Kahshe Lake. Two grandchildren are taken to school by bus and spend much of their time travelling in snowmobiles, power boats and All Terrain Vehicles (ATVs), a striking contrast to the childhood of their grandfather William 75 years earlier, in a log cabin at the other end of the lake.

III SEVERN BRIDGE TO RYDE TOWNSHIP

Just south of the Highway 11 bridge at Severn Bridge, Muskoka Street runs east along the southern Muskoka border. The roads you will see branching off to the south in Muskoka Street's first section lead to extensive cottage communities on the Severn River.

WASDELL FALLS

Farther east a road to the north branches off to Wasdell Falls, where there is a well-preserved power plant, now inoperative. Completed in 1914, it was the first generating station constructed by the Hydro-Electric Power Commission of Ontario. The dam is useful today as part of the system which regulates water levels on the Severn. A plaque outlining the history of the Hydro development has been set in the small picnic area. Visitors may swim or fish below the falls.

Before Severn Bridge had a flour mill, the settlers clubbed together with a row boat, each taking small quantities of wheat, rowed up the Severn to Wasdell Falls, portaged the boat, proceeded by river to Lake Couchiching and thence to Orillia, a distance of about 26 miles.

After you return to Muskoka Street, turn east once more, cross the river, and look next for an Anglican church adjacent to an old cemetery where early settlers were buried and where an annual commemoration service is held in the summer. Beyond the church is a private road to Clearwater Lake where members of the Cooper family have built cottages and sold land. The north end of this Muskoka lake is still crown land.

COOPER'S FALLS

Next comes Cooper's Falls, the focal point of a story that began in Kent, England, in the late 1850s with a romance between Thomas Cooper and Emma, a young lady of the same surname and distantly related.

Emma and Thomas Cooper

Emma and Thomas Cooper began to notice each other when he delivered the meat to Emma's privileged household for his father, the butcher; but Thomas, a hard-working young man, knew better than to stop and socialize in a home where undue pleasantries with a member of the "lower class" would be considered unseemly. Emma escaped the family vigilance by concealing herself in the back garden where

Flying Belle with seven excursionists on Kahshe Lake.

Canoeing on the Black River.

Scale: 1 inch = 2 miles
Roman numerals on maps indicate concessions.

Thomas could not fail to meet her on his way out. Their friendship blossomed and eventually they talked of marriage. When they married on March 24th, 1859, both aged twenty-two, Emma's family disowned her.

Their first child was born within the year and a second child two years later. Emma and her children were ignored completely by her family, who would cross to the other side if they should be unfortunate enough to see her on the street in Woolwich. This miserable situation greatly distressed Thomas, and when he saw posters advertising Canada as the place to make a new life he succumbed to the dream, and they emigrated with pitifully small means. On March 20th, 1864, while the ship bringing them from England was in the St. Lawrence River, their third child was born and named Albert Lawrence.

After a short stay in Toronto, they took the train to Barrie, at the head of the railway, and proceeded by boat through Lakes Simcoe and Couchiching to Washago, where they struck off into the bush for the location of their first land—Lot No. 12, Concession M, Rama township, in the County of Ontario—seven miles away. Intending to build a log cabin and take up immediate residence, they carried with them the baby Lawrence, two-year old Norman and four-year old Ada. When night overtook them in the bush, Emma held the children and covered them with her long, wide skirts, while Thomas fed a blazing fire to keep at bay the pack of wolves lurking nearby. The next morning they reached their location and began the four-day task of building a primitive cabin. Afraid of wolves jumping in the windows, they cut them high above the ground and jammed the cavities with logs at night.

For food they had fish, venison, rabbit and partridge to supplement their meagre supplies, and they planted potatoes and turnips in between the stumps of felled trees. The nearest neighbours were miles away and seldom seen. When the changing seasons, illness or bad storms made hunting and fishing impossible, the Coopers went hungry. The plants and mosses of the forest were used for food and medicine. They made their own yeast, probably from hops, and the children were rationed to one slice of bread each day to conserve the flour supply. The only light they had for years was from candles Emma made with animal fat.

About every six months Thomas Cooper would take animal hides to Orillia to trade for supplies, starting out in the early morning to walk the 25 miles, leading a heifer to haul the supplies back on a stoneboat. To use a heifer as a work animal in 1865 was illegal, just as it is now. Thomas Cooper had acquired her for milking, but the need for an animal to help him plough and haul on his homestead was great, and he used her for this, doubtless straining as hard as the animal he drove. In Orillia he would purchase a barrel of molasses, and some oatmeal, flour and whatever other necessities he could afford, stay overnight and start for home as early as possible.

In view of the conditions in the narrow tracks which served as roads, it was difficult for him to be back at his homestead by dusk, but this was important; for at dusk the brush wolves gathered for hunting. On one trip he was caught in the forest at dusk. He walked beside the heifer, coaxing her forward, waving lighted cedar torches. But this time the wolves closed in. As he scrambled up a tree, the wolves attacked and killed the heifer, not leaving until they had torn into her carcass and eaten their fill. Thomas then fled to the cabin, returning the next day for his supplies.

Thomas Cooper was a decisive yet kindly man who admired and cherished his small, cultured wife. Emma Cooper, a courageous woman who weighed about 100 pounds, gave birth to five more children in that wilderness cabin, attended only by her husband. One baby boy died and was buried there.

In 1876 the Coopers built a house and general store on a lot one-half mile away near a waterfall in the Black River, and this was the beginning of the post office and community of Cooper's Falls, which became much larger during the lumbering and sawmill period than it is today. Some of the Coopers' business came from lumber camps in the northeast which sent drivers with large wagons (or sleighs in winter) to buy supplies. Emma had her ninth and last child at this location when she was 41 years old.

Thomas Cooper had dreamed of opening up a community that would give people an incentive to live good, clean lives, and he was disappointed and aroused when men connected with the lumber camps and river drives came into the village drunk. In support of temperance and prohibition, he addressed groups at home, small and large, and eventually travelled to England, Scotland and Wales on speaking tours.

When Emma came into an inheritance from her family about the time she and Thomas were celebrating their 50th wedding anniversary, they both travelled to England to settle this business. It was a far cry from a lonely log cabin in the frightening wilderness to a comfortable trip back to her luxurious beginnings. Thomas ensured that his grandchildren would know of their early struggles by observing a ritual each Christmas afternoon when he would gather the children around and tell them stories about pioneer days.

A granddaughter, Margaret Harding, when she was 80 years old, described Thomas Cooper to me as "a man of granite, facing whatever trial or test came along and never sparing himself. He had a way of coming out ahead. But when others were involved he was a rock of thoughtfulness, courage, kindness and understanding. I never heard him raise his voice to anyone. He was the magistrate for years. When called on to settle something he would be calm and take plenty of time to talk things over. Almost always folks would make up and settle their difference."

In pioneer days, Cooper's Falls suffered from lack of easy access because navigation on the Black River was impeded by rapids and waterfalls. In 1886 the situation was greatly improved by the construction of the Dalton Road, the basis of today's Muskoka Street, running from the Muskoka Road (Highway 11) to Dalton township on the east. Then the railway stations at Washago and Severn Bridge were more easily reached. Telephones were installed in most Cooper's Falls homes in 1911, and electricity was brought to the community in 1941.

Tom Cooper, a grandson of pioneer Thomas Cooper, and his wife, Doris, come up from California each year to operate a riding stable at their 1100-acre Driftwood Ranch in Cooper's Falls and to holiday in their native territory. Some relics of Thomas and Emma Cooper's days are displayed in the ranch house: a branding iron and a log stamper with the "T C" brand; a muzzle-loading shotgun, powderhorn and shot pouch; a tool for splitting shingles; butter moulds, cheese knives for cutting the curds, etc. One unique relic is a coloured advertising poster which was used in the store, imprinted with "Tho's Cooper, Cooper's Falls". It is a river scene (obviously Germanic) with side-wheeler, sails and barges proclaiming "Dr. Hoffman's German Bitters—The German Cure for Dyspepsia and Liver Complaint".

Visitors to Driftwood Ranch may walk south on the trail to the falls from which the village got its name (the Black River runs parallel to the road on the south side). The iron rings sunk in the rocks high above the water were used by the rivermen in logging days to fasten the chains, ropes and pulleys required to keep the logs running at the waterfall.

East of Cooper's Falls, Muskoka Street follows the Black River for a few miles until it joins Muskoka Road 6, turning north into Ryde township. A rough section of the old Dalton road branching off Muskoka Road 6 goes through Ryde township and ends in about 10 miles at Victoria Bridge. This road is based on the early road used by "cadge" teams to take supplies into Longford township lumbering camps, Longford being the township on the east of Ryde township.

Victoria Bridge, where the Black River falls down several levels and rushes through a narrow gorge between high smooth rocks, is a beautiful place to picnic and swim. (Because it is somewhat remote, there is little or no maintenance service to pick up after the litter louts.)

Litter is not the only environmental problem Muskoka has to contend with. Conservationists have cause to worry where growth of cottage communities has not been planned. The "right" to a lakeside cottage now has conditions: adequate sewage control and the prevention of drainage into lakes and rivers and creeks running into lakes. A large number of motorboats dripping oil and gas in a small lake is also injurious. At least four surface acres of lake per cottage is the present guide.

From Victoria Bridge the course of the Black River is through Longford township (Victoria County) to Muskoka's Oakley township on the north.

The whole of Longford township, consisting of 44,000 acres and including North and South Longford Lakes on the eastern border of Ryde township close to Lewisham, is a private estate owned by Longford Reserve Limited. Even the road allowances in Longford township were sold to the corporation. Consequently, there is no public access to the area.

Canoe trips following the Black River route from Lakes Couchiching and St. John sometimes continue through Longford. Novice campers should be aware, however, that because of the private ownership of the Black River where it flows through Longford township, it is not controlled by dams as the other rivers of Muskoka are. Both floods and drought bring hazards that can spoil a camping trip.

RYDE TOWNSHIP

Ryde township, formed in 1861 and originally part of Victoria County, was named after a seaside resort on the Isle of Wight, off the south coast of England.

The north–south line between the present Morrison and Ryde townships (now wards) was run between July and November of 1835 by a survey party under Lieutenant John Carthew, Royal Navy.

On October 7th, 1861, Robert T. Burns reported that he had completed the internal survey of Ryde township. His field notes and covering letter are on file in the Survey Records office in the Ontario parliament buildings. He concluded: "The approach of the Victoria Road will this winter afford an easy mode of access, and will I think cause a speedy settlement." Today the Victoria Road ends just past Victoria Bridge at the private gates of Longford Reserve.

Licences for cutting timber in Ryde were granted to Cook & Bros. and G. McMicken from 1861 and 1862, respectively. The *Guide Book and Atlas* records no Ryde settlers in 1872, only a few in 1873, but by 1879 settlers occupied much of the land north of Riley Lake and up through Housey's Rapids, and some land around Lewisham. Various lots were occupied by different members of the same family. For example, six different people with the surname Bush occupy lots shown on the map, and three lots bear the name Long, and four the name Brooks. John Henry Brooks, for instance, came to Muskoka first in 1873, took up Ryde land in 1878, stayed for 13 years, then moved to the Bracebridge area, where his life ended in 1924. Some other Ryde township names were Loshaw, Carr, Brass and Rush. The first settlers were so widespread and isolated that it was not unusual for neighbours to be unaware of each other's existence until they heard the sound of chopping in the bush miles away. In 1874 Ryde had one school in operation, shared with Draper township.

The majority of the more than 200 permanent residents of Ryde township today live around Housey's Rapids and Barkway, five miles northeast of Housey's Rapids by road. The other community, Lewisham, about five miles east of Riley Lake, has lost its people; only a few hunting camps remain. About 50 children attend Ryde Central Public School, opened in September 1962, a two-room school on a five-acre lot, reforested with lovely stands of pine; although decreasing enrolment has resulted in serious consideration of closing the school and sending the students elsewhere.

Following District Road 6 north from Ryde's southern boundary, today you will see gravel excavations in a few places, hydro towers and wilderness that is being changed by new house construction.

The road to Riley Lake branches off to the east. Although only a small lake, Riley has 55 miles of shoreline which accommodate the majority of the approximately 300 cottages belonging to Ryde township's summer residents. If you wish to explore the lake, you could launch a canoe at the end of the Riley Lake Road or hire a boat at the marina. The first tourist, a man from Stratford named Saunders, didn't arrive on Riley until 1926. After that the lake was enjoyed by relatively few cottagers until a spurt of building in the 1960s occupied most of the waterfront.

North of the Riley Lake turnoff, you will come to Housey's Rapids on the east side of Kahshe Lake. This was one of the three communities in Ryde populated by early settlers who somehow managed to survive as long as the men could get work in lumber camps. Housey's Rapids was named after the first man to settle in Ryde, James Housey. P. J. Brace came along later to start a sawmill and run the post office. As no road connected Housey's Rapids with Severn Bridge for years, a bridle path cut through the woods was used to transport mail and supplies to the settlement in winter. In the navigation season, people could cross Kahshe Lake by boat, trek out to the Muskoka Road and go south to Severn Bridge.

Sam Coad, a refugee from the big city and a former area councillor, keeps store at the bend in the road called Housey's Rapids. We talked about the reign of terror at the turn of the century that upset this usually quiet community, when a local settler went berserk, held up a stagecoach and murdered three local people. Sam Coad refused to disclose the details of the crimes, but was persuaded to show me the porthole in the front wall of his store where a rifle barrel could be set to cover the road.

Taking the Barkway Road to the northeast from Housey's Rapids, I drove up to Barkway to call on Mrs. Wesley Rebman, a local historian. We talked about the large amount of noticeable swamp in the township, and Mrs. Rebman said that many local people blame the beavers. "When I was young, you weren't allowed to trap them. If you ever were in possession of a dead beaver, you kept it a secret. There was a big fine. You can't get ahead of the things now that you are allowed to trap them, and they are responsible for road flooding in some sections."

"Life in the '30s was OK for us," Florence Rebman said when I asked how they fared during the depression. "My husband had taken over the farm from his parents so we didn't have a mortgage. We had cattle and all the necessities for our children."

The Centennial project of the Barkway Women's Institute was the installing of memorial gates on the pioneer cemetery on the south bank of the Gartersnake River. They were dedicated July 16th, 1967; Ryde council contributed half the required money. One interesting stone, seven feet high, is that for Philitis J. Brace, first postmaster at Housey's Rapids. The township cemetery, north of the pioneer cemetery, was opened in 1911.

When you visit the community, check for activities at Barkway Women's Institute Hall such as Tuesday evening games and Friday evening crafts (under the aegis of the Gravenhurst Recreation Committee).

William Lowe

William Lowe was referred to as the "Emperor of Ryde", Mrs. Rebman told me. One of the early pioneers, he came from Hamilton and settled in Lewisham about 1880. He took a keen interest in public affairs, served on the school board and was reeve for many years. He moved from Lewisham to property at Barkway which he farmed, served as bookkeeper for the Weismiller Lumber Company of Germania Lake for a short time, and then became Inspector of Roads and Bridges, a position he filled splendidly. Many a mile of good road and many a sturdy bridge in Muskoka were built under his supervision.

"He moved from his fine home in Barkway to Bracebridge about 1912 to be more centrally located for his official work. Just as when he was in Ryde, he took an active interest in local affairs and was known as an all-round good citizen, good neighbour and staunch friend. He was known and beloved throughout every section of Muskoka.

"Mrs. Lowe was a good church worker and a good Christian woman. She was often called on in time of sickness and helped to deliver lots of babies in the community. She lived to the age of 96. The Lowes had five daughters and two sons."

Barkway Lake, in the Gartersnake River, was originally called Dedlow Lake or Seahauffer Lake after the families who farmed around its shores. The Seahauffer name was changed to Seehaver. "Louisa Seehaver was married, becoming Mrs. Speicher, from her farm home in 1901 at a big wedding to which all the neighbours were invited," Florence Rebman told me. Her children and grandchildren continued to bring her up to visit the lake where she spent her childhood—even when she was well over 90.

"The lake property came into the hands of a real estate agent who cut it into very small lots and the people who bought them couldn't get deeds. An association was formed which got it resurveyed into proper lots. The lake now has four new cottages and an old farmhouse occupied by a retired policeman, and has been renamed Spring Lake. One wonders if that name will ever really take over, because Barkway Lake describes its location."

Jane and William Merkley and family, c. 1900. The 1879 *Guidebook and Atlas* shows the Merkley property on Gartersnake Creek.

Ernie Merkley

The Lowe family of Ryde Township, c. 1907.

Mildred Rowe, Gravenhurst

Ploughing the road with a 16-horse hitch.

Mrs. Wesley Rebman, Barkway

IV SEVERN BRIDGE TO PORT SEVERN

THE TRENT–SEVERN WATERWAY

Just south of Severn Bridge, the "Canal Road" goes west off Highway
11 to Lock 42 of the Trent–Severn Waterway, which from this point
runs along the southern perimeter of Muskoka west of Severn Bridge
to Port Severn on Georgian Bay, 30 miles away. You can sit on the
wall of Lock 42, which provides for a drop of 20 feet into the Severn
River, and overlook a variety of powered pleasure craft going through
the lock, especially on a summer weekend. Canoeists also use this section
of the waterway, particularly campers from the YMCA's Geneva Park
on Lake Couchiching.

The Trent–Severn Waterway joins Lake Ontario with Georgian Bay
by way of the Trent River, Rice Lake, the Kawartha Lakes, Lakes
Simcoe and Couchiching, and the Severn River, a distance of 240 miles,
33 miles of which are through artificial canals. The remaining 207 miles
are through improved lake and river channels. The world's highest
hydraulic lift-lock (65 feet) is at Peterborough, mile 90. At Kirkfield,
mile 170, the other hydraulic lift-lock (49 feet) enters the summit of
the system, 598 feet above Lake Ontario on the east and 260 feet
above Georgian Bay on the west. In all there are 44 locks and one
marine railway (another means of transporting boats from one level
to another), and it is maintained by the federal government for the
pleasure-boating of tourists and local residents. Inquire about toll fees.

The waterway was first envisaged in the early 1800s as a route to
protect Canadian shipping from exposure in narrow channels in the
Great Lakes because American–Canadian relations were strained by
open talk in the U.S. of annexing Canada. Settlers wanted the waterway
as a means of communication; lumbermen wanted it for transporting
logs. Although it was started in 1833, because of political controversy
and lack of funds the canal was not finally completed until 1920 when
two marine railways were installed on the Severn.

SPARROW LAKE

Soon, at Monahan Point, the Severn River enters Sparrow Lake. Papers
dated 1815 called it Welsh Pool.

John M. Sparrow, Toronto businessman, curious about a lake which
bore his family surname, visited it in the early 1900s and bought vacation property which his descendants retained until 1955. John's older
brother, Dr. Malcolm Weethee Sparrow, a dentist, wrote a paper and

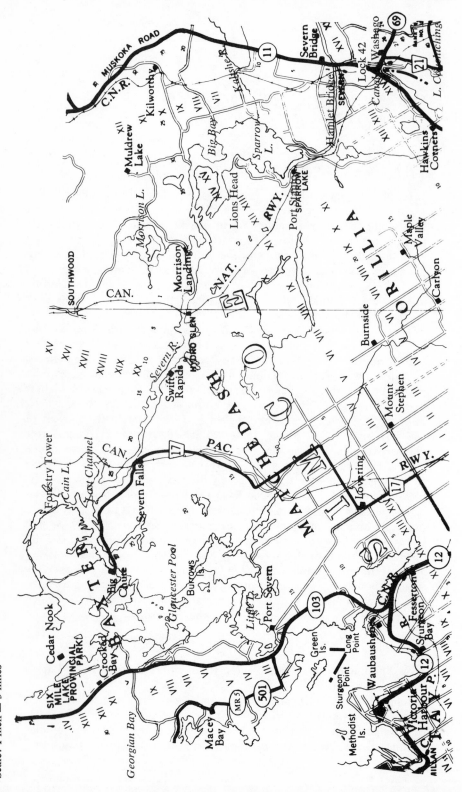

Scale: 1 inch = 3 miles

a long poem in 1924 to record the legends he had collected about the lake, binding his work in brown suede with gold lettering. This volume is now in the family papers retained by Constance Sparrow Trusler, of Toronto.

Malcolm Sparrow wrote that the Indians called the lake Muska-dag-a-ba-sink, meaning "Lake of the Big Fire" because of its wonderful sunsets. When everything around the lake was wild and desolate, an old settler said, William Sparrow came periodically from England to fish and hunt, accompanied by an Indian guide (but not always the same one) hired at the Rama Reserve on Lake Couchiching. They reached the lake by canoe via the Wasdell Falls portage. Sparrow, of good family and wealthy, was apparently in poor health and had a propensity for gambling.

"He was known to the Indians as a very friendly man," Malcolm Sparrow reported, "and seems to have been rather well liked by the few white settlers then on the lake. Nevertheless, one day his guide reported him missing, and as the Indian immediately disappeared, and was never seen again, the supposition was that he had done away with the Englishman, probably after an altercation over cards, and had cleared out to escape justice. As Sparrow was never found, some thought that he might have been disposed of in the lake [and] . . . his name became fixed to the pretty little body of water, first as Sparrow's Lake, then finally as Sparrow Lake. . . ."

Malcolm Sparrow also recorded a different legend about William Sparrow's death as told by an elderly Indian. He said that a white girl once lived on the north shore with her father, a white-haired trapper. It was known that a young Indian was enamoured of her, and this young man often served as Sparrow's guide. "It seems that Sparrow became interested in this mysterious girl, and the young Indian, in a fit of jealousy, shot him." The girl, named Aleeka, said to be an extraordinary person, was shy and elusive, affected the Indian costume and visited the Indian camps to administer to sick children. As she was frequently seen in her canoe on moonlight nights, entirely alone, the Indians spoke of her as Wa-nee-moo-sha, an expression of endearment meaning the Spirit of Moonlight. "Finally the girl and her father disappeared, but her broken, up-turned canoe was found on shore at the foot of Sparrow Lake Rapids, and the Indians, believing that she had been drowned there, spoke of the place afterwards as Wa-nee-moo-sha Portage." (Sparrow Lake Rapids, which once existed where the Severn River leaves Sparrow Lake, disappeared when the Swift Rapids dam farther downstream was constructed to manufacture electricity. During the lumbering era, the rapids were responsible for much loss in kedges, chains and other equipment.)

The Lehmanns from Germany

One of the men who turned up in Severn Bridge in the fall of 1859

Sparrow Lake Station, c. 1912.

Members of the Sparrow family at Sparrow Lake Station, c. 1912.

Sparrow Lake fish
(taken on verandah at Roehl's,
a Sparrow Lake Resort, 1912).

and settled on Sparrow Lake was Adelbert Lehmann, the son of an educated, well-to-do family of the city of Oldenburg, in northeast Germany. Adelbert had decided early to make his career in farming and first worked as time-keeper for the labourers on a relative's farm. Then he went to Holland for a year to learn Dutch because he was thinking of emigrating to South Africa, but he finally decided to go to Canada with his friend, John Everbeck, for the countries of the future, people were saying, were in North America.

On arriving in Canada, the two men spent the summer of 1859 working on a farm in the German settlement at Berlin (now Kitchener), Ontario. After the harvest they set out north and Adelbert bought 200 acres with some lakefront on the northeast section of Sparrow Lake in Morrison township, Concession 7. (He would have preferred a farm on Lake Couchiching but was not able to find a suitable one.) The Sparrow Lake land was not on the colonization road and, therefore, not subject to the same free grant those on the road received. He sent his money right away (oldtimers say it was $1 per acre), subsequently regretting this impetuous action when it turned out that other people who merely squatted on the land received their deeds by grant when the survey was made. While Adelbert built a log shanty and started clearing his land, John Everbeck started on a course that led to building a sawmill on Sparrow Lake at the mouth of the Kahshe River.

In the fall of 1862 Adelbert returned to Germany to find a wife. He soon proposed marriage to Kathinka Bruch, a well-educated young woman, who had spent five years living in Brussels, Belgium, with her uncle, the royal physician to King Leopold. There, while leading an elegant social life at court balls and other such entertainments, she had learned to speak both French and English.

Adelbert and Kathinka were married in April 1863 and left immediately for Canada and Sparrow Lake. He was aged 30 and she was one year younger. Adelbert had intended that a house would be ready for his bride, but the workmen who had undertaken to build it had decided in his absence that building a house for a man who might not return was too risky. The bride and groom, therefore, took up housekeeping in the log shanty and waited many months for a house to be built.

Letters Kathinka wrote to her mother and father in Germany during June, July, August and September, 1863, were preserved by the family but were largely ignored until a new arrival in the Orillia Historical Society asked permission to translate them from German, shortly after the 1967 Centennial celebrations. An Orillia friend, knowing of my consuming interest in Muskoka, hastened to tell me about them, and Kathinka's grandchildren have generously allowed me to cite them.

Kathinka adapted herself courageously and cheerfully to the backwoods, declaring that she had had the gay part of her life and was now ready and willing to settle down. She wrote that her wonderful husband was doing his best to make everything easy for her and that they were living happily together and were very much in love. He was a handsome man, judging from a portrait his descendants have, and he seems to have been charming, gallant and considerate towards his wife.

By the middle of June, Kathinka was making her first butter from the milk of their cow. She had learned to look after the cow and milk it and had developed a fondness for the animal that assuaged her loneliness at least a little. Food was scarce but she and Adelbert had to feed the men who worked for them: a carpenter paid $1.00 per day; a mason paid $18.00 per month; a hired man paid $13.00 per month; and other occasional help. Kathinka baked bread every other day, having been well taught by Everbeck's housekeeper. She served pancakes and potato soup flavoured with ham. She made coffee from bread which had been burned black and wished she could get some chicory to flavour it. Real coffee was a luxury they seldom permitted themselves.

In July she wrote, "We are getting more variety into our meals and are beginning to live a little better. Bread and meat only didn't agree with me at all. My stomach has given me much trouble and I still cannot wear corsets, even if I wanted to in spite of the heat. But I am better now. I used to feel sick all the time." This sickness was probably due to pregnancy, as she gave birth in December. Moreover, crates of clothing, household goods and furniture which would have given her a great deal of comfort did not arrive until July. In the meantime she had feared they were lost forever.

Everbeck, a pleasant conversationalist and good friend, often visited the Lehmanns at the shanty. He would come after dark and sleep in the barn or in the new house on top of the sawdust after they had talked until late. He wanted very much to make an early trip back to Germany to marry his fiancée and bring her to Muskoka, but was delaying as she was only 19 and he was afraid she would find the wilderness life too difficult. His old housekeeper couldn't get along with any of the help and each time Everbeck told her to mend her ways she would pack her things and take off. But she always returned with some excuse, and they would have a grand reunion. She was, however, always generous and helpful to Kathinka.

A preacher from a mission society in northern Germany, who travelled around the country making contact with German immigrants, came to Morrison and brought together all the German families, numbering 20 by this time. Plans for subsequent church services, communions and christenings were made at the meeting. At the first service the minister christened 12 children and Adelbert was godfather for five, all the children of a tailor.

"Evenings, after the work is done Adelbert sometimes rows me around on the lake for a bit," Kathinka wrote. "This is most delightful during the full moon, as it was last week. If we get all our work done earlier than usual, we take along the fishing rod and sometimes we are lucky and catch a good fish for our next dinner. This gives us a great deal of satisfaction. Pleasures over here are of quite a different nature than in Germany. A whole new world opens up to me and I hope I will be able to enjoy it all in time and I hope that you, my dearest ones, will come some day and make everything even more perfect for me."

At the end of September she wrote, "Yesterday Adelbert brought me eight apples, which were very dear, from the Bridge. You all know how I love fruit, and we don't have any. You mustn't think that we always splurge like this, on the contrary, we are always very frugal."

One December day in their first year, Adelbert rushed off to fetch the midwife, but by the time he returned the fire had gone out and Kathinka had given birth in the chilly cabin to Adolph, the first of their five sons.

A combination of circumstances, including a devastating fire in the forest around Sparrow Lake which destroyed much of the beauty that Kathinka Lehmann had enjoyed so much, persuaded the Lehmanns to leave Muskoka and return to Germany in 1871. In 1876, however, they came back to Canada and bought farm land along Lake Couchiching, property on which Maple Drive, in Orillia, is now located. One son had died while they were in Germany; one remained in farming; the other three moved to various parts of Canada to follow careers in chemistry, medicine and teaching.

Other Sparrow Lake Pioneers

Michael Clipsham, the blacksmith, came to Morrison township in April 1865, bought lumber from John Everbeck (whose mill burned down in 1867 while he was on a trip to Germany), and set up shop on the Muskoka Road to shoe horses and do other related work. He soon moved from there to the mouth of the Kahshe River on Sparrow Lake, where, in addition to his other business, he could serve the lumbermen floating logs down from Kahshe Lake by making chains for them and sharpening their pikes, poles and peevees (cant hooks for turning logs). Clipshams still own a lodge on Sparrow Lake.

In addition to Clipsham, names such as Stein, Wiancko and Roehl have a special significance to local people today. Kathinka Lehmann wrote about rowing over to visit the original Roehls in 1863 and being greeted most joyfully. Kathinka admired the young and efficient Mrs. Roehl who served the Lehmanns coffee and bread and butter, knew all about making butter and cheese, and had beautiful vegetables in her garden. Kathinka added that the Roehls were finding the beginning difficult. In addition to some disharmony with another member of the family and their feeling that they had received only a little land for a lot of money, the maid they had brought all the way from Germany had just run away.

Port Stanton

On the southwest shore of Sparrow Lake, in Simcoe County, is Port Stanton, a favoured cruiser stop for supplies and a meal ashore.

The *Lakefield* at Roehls'.

Swift Rapids Lock and Dam.

Thomas Stanton, born in 1842 in Blue Stookes, near Chesterfield, England, came to Canada in 1862 and worked for the Thompson Mills at Longford on Lake Couchiching as Captain of several different steam tugs. He married Ellen Franklin in 1870 and five years later moved to Sparrow Lake, where there were a dozen or so other settlers, including some members of the Franklin family. There he made a living for his six children operating a tug, the *Pioneer*, for the Christie Lumber Company, while clearing land and cutting marsh hay for his stock. During the winter months he cut logs and hauled them to the lake with a team of oxen. About 1890 Ellen Stanton started to provide meals and lodging for fishing parties. Thomas owned a steamer called the *Spartan* which he used to carry mail, supplies and guests to and from Severn Bridge. When business increased, he enlarged his boat and renamed it the *Lady Franklin*, in honour of his wife. He served Orillia township as deputy-reeve, then reeve.

The two eldest sons had a grocery business, operated a sawmill, cut their own timber, and built a steamer, the *Lakefield*, the main means of travel on Sparrow Lake and the Severn River for two decades.

In 1907 the Canadian National Railway came through from Washago and built Sparrow Lake Station near the Stanton's wharf. More people than ever before came to the hotels and boarding-houses around the lake. Typically, the guests at one hotel in 1907 included fifteen "jolly good fellows" from Pittsburgh and a "charming bevy" of eight Toronto young ladies, according to the social column in a Toronto newspaper. (The name of Torpitt Lodge on Sparrow Lake was derived from the first syllables of Toronto and Pittsburgh.)

Various members of the Stanton family built summer resorts around Sparrow Lake, and a grandson of Thomas and Ellen Stanton operated a supply boat, the *Glen Rose*, from 1922 to 1930, serving some 200 cottages on Sparrow Lake.

A small building was erected for use as a place of worship at Port Stanton in the early days through the efforts of Ellen Stanton. When Charles Musson of the Musson Book Company built his summer home in the village, he organized a drive to enlarge the original building and grounds, resulting in a fine summer church—the Church of the Good Samaritan—open during July and August only, which seats 200 persons. It is notable for its stained-glass memorial windows.

SPARROW LAKE TO GEORGIAN BAY

The Trent–Severn course through Sparrow Lake goes north to Big Point, northwest to pass Iron City Point, north into McLean Bay and west into the Severn again. Past Lion's Head and Sparrow Chute, Morrison Creek runs into the Severn from the north. This creek offered a link through various waters which, with portages, provided canoe access to Lake Muskoka in the days before roads. Roads today will take you as far as the government wharf at Morrison Creek; then there is no further road access to the Severn until Severn Falls on the south side of the river. The wharf at Morrison Creek can only accommodate one cruiser conveniently, but stored in nearby slips are the small boats belonging to cottage owners on the Severn whose properties are not accessible by road.

The scenery on the Severn River from Sparrow Lake to Georgian Bay is spectacular. With rock banks as high as 100 feet, secluded cove and peaceful reach, a veritable Eden has been made accessible through the control and conservation of this very fine river.

Portage Bay Cut bypasses the McDonald Rapids, an original impediment to navigation on the Severn. At Hydro Glen, the Canadian National Railways line crosses the river on a high-level bridge.

The lock at Swift Rapids, a little less than 15 miles from Lock 42, was opened in 1965 to replace a marine railway at a cost of $2,500,000, part of an over-all scheme to update the waterway for an estimated $100 million. The Swift Rapids lock accommodates a drop of 47 feet beside a dam and power plant, making even the staircase between the two levels an impressive structure. Boats tied up at the high level of the "Swift" form a friendly community each summer night. Public property beside the lock provides lots of room for exercise, swimming and children's play, and has good washroom facilities. A small store sells food.

At Severn Falls, where there are no falls since the completion of the waterway, you can take on supplies and post a letter. Enquire about the Severn Falls popular non-denominational log church.

Another railroad bridge, this one for the Canadian Pacific line, is 34 feet above the river at Severn Falls, similar in height to the C.N. bridge. Don't try sleeping in a boat at night near one of these bridges, for the trains screaming across will shatter your peace.

Lost Channel branches off to the north about three miles beyond Severn Falls. Up the channel, a very tricky stretch for a boat large enough to sleep people, and past the entrance to Cain Lake on the right (one mile) is a Forest Protection Tower, 85 feet high (standing 150 feet above the water because of the high rock on which it is constructed), with a 10-foot square lookout platform. Unlike the Dorset Tower on the Lake of Bays, however, safety regulations do not permit visitors to ascend. An attractive public campsite with glorious swimming and a good boat dock is on the Cain Lake shoreline across from the tower.

I'm indebted to Lily Smith (Mrs. D. R.), of Severn Falls, for the background material on the tower. "Lost Channel," she says, "has been built up since the war and, naturally, the tower is not isolated as it used to be. Built in 1932, the tower was first manned by William Booth and Lloyd Leatherby, living in tents with their wives. A cabin to provide living accommodation was subsequently erected but is not used now as the men on duty commute from their homes daily by boat. Depending on the weather and degree of fire hazard, the tower is manned daily until

Big Chute marine railway.

A. P. Cockburn, founder of the
navigation company, c. 1868.

6 p.m. from April to the end of September." You will probably notice the air patrols which have taken over much of the firewatching.

Eight miles below the Swift Rapids lock, back on a portion of the Severn where the colourful and imaginative cottage designs are particularly charming, is the Big Chute marine railway, constructed in 1920 to take boats up or down the 800-foot slope to the water level 58 feet below. You steer your boat into a vehicle that looks like a roofless cattle truck; this is lowered by cable down the tracks into the water below. The marine railway has often been subjected to criticism because it takes so long to move the boat traffic and because its capacity is less than other sections of the Trent–Severn. A vessel more than 50 feet in length can't be loaded on the truck. The federal government, however, is building a new $3.2 million marine railway to the right of the present one (facing downstream) which will handle boats up to 100 feet long with 25-foot beam and 6-foot draft, and be able to transfer an average of 40 boats per hour, about eight times the present capacity. It is expected that the new railway will be completed by the end of the 1977 navigation season.

An alternative plan to replace the Big Chute railway with a lock, at less expense, was rejected because the lock downstream at Port Severn, covering a drop of 12 feet, would then have had to be replaced with a marine railway to prevent the spread of Great Lakes lamprey eels which kill game and commercial fish by attaching themselves and sucking blood.

Big Chute can be reached by road. Go to Coldwater (off Highway 12) and follow Simcoe County Road 17 past Severn Falls to Big Chute, about 18 miles.

Below the Big Chute marine railway, you proceed through the fast water of Little Chute (chained timbers along the side provide protection in case your motor should stall) in the approach to Gloucester Pool. Severn Lodge on Gloucester Pool is an old-timer, run by Americans who live there six months of the year.

The course through Gloucester Pool winds through rocky islands into Little Lake; and, if you would go down in your boat to Georgian Bay, Lock 45 at Port Severn will lower you the last 12 feet.

Port Severn

A few grocery stores, marinas, and several hotels with evening entertainment line the road at Port Severn. A long bridge crosses the dam controlling the water flow into Georgian Bay and Lock 45, one of the old, original hand-operated locks of the Trent System. Adjacent to the lock is a park with swimming. Large camping and trailer parks occupy much of the land on the Highway 103 side of the Severn, obviously a preferred location for vacationers trailering boats who want to use the Trent–Severn Waterway.

V GRAVENHURST

TO MUSKOKA TOWNSHIP WITH JAMES McCABE

James "Mickey" McCabe was one of the first seventeen people who met at Severn Bridge on October 1st, 1859. He and his wife made their way farther north than the others out of Morrison township and into Muskoka township where they opened a tavern to accommodate travellers near the south end of Lake Muskoka. The Free Masons Arms, their log cabin, was located near the arch which now stands at the entrance to Gravenhurst. McCabe also put a scow on Lake Muskoka about two miles from his inn at a spot which became known as McCabe's Landing, located on Muskoka Bay near the present boat docks.

The sight of the dim light of the Free Masons Arms glowing through the bush was a blessed promise of food, warmth and rest to the weary traveller searching for land at a time when there were no horses or vehicles on the road, according to one writer who had great admiration for the generosity and good nature of the Irish McCabes. He reported that their log cabin was unpretentious but clean and orderly, that he had been served good food and that many had reason to be grateful to the McCabes. Others were dismayed at the primitive facilities of the one-room log hut in which any overnight guests also had to sleep. The potatoes and onions were dug out of the ground as required, the cooking was done outside, and Mrs. McCabe was likely to use her hand to stir up a quart or two of a refreshing drink made of water, vinegar and molasses for thirsty guests.

Thomas M. Robinson

Another early settler who located on land near Gravenhurst was Thomas M. Robinson (1836–1917), a sailor, from Brampton, England. Robinson first travelled to Canada from England in July 1860 and took the train from Toronto to Barrie to consult an agent for Muskoka lands. From Barrie he travelled by stage to Orillia and then by rowboat to Washago. He walked to Severn Bridge and up the Muskoka road, and long after dark he found the home of a Dutch settler, Frank Webber, where he stayed overnight. In the morning Webber took Robinson a mile farther on to McCabe's inn and then to McCabe's Landing where they found a birch-bark canoe equipped with two paddles, probably belonging to Indians who had left it for their next trip across the water. In the borrowed canoe, Robinson and Webber paddled up the east shore where Robinson discovered land on Cliff Bay that delighted him and which he afterwards acquired. Many years later this land became the site of a sanatorium for tubercular patients.

Robinson then returned to England and brought his young wife and their household possessions to Muskoka in January 1861. He left his wife at Hugh Dillan's inn at Severn Bridge and walked to McCabe's where he met a Mr. Mercier from whom he purchased a 100-acre lot with a small clearing and a log cabin for $25.00. He improved the log cabin and brought his wife to it in the spring. They lived there while he cleared the Cliff Bay land which he reached in a small punt he had bought from Hugh Dillan.

Robinson soon became the most experienced navigator on the lakes. Engaged by a party of surveyors, he managed to find the elusive mouth of the Muskoka River in order to take them up to North Falls (now Bracebridge).

Shortly after this trip, he and his neighbours urgently required seed corn, and they learned it might possibly be obtained at an Indian village on a river flowing into the top of Lake Muskoka. Robinson, in spite of the fears of his anxious wife, set out to find it with William Bradley, one of two young brothers who had settled near them at the mouth of the Hawk Rock River. Early in the morning they started to row up the east side of the lake, searching for the Indian River in the unfamiliar bays and inlets of a wooded shoreline. At last, near sundown, they entered the river and rowed up it to the village with its log houses and cultivated fields, at the present location of Port Carling. Aided by sign language, they bought the corn from the Indians. On the return journey they were drenched and buffeted by thunderstorms but finally arrived home safely about one o'clock in the morning, somewhat wiser about the size and shape of the lake.

During the summer of 1861 Robinson worked for the Severn Bridge innkeeper, Hugh Dillan, as Captain of a large rowboat, plying between Orillia and Washago, which carried the settlers who were beginning to swarm into the district. (A steamer, the *Emily May*, brought the passengers to Orillia from Belle Ewart on Lake Simcoe, the transfer point with the railway.) A young man worked as crew under Robinson and the passengers assisted at the oars. Incidentally, Dillan had procured the boat by arranging with the road contractor, James Cooper, of North Falls, to bring it from Collingwood.

In the autumn, Robinson was able to ready his new house on the Cliff Bay land for occupation.

In July 1862, Robinson made a further exploration of the Muskoka Lakes as the guide of a party of young men from Toronto led by John Campbell and James Bain who had made exploratory trips into Muskoka for adventure and to gather botanical specimens on their vacations in 1860 and 1861. Robinson had met Campbell and Bain when he was working on Hugh Dillan's boat. When he received a letter from them in June 1862 asking him about a proposed trip, he replied, "Since you were here there has been another lake discovered that was not before known to white men and connected to Lakes Muskoka and Rosseau ... and it is said by the surveyors that discovered [it] that it is quite as large as either of the others, and the three are all connected together, merely a fall of 5 feet from the one and 2 feet from the other, which is no serious impediment to the passing of a small or light boat."

The surveyors referred to had been led by Mr. John S. Dennis, sent by the Commissioner of Crown Lands in 1860 and 1861. When they arrived at Lake Joseph on a canoe traverse, they thought they had discovered it, and Dennis named it after his father, Joseph Dennis. Oddly enough, although unknown to all the parties concerned in this tale, it had already been named Lake Joseph years back.

Robinson met the party of four (or possibly five) young men in Orillia late in July with a wagon to transport the boat and tent they had brought from Toronto and supplies of sea biscuit, ham, tea, coffee, sugar, etc. With a small sail mounted on the boat, they pushed off one afternoon, and once again an anxious Mrs. Robinson was left at home to watch and wait. They passed the first night on an island in a thunderstorm, but from then on the weather cooperated admirably.

They reached the Indian village late the next day and hauled their boat up the rapids of the river, where the Port Carling small-boat lock is today. Plagued by mosquitoes, they camped on the shore of Lake Rosseau in the dark. They started out to the west next morning on a course which might easily have taken them to the Joseph River, the connection with the new lake, but they did not find it. Finally they turned south into a long bay on the western shore and sighted a sandy ridge which they climbed and from which they saw water they thought might be Lake Joseph. They decided to make permanent camp on the ridge, now the cut-through at Port Sandfield, and they hauled the boat over it on poles and launched it on the other side. After an early supper, they set off to explore, proceeding westward until they saw the long sweep of water to the northwest which convinced them they had found what they were looking for—the beautiful Lake Joseph.

Within the next several days of exploration they reached the lake head, which became the thriving port of Port Cockburn for a brief era, but they could not find the river connecting Lake Joseph with Lake Rosseau. On the day they lifted the boat back over the ridge, they made another run up the Rosseau shore and this time discovered the two-foot waterfall at the end of the Joseph River. (The rocks at the waterfall were eventually blasted out to allow the safe passage of small boats when the cut at Port Sandfield (1871) had equalized the water levels on the two lakes.) The explorers had accomplished all they had set out to do (how simple it all seems to us today with people to direct us, and charts and powered boats) and they made the return trip to Muskoka Bay bursting with satisfaction. Robinson's employment with the young men provided him with the ready money he urgently needed, and he continued to assist them when required on their subsequent trips.

John Campbell and James Bain, labelled Muskoka's first summer visitors, had formed "The Muskoka Club" with some friends by 1866, choosing Chaplain's Island in Lake Joseph near the Joseph River as a permanent camp.

The first of the Robinsons' four sons was born in the year following the first Lake Joseph trip, and they lived in the Cliff Bay house until it was replaced with a larger one about 20 years later. Thomas Robinson was a councillor of the Municipality of Morrison and Muskoka, which first met on January 16th, 1865. In the first regatta held October 12th, 1870, on Lake Muskoka, sparsely attended because of poor weather, Robinson won the pair-oar race with A. H. Browning and an exciting two-boat race by 13 seconds in his sailboat *Wave*. Thomas Robinson built boats, and he and his wife took in summer visitors, as advertised in a guide book circa 1888:

ROBINSON'S MUSKOKA BAY
Quiet Private Board in retired locality
Terms: $1.00 per day, with the use of boats
T. M. Robinson, Box 186, Gravenhurst P. O.
P.S. A Yacht to charter for cruzing
by the day or week

The *Guide Book and Atlas of Muskoka and Parry Sound* (1879) lists three early boats on Lake Muskoka which could be hired to carry passengers and freight. These were the "first wood boat" introduced by James Cooper in 1862, McCabe's sailboat in 1863 and James Harper's sailboat in 1864.

A. P. Cockburn and Steam Navigation

Then the opportunities in Muskoka drew the attention of A. P. Cockburn, a Beaverton businessman who was reeve of Eldon township, Victoria County. He set aside three weeks in the autumn of 1865 to explore Muskoka and come to a decision about its possibilities.

Cockburn and his companions entered the Lake of Bays at the present site of Dorset, paddled to the portage, crossed it and proceeded through Peninsula and Fairy Lakes to the present site of Huntsville (unsurveyed and unsettled). He paddled and portaged through Vernon, Fox, Buck and Round Lakes to Doe Lake in the District of Parry Sound and proceeded 75 miles through Magnetawan waters.

Cockburn returned by the same route as far as the future location of Huntsville, having encountered only a few trappers making preparations for the fall catch. Striking a trail which led to the most northerly Muskoka settlers, he then walked another thirty miles south to McCabe's where he stayed overnight.

Mrs. McCabe sent him up Lake Muskoka with an enthusiastic description, and he returned after a quick look at Lake Rosseau. The scenery inspired him to proceed with the idea of developing steam navigation on the Muskoka Lakes, even though the total population of all the land he had travelled through numbered only a few hundred, according to the last available census of 1861. As for summer visitors, he knew of only one camping party, no doubt Campbell and Bain. But he had high hopes.

Cockburn sent a report of his observations to his friend, the Hon. Thomas D'Arcy McGee, Commissioner of Agriculture, who in turn presented it to the Coalition Government. It was well received and printed in pamphlet form under the title *A Few Weeks in the North*. (If there is a copy of this in existence, I have not been able to locate it.)

Cockburn received assurances from the government that it intended to pursue a liberal land policy with regard to the settlement of Muskoka, thus practically guaranteeing a large increase in population.

Assurances were also made: first, that early settlers on unsurveyed land would not receive less acreage on the completion of the survey than their original allotment even if survey lines changed their exact location (this would be an inducement to immediate settlement—waiting for surveys would mean delays); and second, that roads would be made and navigation improvements implemented.

Only after receiving these assurances did Cockburn undertake to place a substantial passenger and freight boat on Lake Muskoka.

While his father and a brother, Isaac, began lumbering operations in Muskoka under the name of Messrs. P. Cockburn & Son, A. P. Cockburn opened the first general store in Gravenhurst and began building a paddle steamer. He borrowed the money required to build it from his father-in-law, Mr. Proctor, of Beaverton. Cockburn's wife was given the privilege of naming that first boat, and she chose the Indian name "Wenonah" which she had discovered in the poetry of Longfellow. Wenonah means "eldest daughter", and this name was given in honour of Mary, the Cockburns' eldest daughter.

Cockburn sent word to a settler named Hogaboam, whose land was farther north nearer the location that became Huntsville, to bring some good axemen to Gravenhurst and take charge of the building of the *Wenonah*. Hogaboam gathered Erastus and Nehemiah Hanes and Milan Markle, and they loaded everything they needed in a cart borrowed from Alexander Bailey at his store in Bracebridge. Hogaboam's young son David went with the men to Gravenhurst and returned the borrowed cart on his way home.

On the shores of Muskoka Bay the settlers constructed the *Wenonah*, a 62-ton sidewheeler, 87 feet in length by $26\frac{1}{2}$ feet in width. Practically everything that went into the building of the boat was taken out of the bush without benefit of power-driven machinery; even the planking was all hand-cut, from end to end of the logs, with a whipsaw. On the

The *Wenonah*.

Crew and visitors with the *Wenonah* in the background.

Muskoka Wharf Station, c. 1903.
Excursionists ready to board the
Medora and *Nipissing II*.

Both pictures given to the author by the late Professor J. Roy Cockburn (1879–1964)

Ontario Archives

housing of the paddle wheels "Royal Mail and Express Packet" was lettered. Alexander Bailey's son George, a hunter and trapper, aged about 22 at the time, also worked on the building of the *Wenonah*. George Bailey became a wheelsman on the *Wenonah*, subsequently captained Muskoka Lakes boats for more than half a century and was looked upon as the Commodore of the fleet that grew from the enterprising beginning of the *Wenonah*, the boat with an average speed of ten miles per hour.

The *Wenonah* was launched in June 1866. The community was only sparsely settled; Lake Muskoka and the Muskoka River to the steamer's stop at Bracebridge were uncharted. It was trial and error navigation, and the steamer frequently piled up on unmarked rocks and shoals when none of the usual aids for floating and pulling off a stranded vessel were at hand. The difference of nine feet in the spring and autumn levels of the lakes added to the hazards of navigation. The boat was run at a loss during the first and second seasons, but the events of 1868 justified its existence. That last statement would be deemed controversial by those who did not make a success of settlement in Muskoka, and by their sympathizers. They were known to declare that the 1868 Free Grants Act was fashioned to justify the existence of the *Wenonah* and, with the help of his friends at court, to save A. P. Cockburn from ruin.

GRAVENHURST

Gravenhurst received its name and a post office in 1862. (James McCabe was the first postmaster). "Gravenhurst," also the name of a small hamlet in Bedfordshire, England, was likely chosen by a government official from a book by Washington Irving, *Bracebridge Hall*, published in 1822.

J. D. Cockburn originally owned much of the north part of Gravenhurst, and some of the streets are named after the ladies in his family. A newspaper advertisement of March 27, 1871 states that the village plot of Gravenhurst had been surveyed and that parties wanting building lots should apply to Geo. C. Austin or Dugald Brown.

Dugald Brown, the founder of Brown's Beverages, died in 1885, and apart from his business accomplishments, is remembered for his great confidence in the racing ability of a sorrel mare which he entered in a Dominion Day race. All but one of the other competitors withdrew, considering themselves outclassed, and left the race to Brown's mare and a horse named "Black Dan". Dugald's wild-eyed mare was galloping furiously in a cloud of dust towards the finish line, leading by a nose, when suddenly it left the course, scattering the crowd as it leapt over logs, stumps and a brush pile, and tore back to the starting point. When Dugald was unable to persuade his competitor to re-run the race, he took the place of his rider on the mare's back and raced over the same course to try to demonstrate the horse's ability before a re-assembled crowd. This time the horse reached the finish line but kept galloping madly to its stable. Dugald Brown leapt out of the saddle into the box of a wagon, miraculously escaping injury, just as the mare dashed through the doorway to head for a screeching halt in her own stall.

Today Brown's Beverages has one of the finest plants in the industry and a long-standing contract with Coca Cola; the third, fourth and fifth generations of Browns are current guardians. Local artesian well water is used in the preparation of Brown's popular Muskoka Dry ginger ale.

Gravenhurst progressed from the days of the first steamship and the first of its many sawmills to incorporation as a town in 1887. The first train arrived in August 1875 (see the Centennial plaque at the station) and in November a spur line was opened to nearby Muskoka Wharf where people and goods were transferred to steamboats. The first Agricultural Fair was held in 1876.

J. T. Harvie (1847–1923) was the town's first mayor. Born in Orillia, he had worked for the Harvie Brothers stagelines, moved to Gravenhurst and then branched out into lumbering when the railway reduced the stageline business. Gravenhurst suffered a calamitous fire in September 1887. During three hours in the night at least 45 family homes and about 50 business and public buildings were consumed. Starting in a foundry, "so great was the mass of flames that burning shingles were carried half a mile." Most of the town's homes and buildings were wooden, and insurance covered not more than $75,000 of the $200,000 loss.

The entrance to Gravenhurst's business section today is by Highway 11B. A new section of Highway 11 crosses Gull Lake Narrows and sweeps around the east side of Gull Lake to bypass the town, while the former Highway 11 has been renamed Bethune Drive.

A large fountain depicting a bear and leaping fish is the focal point of the Kinsmen Centennial Parkette at the Highway 11B entrance to Gravenhurst. Near Gravenhurst's traditional arch (a much earlier one was a Lumberman's Arch, constructed by the Mickle–Dyment firm for the Governor-General's visit in 1885), is Corbett's Wildlife Zooette, a private collection including monkeys, deer, pheasant, waterfowl, and peacocks, which our family found most interesting.

With a population of over 3,000, Gravenhurst today has grocery supermarkets, restaurants, Liquor Control Board and Brewers Retail stores, and many shops selling the commodities required by residents and visitors. Apply for tourist maps and information at the Board of Trade office on John Street.

Clipsham Hardware brings to mind the pioneer, James Everett Clipsham (1849–1932), from Lincolnshire, England. He and his brother, Michael, started out as blacksmiths near Severn Bridge. Then James had his own shop at Severn Bridge, after which he moved to Gravenhurst

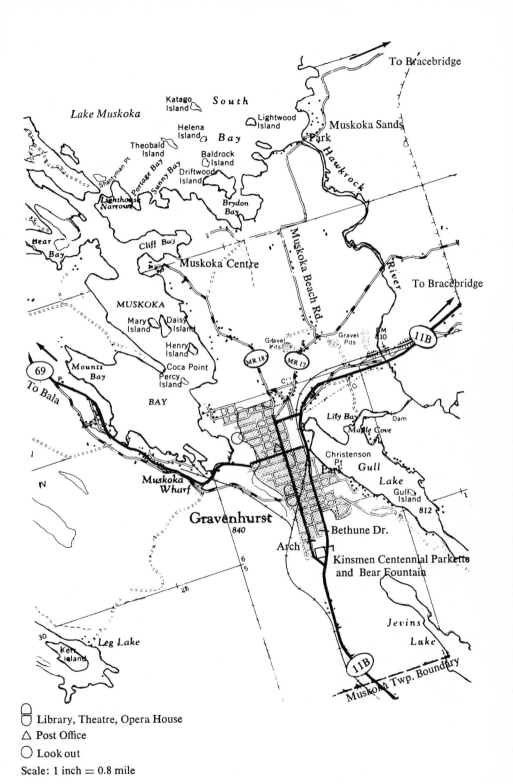

Lake Muskoka

Katago Island

South

Helena Island

Lightwood Island

Muskoka Sands Park

To Bracebridge

Theobald Island

Bay

Baldrock Island

Portage Bay

Sunny Bay

Driftwood Island

Brydon Bay

Hawkrock

Shantyman Pt.

Lighthouse Narrows

Bear Bay

Cliff Bay

Muskoka Centre

Muskoka Beach Rd.

River

To Bracebridge

MUSKOKA

Mary Island

Daisy Island

Henry Island

Coca Point

Percy Island

BAY

Gravel Pits

Gravel Pits

BM 810

11B

MR 18

MR 17

To Bala

69

Mounts Bay

N

Muskoka Wharf

Lily Bay

Maple Cove

Dam

Christenson Pt Park

Gull Lake

Gull Island

812

Gravenhurst
840

Bethune Dr.

Arch

Kinsmen Centennial Parkette and Bear Fountain

6
5

25

Jevins Lake

30

Kerr Island

Leg Lake

11B

Muskoka Twp. Boundary

Library, Theatre, Opera House

△ Post Office

○ Look out

Scale: 1 inch = 0.8 mile

and opened a blacksmith shop and carriage works, manufacturing the first wagons and buggies north of Orillia. He was burned out in the 1887 fire but rebuilt, later selling his business and moving down the street to the present hardware location.

The town's newspaper, the *Gravenhurst News*, is published weekly on Thursdays. Gravenhurst, Bracebridge and Huntsville weeklies will give you and your family a sense of community, news of local government and planning, and announcements of local activities.

The Gravehurst Opera House is on Muskoka Street South. Completed in 1901 at a cost of $10,000, it replaced the Town Hall which had been destroyed by fire in July 1897. When a proposal to demolish it was made about 1965, it was restored through the efforts of a group of Gravenhurst citizens. Muskoka Summer Theatre performances are held at the Opera House, currently under the aegis of the Muskoka Foundation for the Arts. The company's repertoire is also presented at Port Carling's community centre. Among the many other activities the Opera House accommodates are: the annual Oktoberfest, exhibitions of the Gravenhurst Horticultural Society (which hangs and maintains Muskoka Street's flower baskets) and of the Muskoka Philatelic Society (last Saturday in September), Gravenhurst Kinette Club arts and crafts show (October), touring exhibitions such as Prison Arts, and gatherings of such organizations as the Independent Order of Oddfellows. Inquire about a Georgian College summer theatre arts workshop.

Music lovers should seek out the Muskoka Concert Association which began its programming in the fall of 1972 with the appearance of the Hamilton Philharmonic Orchestra. Cyril Fry, Principal of Gravenhurst High School, was the charter president of the Association.

North of the Opera House is a pleasant library in which is the 1914–18 memorial plaque. The names of the fallen from other wars are inscribed on a cenotaph wall between the Opera House and the library.

Gravenhurst has a movie theatre on Muskoka Street South across from the Opera House.

Michael H. Cleary, landscape painter, invites visitors to his studio on Bay Street. He paints in the outdoors, winter and summer. His wife, Pat, is a full-time school teacher and has taken over some of the work started by her grandfather, Claude Snider, giving slide-illustrated talks at the schools on Muskoka's past, one history lesson the local children find fascinating.

Lawrence Nickle, another artist with wide Canadian experience who now lives in Gravenhurst, and Michael Cleary customarily exhibit their work at Toronto's Branksome Hall each November, along with Roberta Haviland, who first attracted attention with pen and ink drawings but has moved into watercolours, and paints and exhibits throughout Muskoka.

Hilary Clark Cole of Gravenhurst works in welded steel, brass or copper, sometimes incorporating stained glass and semi-precious stones. Her works include abstract wall sculptures, animal, bird and human figure studies. She is married to Michael Cole, 1975 Manager of the Gravenhurst Opera House.

Muskoka Ornamental Iron Products, three miles west on Highway 69, designs and produces items to order (if you don't find what you want in stock), in addition to its business of manufacturing and installing metal railings.

An annual summer exhibition of Contemporary Church Stitchery and Banners is held at Trinity United Church, on the east side of Muskoka Street North. This is a positive must for art lovers living in or visiting Gravenhurst, whether or not they ordinarily darken the door of a church. A program describes the exhibited works—selected by a committee from numerous entries—which are hung in the church and its adjacent Browning Hall. The huge dossal curtain behind the altar was hung in honour of Trinity's Centennial (1872–1972). Another work of amazing beauty and grace, entitled "This is my Father's World", which portrays forest, field, mountain, sky and water, permanently decorates the front wall of the balcony.

An aluminum and brass sculpture of contemporary design on the south lawn of Trinity Church depicts Mary, Joseph and the baby Jesus as a universal family in the circle of God's love. Statues of the three wise men are added for Christmas. Ric Green, of Barrie, is the artist. Gordon Sloan, Trinity's organist and choirmaster, is frequently invited to conduct church music clinics in various centres throughout Canada.

Marie Aiken has been the artist behind Trinity Church's notable stitchery activity as well as the instructor for Georgian College's two-week stitchery course held each July in Gravenhurst. She is an internationally recognized fibre craftsman and teacher through her involvement with the World Craft Council, conducting workshops in many countries in addition to Canada. She has taught aboriginal women in central Australia simple crafts that can provide a source of income, and has exchanged techniques with Canadian Eskimo women. She is married to Gordon Aiken, Q.C., county court judge, then Member of Parliament for Parry Sound–Muskoka 1957–72, and author of *The Backbencher*, a book about Canadian political service. They have four grown children and five grandchildren.

In 1975 she opened the Marie Aiken Tower Studio in Gravenhurst on Lake Muskoka, a residence-studio complex ingeniously and artistically created from an abandoned potash factory, constructed about 1915.

The Stuart & Cruikshank building, near Trinity United Church on the southwest corner of Church North and First, is noteworthy for having received an award of merit in an Ontario-wide architectural design competition sponsored by the Ontario Masons' Relations Council. The architects were Howard V. Walker and Anthony C. Campfens, who also supervised the restoration of the Opera House.

While on Muskoka Street North, turn left on George Street where

Steam launches *Wanda, Rambler,* and *Mildred,* with *Medora* and *Nipissing II* in the background at Muskoka Wharf, c. 1904.

Sagamo (destroyed by fire January 10, 1969), and *Segwun,* at Gravenhurst docks, 1964.

there is a sign with the word "Lookout". Four blocks along there is a rough park and a curved stone wall on a height of land from which you get a panoramic view of the docks and Muskoka Bay.

Turn left on Bay Street (Highway 69) at Gravenhurst's post office and drive about half a mile to Sagamo Park on the southern shore of Muskoka Bay. A historical marker in the dock area gives a few details about steam navigation on the Muskoka Lakes. The navigation company took its steamers off the lakes in 1958 after 93 years of operations. The *Sagamo* ("Big Chief"), the company's flagship and "palace steamer", burned in this bay in January 1969 to the top of its steel hull while 12 staterooms were being refurbished for use as a hotel.

The *Segwun* ("Springtime") is the only remaining ship of the fleet. Tied up at the dock it has been used as a floating museum, displaying photographs of Muskoka in days gone by, settlers' effects, navigation and logging relics, and a collection of early outboard motors. The *Segwun*'s hull deteriorated until she was in danger of sinking, and, with the pledge of an Ontario government grant, the *Segwun* Board started a desperate search for the additional quarter of a million dollars needed to save the ship. Help came from an unexpected source, the Ontario Road Builders' Association, which proposed that its member companies and other interested parties underwrite the restoration and refitting. The Muskoka Steamship and Historical Society was founded to provide the organization, including Road Builders representatives, for handling the *Segwun* project. The first task was to rebuild an old shipyard marine railway and carriage in Muskoka Bay to haul the ship out of the water at a cost of $25,000. Her hull was replated, and on June 1st, 1974, the Rt. Hon. Pierre Elliot Trudeau, Canada's Prime Minister, a Liberal visiting a Conservative stronghold, smashed a bottle of champagne against her bow; torches cut the holding irons, and the *Segwun* floated majestically into Muskoka Bay with flags flying. She will be able to cruise anywhere on Lakes Muskoka, Rosseau and Joseph for special events or on charter, as it is not intended to run her on any regular schedule.

The *Lady Muskoka*, a modern cruise boat launched in July 1964, runs on scheduled sightseeing cruises through the Lighthouse Narrows, the island and coves of Lake Muskoka and the Indian River to Port Carling. Reserve in advance if possible, or you might find that the cruise you want is sold right out. The boat can be chartered by groups for moonlight cruises with music for dancing.

Greavette Boat Corporation Limited is on Muskoka Bay west of Sagamo Park. The Greavette name has been synonymous with fine boats since Thomas Greavette incorporated the Greavette Boat Works in 1930. This company advanced the use of "non-pound" bottoms to improve on the old "V" and "round" bottom boats, was famed for its *Miss Canada* speedboats, and internationally sold its fine "Streamliner" craft and built Fairmile upperstructures during World War II. Bruce Wilson, a former Toronto executive who has vacationed in Muskoka all his life, bought Greavette Boats in 1972 and added the Sundance Canoe firm. The company restores antique boats and does general repairs, in addition to building boats.

Another Gravenhurst landmark which must be mentioned is the site of the old Sanatorium on Cliff Bay. Proceed north on Muskoka Street which becomes Muskoka Road 18, pass the Ontario Fire College, and you will come to the gates. Patients came from all parts of Canada and the United States, and sometimes from farther afield, for the treatment of consumption (tuberculosis) at the Muskoka Cottage Sanatorium, completed in 1897. While its building was financed by substantial gifts, including $10,000 from the town of Gravenhurst, it was a private hospital where patients had to pay. To meet the needs of those unable to pay, Muskoka Free Hospital was built nearby in 1902. It has been estimated that these two treatment centres reduced the area's death rate from tuberculosis by one-third in 25 years. Two private sanatoria adjacent to the town were built later. After a fire destroyed the greater part of the Free Hospital, splendid new buildings were constructed on the spacious grounds of the Cottage Sanatorium and opened in 1922. Subsequently the two institutions were merged into one organization named the Muskoka Hospital which grew to accommodate 440 patients while developing model laboratories and operating rooms.

With the development of modern drugs, the need for these buildings as treatment centres diminished until, in 1960, conversion began to a school for retarded girls, as an adjunct to the Ontario Hospital School in Orillia. In 1973 it was detached from the Orillia operation and was named "Muskoka Centre", but it retains the function of caring for retarded girls and women.

If, instead of proceeding north on the Muskoka Street extension, you turn right on Highway 11B, you will soon come to the Muskoka Beach Road, Muskoka Road 17; turn left. The Mickle Memorial Cemetery is on the early part of this road, recalling Charles Mickle, one of the mill magnates of the District, and his wife, Emma Rowe Mickle, residents of Gravenhurst from 1878 until their deaths in 1928 and 1932 respectively. Mrs. Mickle is remembered for the splendid receptions and garden parties given at their elegant home, "Rosehurst" on Bay Street (now Garner Lodge), and for her many good works. (See Muriel Grigg's *Magnetic Muskoka* for more about the Mickles.) A plot in the cemetery was acquired by the Canadian Legion in Gravenhurst in memory of those killed in World War II, and a tall granite cross was erected. Those who have served in the armed forces may be buried in the Legion section.

A large elementary school, Muskoka Beechgrove Public School, is on this road, as well as a number of attractive suburban homes. About three miles from the post office corner in Gravenhurst, just before the Muskoka Sands Inn, is a public park. A concrete sea wall encases a sand beach equipped with barbecue pit, picnic tables, and changing rooms, and the swimming is beautiful.

Almost straight out from Muskoka Sands Inn is Eleanor Island where scores of Great Blue Heron nest each year. Treat this colony with great consideration if you go near.

Past the Muskoka Sands Inn and Rockliffe Ranch (boarding and breeding of horses), the road leads to Bracebridge through an industrial section which starts with Swift's Butterball Turkey Farm #3, and the Alcan Wire and Cable branch plant which opened in 1969.

Gull Lake Park, on Bethune Drive north of the southern entrance to Gravenhurst, has excellent picnic, swimming and drinking-water facilities. The town's swimming program is conducted here. The park's Canadian white pine trees are about 100 years old, and 60 to 70 feet high. The rock bluffs of a long peninsula across from the beach provide a natural grandstand when activities such as water polo championships and speed boat races are staged. Various types of summer Sunday evening programs are presented from the band shell on a barge (sponsored by the Civic Music Association and contributions of local money), while boats lie about in the water and people cover the grassy banks. Queen Elizabeth II and Prince Philip attended the first official performance on July 4th, 1959.

Blue ice, clear as crystal and among the best in the country, was harvested at Gull Lake when natural ice was used for cold storage plants, residential refrigeration and railroad needs. If you're not old enough, you won't remember the days of the iceman and your Muskoka ice arriving by boat. As many as 130 men kept the snow cleaned off Gull Lake ice with wooden scrappers drawn by horse before the days of trucks, tractors and jeeps equipped with blades. Circular saws were used to cut the ice into large standard-sized blocks which were then stored in sawdust in a huge icehouse on the shore or loaded into Canadian National Railways boxcars for immediate shipping.

The Gravenhurst and District Conservation Club owns and maintains a duck and wildlife preserve (370 acres purchased in 1970) on the Doe Lake Road (Muskoka Road 6), north of Gull Lake. The Club has embarked on an ambitious program to establish public parking, lookout points, walking trails, and a haven for Giant Canada Geese, birds with a wingspread frequently exceeding six feet, weighing generally from twelve to twenty pounds and once feared extinct.

Dr. Norman Bethune

Norman Bethune (1890–1939) was born on John Street, Gravenhurst, in the Presbyterian manse of his father's first congregation. He was granted a Bachelor of Medicine degree in December 1916 by the University of Toronto, served with the Royal Navy as a Surgeon Lieutenant, interned in London's Hospital for Sick Children on Great Ormond Street, married, and began practising medicine in Detroit in 1924. When stricken by tuberculosis, he stayed briefly at Calydor private sanatorium in Gravenhurst; then left for treatment at Trudeau Sanatorium, Saranac Lake, New York. There, at his own insistence, he underwent surgery for an artificial pneumothorax, revolutionary at that time. The surgery was successful, and, convinced of its value in the treatment of advanced tuberculosis, he travelled to Montreal to study and become a thoracic surgeon, and was subsequently noted for his improvement of existing surgical instruments and invention of new ones for his specialty.

As a prominent Montreal surgeon, Bethune publicly deplored the lack of medical attention for the poor in Canada. He started the Children's Art School of Montreal in his home for disadvantaged children and supported it largely with his own money. Then he went to Spain and organized the first recorded mobile blood transfusion unit to take blood to anti-Fascists wounded in the civil war, using funds raised in Canada by the Committee to Aid Spanish Democracy.

Later Bethune went to China to organize hospital care for Chinese wounded in the Japanese invasion. His first biographers, Ted Allan and Sydney Gordon, in *The Scalpel, The Sword*, have quoted him as saying in 1937, "In Spain fascism has attacked 24,000,000 people, with the United States, Britain and France embargoing the Loyalists. Now, in China, the attack has spread against nearly one-quarter of the total population of the earth. If the same treacherous policy of blockading the victims and making arrangements with the aggressors is continued, we may well wonder whether any man, woman or child is safe anywhere in the world."

Eighteen months after he went to China, Bethune died there of a streptococcus septicaemia which entered a cut in his finger while operating, without gloves as usual, on a soldier with a head wound which had been untreated for days.

An early Chinese delegation presented the Town of Gravenhurst with a book of Bethune photographs. On July 31st, 1971, the name "Bethune Drive" was given to what had previously been a part of Highway 11 in Gravenhurst. The Ontario government placed a commemorative plaque on the lawn of his birthplace in 1972, but not without evoking controversy. Finally, partly because of the pressure caused by visiting Chinese delegations, the John Street manse was purchased by the federal government for a museum.

In Shih-Chia Chuang, North China, Bethune's tomb and statue dominate the entrance to the Mausoleum of Martyrs. Nearby is the 900-bed Bethune International Peace Hospital, one of the many Bethune Medical Schools, and a Bethune memorial hall. Elsewhere in China are many other memorials.

*   *   *   *

Further information about the Gravenhurst area may be found in *The Light of Other Days*, a book compiled by a committee of citizens in celebration of Canada's centenary, which covers many prominent Gravenhurst people and the history of its churches and institutions.

VI BRACEBRIDGE

THE REAY ROAD

On the way to Bracebridge, about four miles north of Gravenhurst, the Reay Road runs to the east off Highway 11 and is the location of Reay Park KOA, one of the hundreds of "Kampgrounds of America" throughout Canada, the United States and Mexico. Reay Park has over 100 fully serviced campsites and many amenities, and is open all year.

During World War II, the Command of the Royal Norwegian Air Force built a "Little Norway" camp farther along this road to train pilots at Muskoka Airport, which adjoins the property and which they had leased from Canada. The Camp was opened in the presence of Crown Prince Olav and his wife, Princess Martha, on May 4th, 1942. (Another Muskoka camp, "Vesle Skaugum", at the top of Highway 514, had been opened in 1940.) When Norway was occupied by Germany, Norwegians came to Canada from all parts of the world to train. Thor Heyerdahl of *Kon-Tiki* fame was one of those who came.

In 1961 the Little Norway camp was converted to Beaver Creek Correctional Camp, a place where men who have been confined in a federal penitentiary can prepare to return to the outside community. Beaver Creek men go out into the community to help with activities such as setting up Arts and Crafts shows. Beaver Creek Correctional Camp does not, of course, welcome sightseers.

When you are proceeding north again on Highway 11, do not take the first exit to Bracebridge after the Reay Road. Instead, continue north to Muskoka Airport on the right. Owned and operated by the Federal Ministry of Transport, the airport extends down to the Reay Road and the World War II location of the Norwegian Air Force. Air Muskoka offers sightseeing flights, plane rentals, charter flights, and training for pilots' licences.

This airport dates back to 1932, in the depth of the depression, when the Department of National Defence was building emergency airstrips for unscheduled landings between major airports where the land was rough and bushy, and where there were no large cultivated fields. Men who had been "riding the rods" across the country were picked up and offered clothing, room and board, and a small cash allowance for cigarettes or such items, in exchange for work clearing the land. Horse teams were the only assistance given to human labour. The three runways of the triangular airstrip were completed by 1938. The airstrip program was a piece of highly commendable government foresight for,

Scale: 1 inch = 3 miles

while this airport stood more or less dormant upon completion, it provided the training ground in 1942 for the Royal Norwegian Air Force.

MUSKOKA ROAD 4 EAST (*The Peterson Road*)

The official opening of this re-routed road, north of Muskoka Airport, in the fall of 1972, was a tremendous boon to travellers, for it connects Highway 11 at Muskoka Falls with Highway 35 at Carnarvon in Haliburton. It is historically important because it follows the line of the old Peterson Road, although with some variations.

In 1847 Robert Bell explored a line between the Madawaska River and the Muskoka River, and Bell's line became a basic term of reference and was used for the east–west boundary between the Muskoka townships of Macaulay and McLean on the north and Draper and Oakley on the south. When the government was planning a road to give east–west communication to the north–south colonization roads already started, Provincial Land Surveyor Joseph S. Peterson was assigned to check the practicality of Bell's line for a road line. Peterson suggested improvements which were approved by Bell and adopted.

The Peterson Road was built during the five-year period from 1858 to 1863 at a cost of $39,000, and it stretched about 114 miles from the Muskoka Road on the west to a road (the Opeongo Road) connecting it with the Ottawa River on the east. Poorly constructed, the Peterson Road contained long stretches through rough, rocky country which attracted few settlers to help maintain them, and many sections soon became impassable—if, in fact, it had ever been possible for a wagon to travel its whole length. In Muskoka it was kept open from Highway 11 past Prospect and Wood Lakes to the community of Vankoughnet (on the northern reaches of the Black River) named for Philip Vankoughnet, Minister of Agriculture at the time this settlement was established, and Vice-Chancellor of the University of Toronto from 1862 to 1869.

The Peterson Trail Conservation Association has been formed to promote a year-round hiking and nature trail and to develop or preserve beauty spots, waterfalls and pioneer history.

Both Prospect and Wood Lakes have public beaches and Vankoughnet has a village park.

Prospect Lake had originally been named Poverty Lake by construction crews working on the Peterson Road about 1859 when supplies of meat which had been cached were eaten by wolves—leaving the workers hungry and isolated. In 1870, Colonel Francis Cornwallis Maude, C.B., V.C., renamed it Prospect Lake when he arrived with his wife Paulina Susanna, from Hampshire, England, and built a one-and-a-half-storey log house with dimensions of 50′ × 24′ that was the talk of the settlers for miles around. (An account of this is found in the *Herald-Gazette*, April 25th, 1974.)

Colonel Maude was 55 when he arrived in Muskoka with a "liberal retiring allowance" after a distinguished military career. He paid the highest wages in the area to household staff and men clearing the bush, his money often being the only money circulating. He gave many parties for leading members of the community, such as the McMurrays (newspaper editor and entrepeneur), Lounts (division court judge), and Willsons (clergyman). He was a sharpshooter and delighted in hunting parties, the countryside abounding in deer, rabbit and partridge. In April 1872, two years after his arrival, he went for a "visit home" but never returned. From 1876 to 1886 he was Consul-General in Warsaw, and was created a Military Knight of Windsor in 1895.

Muskoka Falls

The road to the Muskoka Falls community branches north off Muskoka Road 4 East very near Highway 11. Muskoka Falls has a public beach and picnic area on the Muskoka River, South Branch, which was first developed as a Draper township Centennial project, and is now the responsibility of the Bracebridge Area Parks Board.

Past the village general store and gas pumps is the Muskoka Falls United Church, one of the three oldest church buildings in Muskoka still in use (the others being Madill United Church and the Port Sydney Christ Church [Anglican]). When the Muskoka Falls Church celebrated its 100th anniversary in August 1969, the Ontario government presented a commemorative plaque. A marker was also placed on the church grounds by the Archaeological and Historic Sites Board of Ontario in August 1969 to commemorate the Peterson Road. A rock cairn with bronze lettering "In Memory of the Pioneers of this Community" was erected here by the Carry-On Club in 1971.

Beyond the church is the Muskoka Falls Public School—a relatively new building occupying a pleasant site overlooking the river—the centre of a community busy with hockey, bridge, Christmas concerts, an annual snowmobile safari to Carnarvon in late February, and the designing of floats for Muskoka parades.

Considered to be the oldest community in Muskoka after Severn Bridge, Muskoka Falls has also been known as South Falls and Muskokaville.

Richard Hanna, a contractor on the Peterson Road, moved his wife and children into a 10' × 15' cabin and became the first Muskoka Falls postmaster in 1860. He died during the Civil War in the United States where he had gone to fight on the Union side, leaving William Hanna, his 13-year-old son, with many family responsibilities. These evidently prepared him for success, for he became a prominent Port Carling merchant. Rachel Hanna, his sister, was born at South Falls May 21st, 1859, and she had a remarkable life.

Trained as a nurse at the Toronto General Hospital, Class of 1891, Rachel Hanna followed the "Trail of '98" to the Klondike to give medical help to gold rush prospectors and their camp followers in answer to a plea for four volunteers. These volunteers became members of the newly-formed Victorian Order of Nurses at a salary of $300 per year. It was reported that "this nurse worked faithfully on, bringing comfort and hope to many a sick, unfortunate, discouraged miner. . . . She has been ready to take the heavy end in everything we have undertaken. She is a grand woman." She returned eventually to live in Muskoka and died there in 1934 from complications resulting from a fall, ironically, on an icy pavement.

Thora McIlroy Mills (Mrs. R. S. Mills, of Toronto and Lake Muskoka) has produced a number of carefully researched newspaper articles about Rachel Hanna in the hope of achieving the same type of recognition of the suffering and courage of pioneer nurses in the Gold Rush as has been accorded Florence Nightingale and the nurses who went from England to the Crimean War.

Returning to Highway 11, you immediately cross the bridge over the falls in the Muskoka River, South Branch, which are unlikely to be noticed by strangers driving at 55 miles per hour. Early tourists rowed or paddled the four miles up the river from Bracebridge, carved their names on the wooden bridge, and expressed their delight in poetry and prose with the original "Grand Falls" or "South Falls." (The original name of Bracebridge was "North Falls".) In lumbering days, logs made the steep descent in a log chute. A power plant has been in operation here since 1909, and now only a small amount of water trickles down the 130-foot drop in summer, the rest being diverted into the Hydro flume.

Thomas McMurray

Thomas McMurray could see no prospect of securing farms for his large family in Ireland, and he decided to emigrate to Canada on the basis of information received from J. A. Donaldson, a Canadian Bureau of Immigration officer for Great Britain and Ireland. The McMurrays set sail from Londonderry on May 10th, 1861, arrived at Quebec on May 20th, and proceeded to Toronto. Leaving his family in a rented house for a month, Thomas McMurray went to Orillia and on to McCabe's and hired McCabe's flat-bottomed boat. He rowed across Lake Muskoka, up the Muskoka River to the North Falls (Bracebridge) and finally chose 400 acres in Draper township on the banks of the Muskoka River, South Branch, about two miles east of where the highway goes over Muskoka Falls today. Donald Ferguson appears to have been the only settler before him in Draper township.

McMurray soon had many irons in the fire, and eventually became the first reeve in 1868 of the United Townships of Draper, Macaulay, Stephenson and Ryde.

When the Free Grant Lands became available in 1868, many intending settlers wrote to McMurray for information, and he started a

Gravenhurst Opera House, today.

Geraldine Coombe

An early sketch of South Falls
by Seymour Penson.

*Guide Book and Atlas of Muskoka and
Parry Sound Districts, 1879*

Ontario Archives

"The Grove," 1874. The residence of Thomas
McMurray, across the street from today's
Bracebridge and Muskoka Lakes Secondary School

weekly newspaper to supply answers to the questions they asked. Printed at Parry Sound, the first issue of the *Northern Advocate* came off the press on September 14th, 1869, at a time when the steamer *Wenonah* was under repair, and thus McMurray had to row 16 miles across Lake Muskoka to distribute the papers. The next year he moved the paper to Bracebridge, as it was more central. He claimed a total circulation of 1,000, including copies sent to England, Ireland and Scotland.

The paper which imparted general, local and market news also offered poetry, inspirational matter, and advice like the following excerpt from a twelve-paragraph column (December 4, 1869) entitled "Maxims for Young Girls":

> If you want to marry, do not court or attract the attention of gentlemen. A little wholesome indifference will be more likely to accomplish this object. Consider, moreover, that it is better to be a woman than a wife and do not degrade your sex by making your whole existence turn on the pivot of matrimony.

The charge for the paper was 3¢ per copy, $1.00 per year if paid in advance. Indebted parties were notified in a January issue that cordwood would be accepted at the *Northern Advocate* office all that month (while the sleighing was good) in payment of accounts.

The short period of general Canadian prosperity from 1867 to 1873 wilted almost overnight in the wake of a depression in the United States which began when Jay Cooke, that nation's leading financier, went bankrupt and wrecked the economy. McMurray, apparently, had over-extended himself and went into bankruptcy in July 1874.

He had been living in a "splendid villa" in the residential part of Bracebridge and got into financial difficulty in the building of the "Brick Block", a three-storey building about 60′ × 60′ with a large one-storey addition at the rear for a printing office. The top two storeys of the three-storey structure were intended as apartments, and the ground floor was a general store in which five clerks were employed. The wide expanse of glass in the windows, the high ceilings, the cashier's box in the central part of the store and the 24-foot long private office with lofty glass partitions elicited some sarcastic contemporary comment, in view of the fact that Bracebridge was hardly more than a backwoods hamlet.

After McMurray's business ventures folded, naturally causing some local disgruntlement, he was appointed Crown Lands Agent in Parry Sound and started another newspaper, the *North Star*. McMurray had been an active proponent of Temperance Societies. On arrival in Muskoka he took up the battle cry, "Keep from the whiskey, the curse of the land," advertising temperance song books for sale and editorializing on crimes and cruelties associated with drink. "If men would but stay at home with their wives and weans, instead of spending their time and their hard earnings at the tavern, we would not see so many broken-hearted wives, nor have to chronicle so many cases of accident and crime," one editorial expounded. Liquor caused such trouble at social gatherings and pioneer bees that men and women who lived careful lives were becoming increasingly offended.

The by-laws passed in 1868 by the council of the United Townships of Draper, Macaulay, Stephenson and Ryde required the payment of a licence fee of $25.00 per year by every tavern, and the number of licences issued was restricted to five. Every tavern was required to have at least four furnished bedrooms for guests, a dining room, a bar room and stabling and feed for at least six horses. General stores which sold liquor were also required to pay the annual licence fee of $25.00 and were forbidden to sell liquor in smaller quantity than one quart or to allow drinking of it on the premises.

One 1870 traveller remarked that the store in Bracebridge had barely $100.00 worth of foodstuffs and household requirements but had what seemed like an unlimited supply of booze. It is alleged that the start of some substantial holdings in Muskoka was considerably reinforced with money made from secret stills. "But that was long ago, and don't quote me," my informant added.

The pressure of temperance groups brought about many changes on liquor regulations in Muskoka, as it did elsewhere. Today all bottled liquors are sold through the Ontario Liquor Board which also licenses and inspects bars, lounges and dining rooms serving alcoholic beverages. Brewers Retail stores sell ale and beer. Liquor and beer stores are always closed Sundays and holidays, and these beverages are served only with meals in licensed dining rooms on Sundays. Some municipalities may still exercise their option of refusing to allow the serving or sale of alcoholic beverages.

BRACEBRIDGE

The pioneer community was made up of such people as James Cooper who occupied land on both sides of the falls and worked on the early roads. His son, Joseph, operated a sawmill, developed a grocery business to supply lumber camps and became a Bracebridge councillor. Hiram Macdonald had a tavern and store on the south side of the river in 1861, when the river was spanned with a large, squared-off pine log to serve as a bridge.

Alexander Bailey acquired land from James Cooper on the north side of the river, above and below the falls, built a gristmill and sawmill at the foot of the falls in 1864, and opened a small hotel, the Victoria, in conjunction with a store and the post office. From Penetanguishene on Georgian Bay, the centre of a large fur-trading operation, Bailey and his son, George, had previously operated a fur-trading post near where the confluence of the Muskoka Rivers, North and South Branches, runs into Lake Muskoka. This fur-trading post is described specifically in Captain Fraser's *History of Muskoka* (1946) as being for the Hudson's Bay Company and at Browning's Bend. In 1865–66 George Bailey helped build the first steamboat, the *Wenonah*, in Gravenhurst, subsequently serving for 61 years as captain and commodore for the Muskoka Lakes Navigation Company. Alexander Bailey also developed a line of stages, evidenced by the following Orillia newspaper advertisement dated December 1st, 1867:

> Bailey's Line of Stages
> Will leave the "Victoria Hotel", Bracebridge, daily
> at 8 a.m. for Orillia. Returning will leave the
> "Royal Hotel", Orillia, daily at 8 a.m. for Bracebridge,
> stopping at Washago, Gravenhurst and Muskoka Falls,
> and connecting with the stage for Parry Sound.
> Charges Moderate.   A. BAILEY, Proprietor

Alexander Bailey moved to land which became the village of Port Carling after selling his Bracebridge land, sawmill, gristmill and other buildings to Messrs. Perry and Myers, from Whitby, in 1870, for $6,000. The sale included all the water power of the falls. R. E. Perry subsequently was postmaster, a reeve of Bracebridge, and warden of Victoria County.

Gilman Willson, William Holditch and A. H. Browning were operating little bush stores in 1866, and then John Teviotdale arrived, and gave the village an impetus when he built the first large substantial store (later acquired by Perry and Myers). Teviotdale, a prominent citizen, was responsible for large improvements in the village; unfortunately he died at age 42 in 1875.

Bracebridge, previously called North Falls, received its name in 1864 when the post office was opened. While it is generally accepted that the name of Bracebridge was chosen by Dr. W. D. LeSueur, the Secretary of the Post Office Department in Ottawa, from the same novel (Washington Irving's *Bracebridge Hall*) from which Gravenhurst got its name, Bracebridge may have been named after a community in Lincolnshire, England.

In 1877 Beardmore Bros., of Toronto, opened a tannery which has been described as the model tannery of the continent, after receiving a $2,000 bonus from the village and a 10-year tax exemption because of the employment it would provide and the fact that it would use local hemlock for tanning hides. Ten years later the village population was 1600.

Bracebridge attained the status of a town in 1889, and its population exceeded 3,000 when, in 1971 Regional Government was introduced, and Bracebridge became part of the larger Town of Bracebridge Area Municipality. It contains the Court House, Registry Office and Administration Building for the District Municipality of Muskoka.

Enter Bracebridge about $2\frac{1}{2}$ miles north of Muskoka Falls. Drive down the hill on Muskoka Road to the river, cross a bridge, and you will be facing Manitoba Street, Bracebridge's main business street. Cross Manitoba Street and turn left to Wharf Road, which descends to the town dock. You will see the falls, about 60 feet high, and the plaque at the powerhouse commemorating the fact that Bracebridge was the first Ontario municipality to establish its own waterpower generating station, in 1894. The grounds in front of the powerhouse have been beautifully developed into a parkette on a height overlooking the river.

Climb back to Manitoba Street and turn right towards the bridge crossing the falls. The flowers in the park just before the bridge are planted in memory of R. J. Dodds, D.D.S., a president of the local Horticultural Society remembered for his creation of flower beds around Bracebridge public buildings. The Bracebridge Horticultural Society was founded in 1932 at the instigation of Mabel McGibbon, wife of Dr. Peter McGibbon, Muskoka's federal Member of Parliament for several years. The Society holds an annual flower show in mid-August.

Across the bridge, on the river opposite the town dock, is Kelvin Grove Park, where public tennis courts were constructed in 1974-75. Follow the road on the south side of the river to reach the "532 Industrial Mall" and some of Bracebridge's manufacturing plants.

Riverside Centre, on the south bank of the river at the corner of Beaumont Drive, was opened in 1973, a development of the Harbridge Corporation, of Etobicoke. It has a 700-foot boat dock, a billiard room intended for family participation, and an eight-lane bowling alley. Check by telephone for current information.

The main shops of Bracebridge line both sides of Manitoba Street, north of the river, starting with Waite's, a popular bakery which attracts many tourists and cottagers from the surrounding summer and winter resort communities.

An Art Gallery at 30 Manitoba Street regularly displays the paintings of about thirty Ontario artists, with an emphasis on Muskoka artists. Robert Scott and his son, Gil, are the entrepreneurs, ably assisted by their wives. Gil Scott takes an active interest in the community, and is responsible, for example, for introducing an art show into the Winter Carnival.

Robert Everett, an artist who radiates joy in his work and has remarkable drive, is prominently featured at the Gallery. Born in Bracebridge in 1920, he started painting outdoor scenes at 14, graduated from the Ontario College of Pharmacy in 1946 and entered his father's pharmacy business. He eventually left pharmacology to devote full time to painting, becoming in 1975 president of the Ontario Institute of Painters. A great Muskoka enthusiast, Gordon Sinclair, Toronto television and radio personality, has commissioned six Everett canvases.

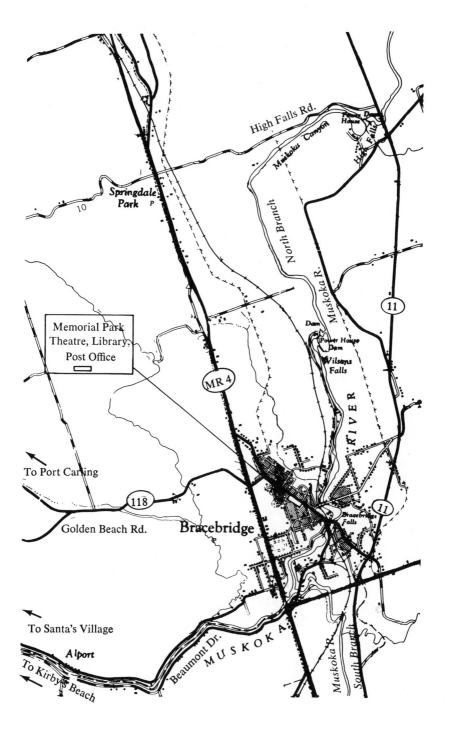

Scale: 1 inch = 0.8 mile

Dorothy Clark McClure, of Aurora and Port Sydney Ontario, who specializes in drawings and paintings of historic homes, buildings, and Muskoka boats, is also displayed. Michael Cleary, Lawrence Nickle and Myron Angus are among the others represented. Myron Angus, born without the use of hands and feet, paints in watercolours and oils by holding the brush in his teeth. His work is admired for its artistic merit, not for its unusual method of production, and he is in demand at centres for handicapped children because his life so clearly demonstrates the possibilities of overcoming handicaps.

Currell's Books and Records next door stocks Muskoka books, pamphlets and maps. Bill Currell has served as President of the Chamber of Commerce. Next to the jewellery and stationery store owned by a member of the prominent Thomas family is Chancery Lane, reminiscent of Chancery Lane in London, England. At the time it was named, lawyers occupied offices and practised their profession behind practically every wall in every building on the hill, this being the District Town.

At the top of Chancery Lane a walk takes you alongside the modern Registry and Land Titles Office and out to Dominion Street. On your right is the Bracebridge Municipal Building; then the Herald Printing Office where the Bracebridge *Herald-Gazette* (distribution 6,000) is published every Thursday morning. The Editor, Robert J. Boyer, was Muskoka's provincial Member of Parliament from 1955 to 1971 and Vice-Chairman of the Hydro-Electric Power Commission of Ontario.

Bus Brazier, who writes a weekly newspaper column on hunting and fishing, is one of Muskoka's best-known personalities. At celebrations and official functions, he plays the role of Chief Mesqua Ukee, after whom Muskoka was named. He is an ardent conservationist and advocate of safety in the woods and on the water. An R.C.A.F. air gunner in World War II, he went overseas and attained the rank of Flying Officer.

On your left, beyond the Registry Office, is the Muskoka District Court House, which has a new wing attached to the original building. Early Muskoka settlers had to travel to Orillia in Simcoe County or Lindsay in Victoria County to settle even minor court actions. In January, 1868, Morrison, Muskoka, Monck, Watt, Humphry, Stephenson, Brunel, Macaulay and Draper townships petitioned the government for a Division Court and Registry Office to be established at Bracebridge, and by June 1869 two buildings for the Registry Office, Court Room, and lock-up were being planned. In spite of various protests in the intervening years, Muskoka did not receive complete jurisdiction for a County Court until 1888.

Along Dominion Street near the river, there's a cosy little bar at the Holiday House, a fine old stone house with modern additions surrounded by beautiful grounds and overlooking Bracebridge Falls.

Back on Manitoba Street, up the hill from the Patterson hotel, is a senior citizens' Drop-In Centre serving 1,200 people. It is open daily for square dancing, woodwork, arts, crafts and games, and some evenings for special activities. (The town's public washroom facilities are located in this building.)

The Chamber of Commerce office is located in the Drop-In Centre, an admirable arrangement because senior citizens provide answering service for the C. of C. telephone. Go there for maps and information about accommodation and activities, such as the annual soapbox derby in October sponsored by the Salvation Army on the Ontario Street hill. Inquire about the summer and winter programs of the Bracebridge Recreation Committee (the Muskoka Shield canoe race from Port Sydney to Bracebridge in June, for instance). Inquire also about the Georgian College Summer School of the Arts courses in Bracebridge, in spinning and dyeing, golf, painting and sketching, hatha yoga and forest ecology.

The Bracebridge library, at the top of the Manitoba Street hill past the post office and Federal Building, exhibits local professional and amateur artists and has special exhibitions from time to time, such as the paintings of Arthur Shilling, an outstanding Indian artist born and raised on Rama Reserve about 15 miles south of Muskoka. The Royal Ontario Museum sends travelling exhibitions, and theatre groups present plays.

Past the library and the movie theatre is Memorial Park with its column in memory of the men of Bracebridge and District who were killed in World Wars I and II and the Korean War. The Royal Canadian Legion Bracebridge Branch No. 161 is responsible for this memorial. It also sponsors the Bracebridge Pipe Band, school children's track and field activities and a social program including shuffleboard and Wednesday night darts. Memorial Park backs on Kimberley Avenue, so named in 1900 in honour of the Relief of Kimberley when the arrival of British reinforcements caused the Boer army to abandon its siege of the diamond-mining town of Kimberley in South Africa.

When Bracebridge celebrated its centenary in 1975, an Ontario historic site plaque describing the founding of Bracebridge was placed in Memorial Park.

Memorial Park is used for various ceremonies and festivities. Santa Claus traditionally distributes colouring books, crayons and candy here the day of the Santa Claus parade, revived after World War II by the Business and Professional Women's Club, passed on to the Lions and then the Kinsmen, and now considered the biggest north of Toronto. The parade floats are entered by businesses and organizations in Bracebridge and nearby communities and prizes are awarded. School bands are big in Muskoka, and they provide the lively music. Opening ceremonies for the Winter Carnival and some of its activities are held here.

The Bracebridge Community Fountain (unveiled July 1970) is one block north on the corner of Manitoba and McMurray Streets. McMurray Street reminds us of Thomas McMurray, his newspaper and business ventures. The land for the fountain was donated by Reginald Kirk, a descendant of Macaulay township pioneers.

The South Muskoka Memorial Hospital is on Ann Street, which runs east off Manitoba Street south of the supermarkets, liquor and beer stores. The South Muskoka Hospital serves the area north of the Soldiers Memorial in Orillia and south of the Huntsville District Memorial Hospital.

The Bracebridge Memorial Community Centre, opened in February 1949 in commemoration of war heroes, is on James Street (east of and parallel to Manitoba Street). At the indoor hockey arena, try the Ladies' Skate and Coffee Break every Thursday morning in winter. The Bracebridge Auto, Boat and Home Show (the 1975 show was the nineteenth) and the Cavalcade of Colour Muskokafest are held here.

Boys' hockey in Muskoka has produced several National Hockey League players. Among these is Irvin "Ace" Bailey, born in Bracebridge 1903, and elected to the Hockey Hall of Fame in 1975. His career with the Toronto Maple Leafs was relatively brief, ending on December 12th, 1933, when he suffered a nearly-fatal fractured skull as a result of a collision during a game in Boston, but he is remembered as an outstanding scorer and a super defensive star. Roger Crozier, a Bracebridge Bantam player in 1955, described as the "Daredevil Goalie" in the book written about him, played for the Buffalo Sabres in the 1974 Stanley Cup finals.

The Muskoka Arts and Crafts large exhibition and sale is held annually in July in Williams Park on the outskirts of town. This show is bursting with new ideas, crafts and talent. Paintings hang from fences, quilts from trees; artists demonstrate their work, some help children try painting, weaving and pottery. Leather, macramé, puppetry, pottery, pets, and revived pioneer skills, all vie for attention. The Ministry of Natural Resources and the Royal Ontario Museum have displays; the Gravenhurst and Bracebridge schools for the retarded exhibit their crafts.

The Victoria Street School in Bracebridge has about twenty-five pupils, ranging in age from five to twenty-one, who are receiving special attention because of retardation, as part of a program to enable mentally handicapped children to live at home and receive teaching at school in self care, home skills, woodworking, crafts, music, and physical education, in addition to as much academic education as they can absorb. The School was started in a church basement by the South Muskoka Association for the Mentally Retarded in the early 1960s, and gradually acquired community funds and grants needed to build.

Jubilee Park occupies the block between Victoria and Wellington Streets—Victoria, of course, named after the British queen; Jubilee Park after her Diamond Jubilee in 1897; and Wellington after the Duke who defeated Napoleon in the battle of Waterloo in 1815. (From Manitoba

Street, take McMurray Street, passing the Bracebridge and Muskoka Lakes Secondary School and the Victoria Street School.)

The Bracebridge Fall Fair, dating from 1867, is held about the middle of September at Jubilee Park. Prizes at the Fair are awarded in a wide range of classifications from grains to gladioli, horses to hens, pickles to portraits. The Bracebridge Agricultural Society includes a Junior Fair within the larger Fair, sponsors the 4-H Club, and invites the public to an annual spring country supper and social evening. Apart from local Fall Fairs run by Agricultural Societies, Muskoka farmers often do well at the Royal Winter Fair in Toronto and are active in such organizations as the Muskoka Soil and Crop Improvement Association.

Annual Kinsmen Victoria Day fireworks have also been held at Jubilee Park. The Rotary Club holds a three-night fair here in early August.

Bracebridge's Centennial Centre, housing an 82' × 42' six-lane swimming pool, a hall large enough to seat 500, and a stage, is in Jubilee Park. Devoid of obstacles such as stairs, which inhibit handicapped persons, the Centre includes specially equipped changerooms and a ramp to allow entrance into the pool by the physically handicapped. Snorkel diving and other programs are available. The $652,000 building was financed by a $250,000 Bracebridge Area Municipality debenture, government grants, $80,000 from three service clubs, and generous donations from business, industry and private citizens. It was "Give a Birthday Present to Bracebridge" time (it's never too late) and, although planning had not begun until mid-1974 and the contract was not awarded until November 23rd, 1974, amazingly the Centre was opened on June 28th, 1975.

Starting a few days earlier, a Bracebridge old-home week drew many celebrants to the high school reunion, Centennial Ball, dances (one with Rudy Meek, champion fiddler), concerts, socials, picnics, barbecues, and a long list of other events including a Dominion Day regatta sponsored by the Bracebridge Power Squadron. (Power Squadrons throughout Muskoka hold classes and Canadian Power Squadron annual examinations.) A Bracebridge Centennial Day was presented at Ontario Place, Toronto, in 1975, with performances by student bands, choirs and thespians.

The bell on St. Thomas Church, on Mary Street (opposite Memorial Park) is the church's third, installed in 1904 in memory of Robert Mortimer Glover Browning, a prominent businessman in Muskoka's lumber industry at the turn of the century. The first two bells broke while sounding alarms in earlier days when the St. Thomas bell served also as a fire bell.

The Pines, Muskoka's home for senior citizens, is on Pine Street, reached from the Highway 118 exit to Highway 11. An auxiliary, aware of the need for the residents to participate in the community, encourages social and cultural activities. As Muskoka has the highest ratio of population over 65 in Canada, partially due to people who leave the District during their working years returning when retired, additional accommodation is being planned.

The District Municipality of Muskoka Administration building, which houses the offices of the District Treasurer, Welfare Administrator, Director of Planning, Engineer and Clerk, is also on Pine Street. The highlight of the official opening on September 23rd, 1972, was the deposit of the colours of the 122nd Muskoka Battalion, handmade by Muskoka ladies for original presentation in 1917. The Battalion under the direction of Colonel D. M. Grant, of Huntsville, sailed for overseas on June 2nd, 1917, with 26 officers and 686 other ranks, and was transferred to the Canadian Forestry Corps shortly after their arrival in England. On Colonel Grant's request, the colours were placed in St. George's Chapel at Windsor Castle, the first from any military unit outside the United Kingdom to receive this honour. When the Battalion returned to Canada the colours were deposited in the Court House, in Bracebridge, the central public building in Muskoka before the opening of the Administration building.

The Society of St. John the Evangelist (Anglican) has a unique institution in the monastery of the Cowley Fathers, founded in 1928 under the direction of Father Roland Palmer. On a 10-acre site off Maple Street in the north-eastern section of Bracebridge, recently affiliated with the St. Leonard's Society (which provides halfway-house services for ex-prisoners and parolees), the Society has had the care of rural Anglican mission churches in Muskoka, attracting many visitors to its Mission House and Collegiate Church.

The John and Margaret Ann Wilson McConnell Memorial Foundation was established by John Wilson McConnell in memory of his Muskoka parents, Monck township pioneers. John Wilson McConnell, the youngest son, became a wealthy Canadian financier and established the fund in 1957 with $500,000, which had increased to approximately $750,000 by 1975. It provides bursaries in Muskoka for high school students, aids residents with heavy expense due to illness, and makes annual grants to charitable organizations and hospitals. A total of $36,900 was distributed in 1974 by the directors.

Recreation Areas

Bowyers Beach Park, where the clean, firm, wave-rippled, sandy bottom of Lake Muskoka slopes gently until deep water is reached, is an excellent playtime beach for children and provides good swimming. Turn left on Highway 118, a few blocks north of Memorial Park. Pass Rainbow Ridge and turn left on Golden Beach Road. In one mile you come to Bangor Lodge where you make a sharp left turn. The property between Bangor and Morrow's Marina is Bowyers Beach Park, site of the 1976 winter carnival Polar Bear dip and dog sled races.

South Muskoka Curling and Golf Club, an 18-hole course surrounding a new residential area, is a short distance to the northeast from Bracebridge's northern supermarkets. Enter off Liddard Street. Inquire about pay-as-you-play golf privilege. The nucleus of the new Curling Club was formed by the members of the former Curling Club on James Street.

High Falls, the highlight of picnic sites around Bracebridge, is 5.2 miles north via Muskoka Road 4, a route I recommend over the prosaic jaunt north on Highway 11. Proceed north on Muskoka Road 4 from the intersection with Highway 118 for 2.6 miles and turn right at the High Falls sign. A roadside park and picnic area on Muskoka Road 4 (with a ¼ mile warning sign) easily identifies the southeast corner of the High Falls road, which winds up hills with a view and down through pleasant valleys. Soon through the trees is a panoramic view of the falls on the Muskoka River, North Branch, where the water drops into that part of the river known as Muskoka Canyon. Cross a little bridge, climb one last long steep hill to the Ministry of Natural Resources headquarters and turn south (right) on Highway 11. A few feet after crossing the highway bridge turn right into High Falls picnic area and park your car near the river or at one of the barbecue locations. Walk on a carpet of pine needles between rock ridges, stand on high rocks and watch the water break over rock shelves in a series of waterfalls. Every season has its reason, as the vacation resort admen say, and it's well worth a special visit to see High Falls when the spring run-off is roaring over the rocks. The Hydro plant and its diverted water is on the north side of the river.

A rock cairn in the park honours Aubrey White (a Companion of the Order of St. Michael and St. George), known as the Father of Forest Protection in Ontario and responsible for the first system of fire ranging in Ontario in 1885. Appointed Assistant Commissioner of Crown Lands in 1887, he continued to serve as Deputy Minister of Lands, Forests and Mines until his death on July 14th, 1915. The plaque on the cairn also notes that Aubrey White came to Muskoka in 1862, worked on the early steamboats and was Crown Lands Agent for Muskoka in 1878.

The Ministry of Natural Resources High Falls Office is responsible for administration of water levels, timber management, fire prevention and protection, and fish and wildlife conservation, stocking and control. Courses and examinations are held in hunter safety, in September and/or October, by appointment. In co-operation with at least nine snowmobile clubs, 250 miles of interconnecting trails have been assembled stretching from Gravenhurst to Huntsville and points east and west (negotiations with some private landowners still pending). It is also conceivable that these trails will be expanded for use by hikers, cross-country skiers and cyclists. Extensions to Orillia and North Bay are being planned, with the Ontario government providing some $30,000 annual maintenance support.

Visit the office or write Box 1138, Bracebridge, to obtain "South Branch Muskoka River Canoe Route", a free folded card which gives portage, water and crown land camping information from Baysville to Bracebridge; ask about any other routes.

Of 227 licensed trappers in the District, about 13 have registered trap-lines on crown land, and the remainder trap mostly on private land with the permission or at the request of the owners. As damage done by Muskoka beavers, estimated to number 11,500, is regarded as serious, area trappers have been warned to fill their quotas or risk losing their licences. When beavers dam up watercourses, flooding the surrounding forest, most trees eventually die because their roots cannot get air, and an unsightly landscape of blackened tree trunks in a swamp results. The harvest of 4,500 beaver pelts should be increased—probably to 7,500—with a corresponding revenue increase. Do not assume that the Ministry does not consider the views of naturalists. It does.

Trapper courses in methods of handling fur to produce a top quality pelt and on humane trapping methods are held periodically. Trappers bring animal pelts to the office once a week to have them stamped and recorded prior to selling. The value of furs taken in the District during the 1973–74 season was estimated at $115,000.

At Cooper's Pond, off the road to Windermere, Ministry personnel have been conducting a duck-banding project for over ten years while baiting the 200-acre pond, controlling predators, and providing nesting boxes for wood ducks because natural cavities are too few. As management of Cooper's Pond continues, it may well become one of the best waterfowl areas in Ontario.

The Bracebridge Resource Management Area, approximately two miles north of the intersection of Highways 11 and 117, is a 1500-acre conservation and study area. It is not intended as an average picnic ground, but there are three nature trails (two of $1\frac{1}{2}$ miles and the third twice as long) with signs marking the highlights. A network of winding roads enables one to drive or snowmobile through the park, but one should first study the area map.

The Georgian College summer course "At Home in the Forest" uses this facility. National Forest Week in May is celebrated with a Sunday (probably Mother's Day) guided tour. Junior Rangers from across Ontario (all aged 17, both girls and boys) work summers in the Resource Area. The Ministry can demonstrate here how to thin trees properly on the request of any property owner.

Forest products have always played an important role in the Muskoka economy. In 1974 there were 30 million board feet of lumber produced in the Bracebridge forest district, as reported in the *Herald-Gazette*, May 8, 1975.

Wilson's Falls are on the Muskoka River, North Branch, above the Bracebridge Falls and below High Falls. To drive there, turn off Manitoba Street at the Patterson Hotel corner in Bracebridge, pass the railway station and stay on River Street (which borders the river closely) right to its end at the power plant at Willson's Falls. The falls are named after the family of Rev. Gilman Willson who settled there in early days. He was operating a little bush store in 1866 and was the licence inspector in 1868 at a remuneration of $5 per annum.

Kirby's Beach is on Lake Muskoka. Start off for Kirby's Beach on Beaumont Road on the south side of the river. Beaumont Road, which begins as a fine residential area with farmland behind and the river in front, leads to Bracebridge Camping and Riding Stables and the Trans-Canada Pipelines Compression Station. A six-mile course behind the Compression Station through some beautiful trails and up and down some interesting hills provides the locale for the Winter Carnival Skokie Loppet, a cross-country ski race. Continue past Stephen's Bay road until on the other side of the river you see Santa's Village; then take next left turn to Kirby's Beach.

Annie Williams Memorial Recreation Park is on the north bank of the river below Bracebridge Falls. It is just past Bracebridge Lumber and may be reached by following the signs to Santa's Village. The park has picnic tables, a barbecue pit and wide-open playing fields. The Muskoka Arts and Crafts Show is held at this park in July. The Bracebridge Lions Club holds an "Annual Steak Bar-B-Q" around August 1st, serving 700 or more steaks and quantities of hot dogs to a capacity crowd. Funds are raised in this way for new park equipment and maintenance since the Lions Club is a co-sponsor of the park with the trustees of the Williams Estate, the Rotary and Kinsmen Clubs of Bracebridge, and the Town of Bracebridge.

Dr. James Francis Williams (1859–1926) moved to Bracebridge with his wife, Gertrude Annie Williams, in the 1890s, set up medical practice, served as Magistrate for some years, and provided the memorial park in his will. In a rectangular plot enclosed within an ornamental iron fence and shaded by trees, one large stone marks the graves of Dr. and Mrs. Williams and their only child, a son who died at the age of one.

Apart from the Memorial Park, Dr. Williams is notable in local history for planting thousands of red pine seedlings on a 300-acre site in Oakley township in co-operation with the Ontario Forestry Branch, now the Ministry of Natural Resources, when he was well past age 65. "Who else, other than a completely unselfish man, will plant a crop which takes 80 to 100 years to mature, and whose maturity he will never live to see?", wrote one journalist. Logs harvested in this plantation in late 1973 caused a sensation. Only 50 years old, measurements indicated that one was 85 feet high and 16 inches in diameter at chest height. According to experts in the Ministry of Natural Resources, this tree should have been at least 95 years old, or nearly double its age.

Also benefitting from a trust set up by Dr. Williams's will are Muskoka residents with cancer or tuberculosis who are being treated in their homes. In 1974, 19 such persons received assistance totalling $12,460.

Santa's Village, the children's delight, began operations in 1956 and is about $3\frac{1}{2}$ miles down the river from Bracebridge on the north side. As the 45th Parallel of Latitude runs through this area, it is imaginatively described as being "halfway to the north pole". The attractions include Santa himself, toy shops where Santa's elves and gnomes are at work,

Bracebridge, sketched by Seymour Penson.

Santa's Village.

Port Carling Road, looking towards Beaumaris, c. 1905.

ferris wheel, merry-go-round, boat rides, a covered wagon ride, a train ride on the Candy Cane express, a free Moon Walk and playgrounds in the Enchanted Forest. Goats, rabbits, ducks, deer, chicken and sheep inhabit the village in suitable enclosures, some illustrating nursery rhymes. Take your lunch-basket and enjoy a picnic in Santa's Picnic Grounds beside the river or go unencumbered and purchase refreshments at Alice's Tea Room or the Railway Lunch. Older children and conservationists will be interested in the erosion control methods taken on the river bank. Open daily from about June 16th, 10:00 a.m. to 6:00 p.m., admission is $1.50 per adult and 25¢ per child under 12; season tickets and special group rates are available. Public school week in June 1975 brought close to 2,000 children and their teachers.

Bracebridge Boat Cruise

The M.V. *Mildred* offers regularly-scheduled trips from Bracebridge dock, a pleasant excursion on a summer's day. A cruise on this boat takes you down the Muskoka River, North Branch, past where the South Branch joins it, past Santa's Village and around the bend of the Devil's Elbow.

The river divides and empties into Lake Muskoka in two channels. This was a convenience in logging days when the main channel would sometimes be clogged with logs; then boats could take the "Cut", later called the Patterson-Kaye channel when the lodge by that name was built in 1936 by William J. Patterson, his wife Mabel Kaye and her sister Phyllis Kaye. The Kayes were Monck township residents, whereas Patterson had been born in the United States, and he and his wife lived in Detroit until their interest in the summer resort business led to the lodge. Since 1960 it has been owned by Frank Miller (M.P.P., Muskoka), who is also President of Santa's Village. Ross Miller, Frank's son, bought the 235-acre pioneer Fitzmaurice farm near Bracebridge in 1973 and intends to make farming his career. This gives the family an interest in three different sectors of Muskoka's livelihood and produces an alert M.P.P., who became Minister of Health in 1974.

Travelling northerly on Lake Muskoka towards Beaumaris, you soon come to the famous "Millionaires' Row", and here on the mainland and islands are fabulous summer homes, sometimes called "Little Pittsburgh" because many of the early moneyed people who built mansions here were from that city in Pennsylvania. Sumptuous yachts may be seen on the waters and in boathouses, and the buildings are surrounded with masses of flowers and landscaped grounds.

Some of the islands have interesting characteristics—a profile of an Indian on the rock at the end of Idlewylde Island, and the shape of an island called "Flower Pot". The tremendous rock cliffs that form the shores of the lake and the peaks that rose up in its midst to become islands were formed when volcanic action threw up part of the Laurentian Shield.

On the way back to Bracebridge, you pass one of the oldest summer homes in the area, built by the Bird family, owners of the early woollen mill. Henry J. Bird, son of the founder, was Mayor of Bracebridge in 1922, held high offices in the Masonic Order and Rotary Club and was a strong supporter and officer of the Bracebridge (later South Muskoka) Memorial Hospital from the time it was instituted in 1928 until his death in 1949. One daughter of H. J. Bird, almost 100 years old, is in the Pines, Bracebridge, and one of two surviving grandsons rents the cottage. Gil Scott writes, "the family is anxious to drum up interest in the house as they are worried about its future."

Fraserburg Road (*Muskoka Road 14*)

Muskoka Road 14 (Fraserburg 9 miles) runs east off Highway 11B about 1,000 feet north of the Bracebridge business section entrance. It takes cottagers east to McKay, Healey and North Healey Lakes, goes through Fraserburg and ends at Pine Lake. The Fraserburg community was named after the pioneer family of W. C. and Isabelle Fraser. Other early family names are inscribed on tombstones in the well-kept cemetery at the United Church.

"I came here in 1954, after 37 years with the C.N.R., to get away from traffic lights and No U Turns to fresh air and clear water," George Allen, Fraserburg storekeeper, recalled twenty years later. "The settlers left when they couldn't make a living after the pine was cut, many of them for Western Canada. This land was only good for hay or oats. Spring frosts come very late. When I first came I tried to garden, but my asparagus was frozen three times before I got a cutting, and I've had strawberries frozen solid."

A poem which Mrs. Allen salvaged from old records at the Fraserburg post office ends:

> There's a bridge across a river
> On which to muse and dream—
> In the shadow of the moonlight,
> At Fraserburg, all serene.

"This was obviously written by a tourist," George Allen said. "I can't see a disillusioned farmer musing and dreaming on the bridge."

Big Canoe, a United Church camp nearby on the Muskoka River, South Branch, accommodates about 90 young campers from Markham, Richmond Hill and Thornhill.

The McVittie Red Pine Plantation near Fraserburg is expected to provide the best Red Pine in the province. John Phillips McVittie, of Bracebridge, purchased the plantation in 1945 from the estate of Dr. J. F. Williams. As well as carefully preserving the Williams plantings, Jack McVittie has planted more than 250,000 trees in the townships of Stephenson, Macaulay, McLean, Draper and Muskoka.

VII *PORT CARLING*

BRACEBRIDGE TO PORT CARLING

Turn left off Manitoba Street at the northern end of Bracebridge for the 15-mile scenic drive to Port Carling along Highway 118. Rainbow Ridge ski area, one mile along, has an annual snowfall of over 350 cm plus equipment for making artificial snow, lighting for night skiing, T-bar and rope tows. The Bracebridge Ski Club and four nearby public schools use it for their skiing program—one of the advantages enjoyed by children attending school in Muskoka.

After dropping from the Bracebridge and Rainbow Ridge altitudes, the highway begins to run along Lake Muskoka's eastern shore, and roads branching off to the left lead to lakeside resorts. Tamwood Lodge, on Highway 118 six miles out of Bracebridge, open all year, is a fine example of an exceptionally large building made of local logs. It has a heated pool. Aston Fairways 9-hole course across the road offers good golfing terrain and in the fall presents a splendour of colour that I often recall with particular pleasure. Beside Aston Villa, one of the chain of Grisé resorts, the highway climbs a hill to give a stunning view of Lake Muskoka.

Roads in to Leonard Lake now appear on your right. Leonard Lake, about 1½ miles in length and 1 mile at its widest, stands alone on an altitude about 100 feet higher than Lake Muskoka. Its shores and islands dotted with private cottages and several cottage resorts, like many other small Muskoka lakes it offers excellent swimming and canoeing and colourful sunrises and sunsets. Because it is small, Leonard Lake is one of the first to freeze in winter and is popular with ice fishermen eager to get a fish hut on a lake.

The road to Beaumaris goes off Highway 118 to the left, crossing a bridge to Tondern Island where Edward Prowse built Beaumaris Hotel in the 1890s (destroyed by fire July 1945). Edward Prowse is also credited with laying out the first Muskoka golf course in 1879. The Beaumaris road passes the 18-hole golf course ending at the Beaumaris Boat House and the large government dock originally built for steamers. Nearby on the shores and islands are the vacation estates which gave this section of Lake Muskoka the name of "Millionaires' Row". (Many of these summer homes may be seen on the *Mildred* cruise out of Bracebridge.) The Muskoka Lakes Association Junior Sailing Program conducts a course at the Beaumaris Yacht Club.

While you are on the Beaumaris road, look for Francis Fowler's two

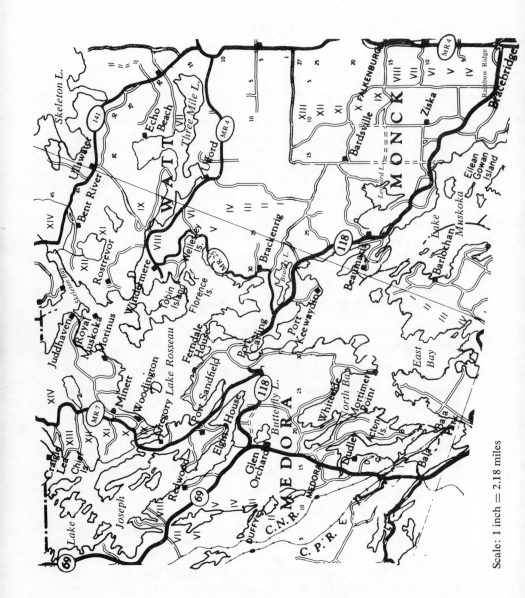

Scale: 1 inch = 2.18 miles

Steam yachts at Beaumaris dock, c. 1905.

Canoeist beside the 11-acre Cinderwood Island, the summer home of Ruth and Carl Borntraeger. He had camped on it, named it Cinderwood because it had been burnt over, and arranged its purchase in 1896 before he was 21. Cinderwood was sold in 1969 after Mr. Borntraeger's death. The Borntraegers were noted for their generous support of the Bracebridge hospital and other community activities.

The *Ida II,* owned by the Borntraegers of Pittsburgh, Pa., c. 1905.

boathouses made from the hull of the *Newminko*, a supplyboat which used to be operated by William Hanna, of Port Carling. Fowler turned the hull upside down, cut it in two and added some shingles to make what could be called real "boat" houses.

Now bypassed by Highway 118, the community of Milford Bay is on the mainland opposite the northerly part of Tondern Island. Former professional hockey player, Gordon Reid, bought the Milford Manor resort and started expanding it in the 1940s to accommodate 300 guests. "A resort for the young at heart", it has two- and three-bedroom cottages, swimming pool, golf, tennis, evening adult entertainment and enough activities to keep children happily occupied. Roseneath Manor in Milford Bay (which has one of Muskoka's night spots for dinner, music, dancing, entertainment) was proud to be chosen as the location of a recent Ontario Association of Telephone Distress Centres symposium. Library, bingo and other activities are held at the Community Hall. Milford Bay firemen hold an annual pancake and maple syrup weekend in April. The Milford Bay Snow Bombers, a snowmobile club, and the Winter Carnival Committee keep things humming in the winter.

At about mile 10 from Bracebridge, as you bypass Milford Bay, Highway 118 passes through the Huckleberry Rock Cut, 4/10 mile long, with walls up to 40 feet high. When the road builders began their dynamite blasting into the granite ridge in 1962, the natural sculpture of the inner rock was revealed in its primitive splendour, a vibrant pink in colour. Dorothy Duke, of Port Carling, expressed a common reaction to the beauty of the completed cut when she said, "The first time we drove through those walls on the newly-laid highway I wanted to stop the car, jump up on the hood and sing 'O Canada' at the top of my voice."

When you emerge from the Huckleberry Cut, look to the left for another view of Lake Muskoka. At the bottom of the hill is a park where you can picnic on the shore and go swimming.

PORT CARLING TODAY

Past Brandy Lake and Muskoka Road 25 (a very good road to Windermere) both on your right, you reach the outskirts of Port Carling, population 600 or thereabouts, at mile 15. Highway 118 continues through Port Carling as Joseph Street.

Soon a road on your right leads into Silver Lake, only a block away. In the cemetery on the left-hand side of Joseph Street, you may see tombstones of some of the early people mentioned later in this chapter and one in remembrance of a son who died in 1892, which is touchingly inscribed:

> How short is life: how shure is death.
> Our days alas: how few.
> This mortal life is but a breath,
> 'Tis like the morning dew.

Charles S. Smith, Walker's Point

A steam automobile driven from Pennsylvania to Muskoka c. 1905.

Ontario Ministry of Industry and Tourism

Huckleberry Cut.

The curling club off Joseph Street accommodates the annual Hobby and Craft show early in August. The Municipal Office, formerly the elementary school until the building of a central school at Glen Orchard, marks the corner of Bailey Street, named after the family who originally owned most of the village site. The village dock at the end of Bailey Street on the Indian River is the location for Red Cross swimming classes in July and August. Beside the dock is Hanna Memorial Park, named after William Hanna, who came to Port Carling in 1881 to operate a general store, served as postmaster for 25 years, and was village reeve for several years.

Because the Indian River flows out of Lake Rosseau on the north and winds through Port Carling towards Lake Muskoka on the south, Port Carling, known as the Hub of the Muskoka Lakes, is almost surrounded by water which sparkles on sunny days and gives an "Island-in-the-Sun" feeling in summer.

Muskoka people had to think big to push for the two new hockey arenas, one of which is at Port Carling—opened in January 1974—on Bailey Street. (The other is at Bala.) Township debentures for $125,000 provided the basic financing of the Port Carling arena, and the provincial government granted $10,000, leaving about $90,000 to be raised locally. The Port Carling Lions Club pledged $15,000 and the members' wives helped to raise the money. In addition to hockey league activity, the new arena provides headquarters for the annual Winter Carnival in February, the figure-skating club (four hours' instruction every Saturday morning), and roller skating when the ice is out (rental skates available). The arena is also used for such activities as the Lions Club carnival—two big nights of fun at the beginning of August—and the Legion giant flea market later that month.

The Memorial Community Centre, on Joseph Street past Bailey, contains an auditorium used for the summer theatre (now under the aegis of the Muskoka Foundation for the Arts) which traditionally attracts people in boats and cars from all over the lake district. The Centre also accommodates such activities as the annual Thanksgiving dinner organized by the Lions, assisted by the Port Carling Women's Institute and many other community women, and attended by about 700 cottagers and residents; a Lions Millionaires' Night (tickets $25.00); and a New Year's Eve Ball sponsored by the local fire department.

The Public Library in the Community Centre is an expanding resource centre with current periodicals and a variety of records and films, and rotates books with its branches at Windermere, Bala, the Peninsula and Milford Bay. Check for hours of operation.

The post office and John Rennie's art gallery are on the other side of Joseph Street. John Rennie, a scholarship student at the Ontario College of Art who studied later at the Art Students' League in New York and then in Mexico, has exhibited widely. Several large canvasses by him depicting Royal Canadian Engineers in action, commissioned during

World War II, hang in the Engineers' Headquarters in Chiliwack, British Columbia. Many of his wild flower studies have been used by the Audubon society, and one hangs in Ontario House in London, England—trilliums, Ontario's floral emblem, naturally. John Rennie shows works of many accomplished artists, in addition to his own. A New York gallery handles many of Rennie's abstract and non-objective pieces. The Rennies stay in Port Carling for the summer and autumn until Thanksgiving, then head south for a winter of painting and sightseeing.

The Village Place nearby is new and outstanding, a showcase of enchanting French patio and high-style imported furniture, some antiques (Canadian pine is favoured), watercolours, acrylics, prints, carvings, terra cotta figures, pottery, bronze bird forms, maple products, herbs, Muskoka books, and numerous other items.

Joseph Street goes downhill and crosses the Indian River and Port Carling lock on a two-lane bridge, a million-dollar project begun in 1973 to replace the traffic-congesting one-lane swinging bridge which has been part of the Port Carling scene since the first lock in 1871. Nearby on the river, the Duke Boatworks, operated by descendants of one of the early families of Muskoka boat builders, builds a variety of pleasure craft, restores antique boats, and carries on a boat-servicing and supply business. The firm manufactured 27-foot motor cutters and small craft for the Navy in World War II.

The former Tourist Information Centre office was demolished in the new bridge construction; inquire about its new location. More Port Carling shops line the steep hill rising on the other side of the river. The Muskoka Homecrafts shop, supplied by local artisans, is at the Cavers Inn.

Turn left at the top of the hill along Medora Street (leading to Port Sandfield, Bala and MacTier) to find the liquor store and the exclusive sports wear shop founded by Canada's famous golfer, Ada MacKenzie, a Muskoka habitué, who died in 1973. If you are shopping for woollens and sport clothes, don't overlook Mildred Wright's near the post office.

Snowmobilers might inquire about the Port Carling Snow Drifters Club which supervises the maintenance of over 50 miles of trail created with the help of a federal government local initiative grant.

Port Carling, unlike Gravenhurst, Bala, Bracebridge and Huntsville, has never been served by railroad. The early steamboats provided the link with the railroad, and now good roads, trucks, and cars obviate the necessity.

There are two locks on the Indian River in the Port Carling business section, one for large boats and one for small boats, which permit passage between Lake Rosseau (742.5 feet above sea level) and Lake Muskoka (739 feet above sea level). The large lock was originally constructed between 1869 and 1871 in a channel excavated for the purpose, which created an island between the lock and the semi-circular course of

In the Port Carling Pioneer Museum.

Antique boat show in Port Carling Lock, 1973.

the river. Enlarged in 1902, rebuilt in 1922, it was reconstructed in 1953.

The smaller lock, first installed in 1921, replaced in 1940, and rebuilt and mechanized in 1963, is on the original river course beside the dam controlling water levels. Before mechanization, small boys hung around this lock to turn the wheels which opened and closed the gates and then dived happily into the water for the coins which were tossed in appreciation. Great was the rejoicing, for everyone but the boys, when the mechanization afforded faster locking.

The plaque near the locks, unveiled on September 26th, 1956, and the first erected under the authority of the Ontario Archaeological and Historic Sites Advisory Board, notes that the village was named in 1869 and incorporated as a village in 1896.

While in this vicinity, stroll up the hill in the island park beside the locks to visit the Port Carling Pioneer Museum, open during July and August from 11:00 a.m. to 5:00 p.m. and 7:00 to 9:00 daily, and from 2:00 to 5:00 p.m. on Sunday. (Inquire about June and September hours.) Port Carling residents joined forces with many in the summer colony to make the collection which is displayed in the museum. The building was a Canadian Centennial project, opened July 2, 1967. The Ontario government gave a 99-year land lease (for the token fee of $1.00) on the island park; the federal and provincial governments made grants of money—the federal also promised an annual maintenance grant of $600; and Watt and Medora townships turned over their Centennial grants. Port Carling contributed its $1,058 Centennial grant, matched it with $1,058 and added $2,500, and the Directors of the Museum Board set about raising the considerable balance from private sources. The building's inscription reads: "To honour the settlers who cleared the forest with their axes and with their hoes planted the seed of Canada's future greatness."

In 1974 the Catto Wing was added, honouring two summer residents, Lieutenant-Colonel and Mrs. Douglas E. Catto, for their deep involvement in the historical society and the building of the museum. Douglas Catto (1899–1973) went overseas as a gunner in 1916, graduated from university with a degree in architecture after his return, and later designed many famous buildings including Sunnybrook Hospital in Toronto. During World War II Lieutenant-Colonel Catto went overseas with the Royal Regiment of Canada and was its commanding officer at the time the unit took part in the disastrous raid on Dieppe, where he was taken prisoner. He was a past-Commodore and Honorary President of the Muskoka Lakes Association and had served as a director of the South Muskoka Memorial Hospital.

Hand-hewn pioneer furniture is arranged in room groupings, contrasting with family heirlooms of fine china and beautiful silver brought from the places of the settlers' origins. There are mementos of early tourist days and a patchwork quilt made by Rosseau village ladies about 1900 from hundreds of small diamond-shaped patches, each embroidered with the name of a member of the community. A collection of photographs, trophies and models belonging to Harold Wilson, the speed boat racer, and a boat with the disappearing propellor invented by W. J. Johnston, Jr., of Port Carling, are displayed in the Catto wing. In 1976, a second wing will be added to the museum.

Among the numerous Muskoka people who through the years have made interesting and outstanding careers in the larger world, several Port Carling examples come readily to mind. James Karl Bartleman, who attended the now-closed Port Carling Public and Continuation School for 12 years, is remembered as a brilliant student. He was Acting High Commissioner in Bangladesh from August 1972 when he was 32 years old. In his career with the Department of External Affairs, he has also served at the United Nations and in Bogota, Bangkok, and Brussels.

Bernard A. Ennis, General Manager, Administration, Bank of Nova Scotia, born in Port Carling and educated in Muskoka schools, joined the staff of the Bank of Nova Scotia at Port Carling when he was 19. In 1966 he became the bank's chief accountant at the age of 32, then the youngest man ever to hold this position for any chartered bank in Canada. Bernie Ennis is also an active outdoorsman, whose activities include flying, boating, fishing, golfing, snowmobiling: "a natural instinct for anyone born and raised in the Muskoka area," he remarks.

Dr. Douglas E. Cannell was born in Gravenhurst 1902 and shortly thereafter moved to Port Carling with his parents. He attended Port Carling and Gravenhurst schools, then Oakwood Collegiate, Toronto, and the University of Toronto, and served in the Royal Canadian Army Medical Corps from 1939 to 1943. During a distinguished career, he was Professor of Obstetrics and Gynaecology at the U. of T. from 1950 to 1965 and since then has been Medical Director of the Ontario Cancer Treatment and Research Foundation. In May 1973 the U. of T. conferred upon him an honorary degree of Doctor of Laws. He spent vacations at Port Carling during his school years and continues to summer in the village.

PORT CARLING HISTORY

Before the township of Medora was surveyed and opened for settlement by the white man, the Indian village of Obogawanung lay within the present bounds of Port Carling. In the early 1860s it consisted of some twenty log huts on the Indian River and nearby Silver Lake with a good deal of cleared land where the Indians grew potatoes, corn and other vegetables. They had no domestic animals but dogs and no boats but numerous birch-bark canoes. Musquedo, the 80-year old Medicine Man of the village, wore a silver medal conferred upon him for bravery by the British at the battle of Queenston Heights in 1812. The Indians were squatting on land to which their title had been signed away by treaty, and they were moved to Parry Island on Georgian Bay with the coming of the settlers, but Indians have come back sporadically to summer houses on the river bank at Port Carling to sell their handicrafts.

In 1865 a trading post was established at Obogawanung (which became known as Indian Village) near the present Port Carling locks by Donald Cockburn, a relative of the lumbering and steamship Cockburns. When the lock was completed in 1871, he became its first lockmaster.

The part-Indian and part-French Bailey brothers, Alexander and Michael, are believed to have been the first settlers in the Port Carling area, arriving in 1865. Alexander came from Penetanguishene, had engaged in fur trading in Muskoka, and had operated a trading post, store, sawmill and gristmill at Bracebridge. Most of the land of the village of Port Carling, as incorporated in 1896, was originally owned by the Bailey brothers. The George Bailey who became a Captain for the Muskoka Navigation Company was a son of Alexander.

Benjamin Hardcastle Johnston, with his four sons, came to Muskoka from London, Ontario, in 1866, settled originally near Windermere, and subsequently built a house at Indian Village beside the rapids on the river. This house became the first post office when Mr. Johnston was appointed the first postmaster, a position he filled for almost 30 years.

Realizing the importance of having a canal dredged to connect Lakes Rosseau and Muskoka with a lock to raise and lower passenger and freight boats, Ben Johnston obtained the signatures of the settlers around the lakes on a petition and took it to the provincial government at Toronto. Some of the Members laughed at the idea of undertaking such a venture to connect "two frog ponds". But A .P. Cockburn, the man who owned and operated the steamship *Wenonah* out of Gravenhurst, was the Federal Member for Muskoka and Parry Sound, and he proved to be a powerful ally, especially as navigation aids had been promised to him in 1865. The building of the lock was started in 1869, but was not completed until almost the end of the navigation season in 1871.

When Mr. Johnston was asked to name the village, he called it Port Carling after his friend John Carling (later Sir John), Ontario's first Minister of Public Works and Agriculture, who was on a fishing trip in the village at the time. So Port Carling, until quite recently a "dry" village by "local option" (which meant you couldn't buy liquor either by bottle or glass), was named after a rich and powerful brewer.

Mr. and Mrs. James Martin Tobin came to Muskoka with their four sons and six daughters from Glengarry, Ontario, in 1867, and settled on a large island in Lake Rosseau north of Port Carling which became known as Tobin Island. Until their own log house was built, the Tobin family lived in a couple of log cabins left by the lumbermen who had taken off the pine. Two more sons were born on the island. The Tobins owned the first cow and the first team of horses in the area and built one of the first summer resorts, calling it Oaklands Park. Each year they cultivated more land and grew more garden produce to supply the tourists who were building summer houses nearby. Mr. Tobin lived to be 82 years of age and Mrs. Tobin to be 78, and they left many descendants.

Tobin Island is familiar to those who remember Wigwassan Lodge, perhaps as summer visitors. When Wigwassan grew old and in need of large capital expenditure, the large property was sold and the buildings were demolished.

Penson, Adams and Rogers

Richard George Penson of London, a lithographer and well-educated man, accompanied by his wife and seven children, set out from England in May 1869 for Muskoka. On board ship the Pensons met Captain Adams, of Whitstable, England, with his wife and four children, who were also emigrating to Muskoka.

The Pensons and Adams made their way to Washago, where the women and children were left while the men went on to Bracebridge to locate land. As all accommodation had been occupied by the rush of immigrants, Captain Adams and Richard and Seymour Penson slept on the floor of the hotel. After they learned the location of available land, they went back to Washago and brought their families to Bracebridge. Because they were still unable to get accommodation in Bracebridge, they took all their possessions down the river to a deserted lumber camp and made themselves surprisingly comfortable alone in the woods.

Medora Township had been surveyed the year before and Penson and Adams set off to locate their land near the Indian Village (now in Port Carling) by following the surveyors' stakes. After erecting two hemlock tents for shelter, they returned to the lumber camp for their families. All boarded the *Wenonah* at Bracebridge, travelled down river to Lake Muskoka, up Lake Muskoka and the Indian River, and disembarked near the Indian Village. On the other side of the rapids (now the site of the small boats lock), they transferred to a large rowboat available for passenger and freight service on Lake Rosseau and landed at the Adams' location.

On the south shore of Lake Rosseau, just west of the head of the Indian River, is Adams Bay, named for the Adams family who settled on the land surrounding it. The Pensons settled on adjoining lots to the west of the Adamses on the bay they named Ferndale Bay. When 17-year-old Seymour R. G. Penson started to chop down trees for a log house, one of the Tobins came over from Tobin Island and said that he should "get a bee". Seymour had never heard of a "bee", but Tobin arranged one and the men of the community quickly put up a house.

Seymour continued to help his family, walking to Orillia once, for instance, to drive back two cows. Later, in an effort to find a way to earn more money, he walked right down to the Michigan woods but took ill with "malaria" and had to return penniless.

Two more children were born to his father and mother in Muskoka, the first of whom was Herbert, on Christmas day of 1869. Herbert, who died in infancy, was the first child born to settlers in the area. Mrs. Penson was pregnant when she left England in May with seven children to take up life in the backwoods, yet she is remembered as being cheerful and loving Muskoka. The ninth and last child, a son Harold, was born in March 1872.

Seymour Penson, who had served an apprenticeship in England to a lithographic artist, illustrated the *Guide Book and Atlas of the Muskoka and Parry Sound Districts* (1878), which John Rogers had induced the publishing company of H. R. Page, Chicago, to finance. Penson's 24 drawings in the *Atlas*, splendid examples of lithographic art of the time, depict lake scenes and waterfalls, the old steamer *Nipissing,* farms, houses and villages.

John Rogers (1846–1926) was born in Derbyshire, England, the oldest of a family of four. He worked for a railway briefly and then studied law for three years before deciding that this career did not appeal to him. A London firm which manufactured diving and condensing machinery sent him to Aden in Arabia where he was placed in charge of a sea-water distilling plant, at that time the largest of its kind in the world. He was sent to the east coast of Africa to manage the distilling apparatus which supplied drinking water for the British during the Abyssinian Expedition. This expedition disembarked in January 1868 and advanced into the interior to attack Theodore II, crowned ruler of Ethiopia who had stubbornly refused to liberate the British envoy, C. D. Cameron, imprisoned with some other British subjects and European missionaries, after having falsely accused Cameron of participation in a supposed Egyptian plot to overthrow him.

Next, John Rogers spent 94 days on an old clipper ship sailing to South America, and he then sailed from Peru to Antwerp (a 122-day trip) on another vessel as its engineer. He returned to London in August 1870.

The following spring John Rogers left for Canada with the intention of settling down in Hamilton, but on the way over he met a young couple who had recently settled in Muskoka. They gave him such glowing accounts of their new home that he changed his original plan and went with them to Gravenhurst. They took the boat to Port Carling and went to the young couple's farm on the Joseph River via the new cut at Port Sandfield (which had not yet been cribbed in). Rogers stayed with them for a year and a half, felling trees, burning timber and clearing land. Then he left for Toronto (where he met the Cox family, as related in the Port Sandfield story) and worked for a wholesale book firm.

In 1878 Rogers was back in Muskoka to work on the *Guide Book and Atlas.* He was to do the mapping and was also responsible for selling the finished product. Before Rogers had finished the mapping, he had walked every road between the Severn River and Lake Nipissing, checking existing maps and correcting errors. Penson joined him in July. Some days they walked 40 miles; some days they paddled that distance or more in their birch-bark canoe. The 10″ × 12″ *Atlas* contains a full-page map of each of the townships of Muskoka and Parry Sound with the names of all the landowners marked on their respective lots. W. E. Hamilton, the Emigration Agent at Bracebridge, wrote the territorial description for the *Atlas*, giving many details to inform intending settlers and sportsmen. When a limited edition of 1500 copies of the *Atlas* was reprinted in 1971, you had to move quickly if you wanted a copy.

Soon after the completion of the *Atlas*, John Rogers married a daughter of Enoch Cox of Port Sandfield and settled down at Hemlock Point on Lake Joseph. He owned and operated several boats and then built a larger one, the *Edith May*, named in honour of his wife, which he ran for 10 years as a supply boat for a Rosseau firm. Then he purchased the *Flyer*, a steam yacht—said to be the fastest of its day on the lakes —which he ran as a passenger boat. During these years he prepared a directory of the lakes with maps on which he marked accurately every known shoal.

R. G. Penson (Seymour's father), seeing that the summer resort business offered opportunity, built the first Ferndale House in 1879. The following is an extract from an advertisement for this resort in the *Canadian Summer Resort Guide*, published in Toronto, in June 1894:

> The Ferndale House stands on a high bluff and the grounds are well shaded. There is accommodation in the house and the cottages near by for seventy or eighty people. From the summer cottages on the high cliffs very extended and pleasing vistas are to be seen. The farm in connection with the hotel supplies fresh milk and eggs, vegetables and small fruits. There is a fine spring of pure ice cold water. The grounds are well laid out and there are many charming walks near by. There is also a good boathouse and a plentiful supply of boats. . . .
>
> Deer and bear hunting and partridge and duck shooting are also to be had in the fall. There is a cluster of thirteen islands around Ferndale and the cottagers on these islands add considerably to the life and gaiety in the hotel attending the semi-weekly hops.

After the production of the *Atlas*, Seymour Penson became a scenic designer and artist for two Toronto theatres. This work developed into a position with Hand and Teale, the fireworks company which staged pageants at fairs and historical celebrations in Canada and the United States. Seymour Penson designed and executed the scenery for such entertainments (including the Canadian National Exhibition in Toronto for almost 40 years) where fireworks would climax the presentation of, for example, a historical drama about a city under seige.

Concurrently, he took over the Muskoka hotel business from his father in 1895, replacing the first hotel with a new one in 1899. Most of the property originally owned by the Pensons now belongs to the Canadian Keswick Conference, an interdenominational religious organization, which accommodates both ordinary vacationers and religious conferences.

To reach Ferndale Bay today, make a right turn off Medora Street to Ferndale Road and follow it to the site of the Canadian Keswick Conference and resort complex.

Elizabeth Penson, eldest daughter of Seymour, was a loved and respected member of the Port Carling community, especially after her retirement. She began her teaching career at 18 in Port Carling, obtained an M.A. degree at Queen's University, taught at Orillia and later at Georgetown for more than 20 years. She died in 1974 in her 90th year.

The Early Steamboats

When the Port Carling locks were started in 1869, settlement was growing, an American William H. Pratt was planning to build a large hotel at the top of Lake Rosseau, and A. P. Cockburn wanted to get a steamer on Lake Rosseau without delay. He could not wait for the completion of the locks that would join Lake Rosseau with Lake Muskoka; so he went to Belle Ewart on Lake Simcoe and purchased the *Dean*, a much smaller steamer than the 85-foot *Wenonah*. Cockburn had it brought up from Lake Simcoe to Gravenhurst by sleighs during the winter's snow, no small accomplishment on the Muskoka Road of 1870. He renamed it the *Wabamik*—the Indian name for white beaver—and sent it up Lake Muskoka and the Indian River to the rapids at Port Carling. All the available men in the area formed a bee to warp the *Wabamik* up the rapids so that it could ply Lake Rosseau for the 1870 season.

Cockburn then planned to build a new and larger steamer in anticipation of completion of the locks. The new 123-foot steamer, the side-wheeler *Nipissing*, was built on Muskoka Bay at a cost of nearly $20,000. Decorated with a gold beaver on the cupola-shaped roof of the wheel house and a gold sunburst on each paddle, she was launched on Lake Muskoka for the opening of navigation in 1871, but the locks were still not completed. As "the lock construction was still dragging wearily on," to use A. P. Cockburn's words, he once more had a steamer warped up the rapids of the Indian River, this time the *Wenonah*. The locks were completed just before the end of navigation in 1871, barely in time to bring the pioneer *Wenonah* down through them to winter quarters at Gravenhurst. The cut at Port Sandfield between Lakes Rosseau and Joseph was completed by this time.

When the *Wenonah* was about 20 years old, A. P. Cockburn transferred her machinery to a new boat, also called the *Wenonah*. According

The *Nipissing I* in Port Carling Lock, c. 1873.

The Snider Lumber Co. tug *Rosseau,* c. 1905.

World War I troops on Port Carling dock.

Building a new lock at Port Carling, 1922.

STRATTON AND PORT CARLING HOUSE—PORT CARLING, MUSKOKA.

Stratton House (burned in 1912) and Port Carling House, both owned by Mr. and Mrs. George Cannell.

to Professor J. Roy Cockburn (until his retirement in 1950, the Head of the Department of Engineering Drawing at the University of Toronto), the new *Wenonah* was the only boat of its kind on the continent that was propelled by both paddles and screw. It worked as a freight and passenger steamer on the Magnetawan River in the Parry Sound District, where its special design enabled it to make the tight turn at Fiddler's Elbow.

The first *Nipissing* burned at Port Cockburn in 1885. "I thought it was the end of the world when my sisters told me the *Nipissing* had burned," Professor Cockburn recalled. Although only seven years old at the time, he had been closely involved with his father's boats, and travelled in the engine room or the pilot house.

This *Nipissing* had carried the vice-regal parties of Lord and Lady Dufferin in 1874 and Lord and Lady Lansdowne in 1885 on their trips through the Muskoka Lakes. Lord Lansdowne instructed his Aide to write "that he could not have seen that beautiful region under pleasanter conditions."

The new *Nipissing* had a metal hull made in Scotland on Clyde Bank. The wheelhouse roof was decorated with a phoenix, carved by George Bailey. When the *Nipissing* was rebuilt in 1925 and re-named the *Segwun*, the phoenix was transferred to the wheelhouse roof on the *Sagamo*, when it was being rebuilt after a fire. The phoenix itself was finally destroyed by fire in January 1969 when the *Sagamo* burned down to its steel hull at Gravenhurst.

Sarah McCulley Brady (1861—1958)

When Mrs. William Brady was a fragile 94 and the oldest resident of Port Carling, she had clear memories of early days but explained that she had not suffered the hardships of isolation in the wilderness. She had arrived ten years after the first settlers, and by this time the railway had reached Gravenhurst and the navigation company was operating regularly scheduled boats through the Muskoka Lakes.

At the age of 15, Mrs. Brady (born Sarah English McCulley) came to Port Carling with her father and mother, Mr. and Mrs. Charles McCulley. Originally from Ireland, they had been living in Moorefield, Ontario, about 30 miles northwest of Guelph. Before settling on their Muskoka farm, the McCulleys lived three years in a house left by Indians who had been moved to a reservation on Parry Island. The family subscribed to Guelph and Montreal papers which arrived by twice-weekly mail.

The McCulleys and other farmers raised cattle and sheep. The wool from the sheep would be taken to Bird's mill at Bracebridge to be made into rolls; then the women spun the rolls into yarn—some coarse and some fine—and the yarn would be taken to the weavers to be made into material.

The *Lady Muskoka,* first boat to pass the new
lift bridge at Part Carling, September 12, 1975

Tilting contest at the M.L.A. Regatta, 1975.

The *Nipissing I* at Port Cockburn, where it burned in 1885.

The District was well suited for raising sheep. As the tourist industry grew, quantities of lamb were used to feed the summer visitors, and large amounts were transported for sale elsewhere since Muskoka had become famous for its lamb as far away as New York where it was featured in restaurants.

Sheep-raising in Muskoka later diminished until it was practically non-existent, and I discussed this with Sarah McCulley Brady. We concluded that it was because the farmers began to lose so many of their sheep through attacks by bands of dogs and wolves that it did not pay to attempt to replace them. Another woman recalled to me a night when her brother lost twenty sheep. Although wild dogs and wolves have never been a problem to the Muskoka visitor, there are areas where they can survive without interference and run at night into the ranch areas to attack the sheep. When travel conditions allowed easier transport into the District and the farmer's wife no longer had the same urgent need for the wool, there was not the same incentive to continue fighting a losing battle to protect the sheep. Today, however, sheep-raising in Muskoka is again increasing.

In the year of her arrival in Muskoka, young Sarah McCulley attended her first dance on the occasion of the Port Carling Fall Fair. People from all around the lakes converged on the village, and A. P. Cockburn ran his boats to full capacity. The tourist business was growing, and each spring Sarah took the first boat to the top of Lake Joseph to work at the Summit House, one of the early resorts.

Sarah's first marriage was to Hugh James, the son of Port Carling pioneers who had arrived in 1869. A few weeks after the wedding, Hugh died of typhoid fever. He was one of eight children, five of whom survived him; two had died in infancy. Sarah later married William J. Brady who had come with his family from Battersea, England, and bought a farm at the top of Lake Joseph and later became the first Clerk-Treasurer of the village of Port Carling.

In the absence of any other nursing care, the women of the community did what they could for the sick. Sarah McCulley Brady recalled nursing one of the women of the Duke family who became seriously ill with influenza one Christmas Eve in the early days. The steamers did not run at that time of year, and the nearest practising doctor was at Bracebridge, a round-trip drive of three or four hours. Luckily there was a doctor living on Lake Joseph, in retirement (because of an alcohol problem, it was said), and a boat was sent from Port Carling to get him. This doctor stayed right at the house for two weeks until the patient recovered.

The Plaskett Family

At the same time the farming family of McCulley came to settle in Port Carling in 1876, tourist families were arriving to take up land for summer homes. The Plaskett family was among the early tourists, and Miss Josephine Plaskett has written an account of their early days. Her father, John S. Plaskett, first came to Muskoka in 1876 and soon purchased from the government the island called Bohemia, situated off the lower end of Tobin Island, within calling distance of another small island called Vacuna (named for the god of idleness) owned by his friend, Mr. Scadding.

Bohemia and most of the surrounding islands had been burned over, and the Plasketts found a young growth of wild cherries, blueberries and softwood trees. Many burned trees still stood and these, together with charred stumps of pines which had probably been hundreds of years old, gave the place a desolate appearance. In subsequent years the growth which had followed the fire was gradually replaced with evergreen pine, cedar and hemlock, hardwood oak and maple, and low growths of ground hemlock and junipers.

In June of 1877, John Plaskett arrived in Port Carling with his nine-year old son, Dick, and seven-year old daughter, Mary. Although it was nearly midnight, black as pitch and blowing a gale, he put the two children in the bottom of a small row-boat and rowed the two miles out to Vacuna, where they stayed a few days until he had pitched a tent on Bohemia and erected a rude shelter of brush and boards in which to have meals. They ate and drank from plates, cups, saucers and spoons made of the durable tin manufactured in those days, and used lights made from the pitch of pine trees.

John Plaskett built his cottage on the highest point of the island facing east, about 50 feet above the lake level, using oxen brought to the island to draw the lumber up the 200 yards from the water. The lumber was rough pine boards about 12 inches wide, and the cottage was built straight up and down and battened over the cracks. The nails were called "cut" nails, as they were cut out of iron. There were no locks on the doors—just sliding wooden latches.

John Plaskett built tables, benches and bunk beds. The mattresses were made of ticking filled with hay, which would be emptied on the floor before leaving the cottage for the season and the ticking hung up to keep it from destruction by mice and squirrels. The first job on arrival the next year would be to refill the mattresses.

Josephine, the youngest of the six Plaskett children, wrote fondly of the Muskoka experience at the family cottage in the last 20 years of the nineteenth century:

> My early memories were of the anticipation of school soon closing and the excitement of Muskoka in the near future. On our arrival we children were bereft of our shoes and stockings. Bare feet was the vogue until our return to the city and many times did we stub our toes painfully on the rocks,
> The shores of our island were littered from five to ten feet

with dead trunks of trees, drift logs and debris. We had many a large bonfire and used to dance and sing around the fire like wild Indians.

The men wore grey flannel shirts and we took all our old clothes and wore them out. The good old days of the grey flannel shirts were the real days in Muskoka.

In the early days practically all our utensils were taken up and brought back to the city at the end of the holiday as our cottage would be broken into and we could not afford new things each year. Consequently, we had a load of luggage, a tub, axe, saws, trunks, nail kegs packed with utensils, altogether about 14 pieces.

I can remember my father riding down to the station sitting up beside the expressman with the load and my dear old field spaniel "Bounce" sitting up beside father. Then I knew we were really ready to go to the place which was heaven to the children.

I have often wondered how our parents ever accomplished so much, getting the children ready for the trip and such a trip, leaving the city early in the morning and not arriving at "Bohemia" until midnight. I can remember helping to put the hay into the ticking on arriving, and occasionally a thistle would prick your fingers.

The express wagon which picked up the Plaskett luggage from their Toronto house was, of course, horse-drawn. The Plasketts took the early morning train for Muskoka and transferred at Gravenhurst to the steamship *Wenonah*, which first went up the Muskoka River to Bracebridge. Here delays would be encountered. The lumbering business was very active, and the steamer would often be jammed for hours in the logs floated over the Bracebridge falls and down the Muskoka River before it could get back out on Lake Muskoka to make the trip to Port Carling.

As it was difficult to secure supplies for several years, the Plasketts brought seven or eight smoked hams with them which were hung to the beams of the cottage ceilings. Fish were so plentiful one could see them swimming in the water. Blueberries were abundant. Among the food supplies was a large box of "hard tack", round sea biscuits about four inches across, three-quarters of an inch thick and exceptionally hard. These were given to the children to gnaw on when they got hungry between meals.

There were no cottages on the river between Lake Rosseau and Port Carling then—just the small log house built by the Adams family. When campers began to come to Muskoka, "it was pretty to see the tents on the islands", but they were thought to be the cause of the burning of many of the beautiful islands. Today all the land is private property and not accessible to campers.

After the Plasketts had been on Bohemia for some years, Frank Forge, a farmer who had settled near Windermere, began to bring them supplies. He sold lambs, vegetables, butter, eggs, milk and ice from a leaky, overloaded rowboat. Twice a week he would row past the Plasketts, through the Port Sandfield cut to Lake Joseph, up Lake Joseph and return, a total distance of forty miles, having risen at four o'clock in the morning to kill the lambs and get his boat ready. The Plasketts would hear him rowing home past Bohemia late at night, singing—so that his wife, always anxious about him, could hear him over the water and know he was safe. All this work apparently agreed with him, for he lived to be 92 years of age.

The summer visitors (generally referred to as the tourists) also took their families on long rows, some families having canopied rowboats with three pair of oars. People in rowboats, canoes and dugouts went to Port Carling for mail, often in procession and singing together as they travelled. The two tugs, *Rosseau* and *Joseph*, moving slowly and lazily along the steamboat channel and towing logs or tanbark, added a picturesque touch.

Soon the grey flannel shirt was *passé* and to dress in pretty summer clothes and row to Port Carling to meet friends and watch the steamers go through the locks was the popular thing to do. The women wore long white or coloured starched dresses (an ordeal to launder) and the men wore white duck trousers, striped blazers and yachting caps.

"The early days of Muskoka," Josephine Plaskett concluded, "were perhaps not as easy, lacking conveniences, but the satisfaction of accomplishing and overcoming difficulties made character, and people enjoyed the simple way of living and the beauties of the country to a much greater extent, compared to these days of combustible locomotion and speed." (Those words were written in 1945.)

Windermere

Thomas Aitken, a young pioneer Scot, settled across from Port Carling on Lake Rosseau at the place that became known as Windermere. He began accommodating stray adventurers and sportsmen in search of new fishing grounds, and eventually his first small house grew to be the Windermere House of today.

By 1890 the Windermere main building and adjoining cottages had accommodation for 220 guests. The rates were around $1.50 per day, with special rates for families. The main dining-room could seat 200, and children and their nurses ate in a separate and smaller dining-room. Long verandahs or "piazzas" of over one-eighth of a mile in extent surrounded the building, affording comfort and shade at all hours of the day and pleasant views of the lake. A sand beach for bathing (safe for ladies and children in their cumbersome 1890 bathing costumes), tennis, croquet, quoits and the good old English game of bowls provided recreation. Guests hired horses and buggies for driving, and a favourite drive was five miles along the government road to Skeleton Lake. All the rivers and lakes of the surrounding country provided good fishing.

An important attraction to visitors of that era, the nearby Mechanics' Institute contained volumes of philosophy, mechanics, science, art, history, poetry, biography and general literature, and provisions were made for the giving of lectures and other literary entertainments. The Free Reading-Room was furnished with draughts, dominoes, periodicals, standard magazines, the Toronto newspapers and several of the New York and Chicago dailies.

Several pretty walks were recommended to Windermere guests when they visited Port Carling—one through the woods to Ferndale, the Pensons' resort; another to the Indian burial grounds; and one to Silver Lake which had a local reputation for its fishing, its black bass ranging up to seven pounds. About half a mile beyond this 140-acre lake was a morass filled with the intriguing pitcher plant which traps and digests small insects (the floral emblem of the province of Newfoundland).

Equipment at Windermere House was constantly updated. The kitchen was rebuilt; the wooden verandahs were replaced with handsome stone and an enclosed sun room in the 1930s; a bar and outdoor patio were added to the restaurant on the lower level; and in 1972 "The Terrace" was opened, a new building adjacent to the main lodge, each of its ten luxury suites named after a Canadian province. Mary Elizabeth Aitken, today's owner, has since built a number of winterized efficiency units, named "Settlers' Bay", on the adjacent property. This new development is situated on the property where Fife House, a resort built by pioneer David Fife, stood before it was demolished about 1970.

The activity in Windermere village today revolves around Windermere House and the popular Baldwins Resort, water-skiing school and exhibitions, the golf course, Lions Club pancake and maple syrup festival in April and regatta day in summer, Thanksgiving dinner for 500 or more at the United Church, winter carnival early in March (snow-sculpturing, bean supper, and the snowmobile 10-mile "Poker Run"), and the Community Centre activities.

Cindy Nicholas, the 16-year-old Toronto girl who, in August 1974, set a record time for swimming across Lake Ontario (15 hours and 15 minutes, accomplished by maintaining a pace of 72 strokes per minute for much of the approximately 32 miles), trained at Windermere and nearby. Her coach was Al Waites, director of Windermere swimming classes.

A memorial window in Windermere United Church honours the three pioneers, Thomas Aitken, David Fife and Francis Forge. Frank Forge, the singing boatman who sold farm produce, owned the land south of David Fife's and worked for Timothy Eaton, the wealthy Toronto merchant who built a summer residence at Windermere. The Burton family (Robert Simpson Company) and Albert Matthews (Lieutenant-Governor of Ontario 1937–46) have also been active in the Windermere community as summer residents.

The wheelhouse of the
Nipissing II.

Windermere, c. 1900.

Windermere, 1974.

The Muskoka Lakes Association

Motivated by concern about the high freight rates being charged by railways and steamboats, the need to get involved in legislative matters, heavy steamboat and other traffic on the lakes, and to encourage aquatic skills, especially safety, the summer residents on Lakes Muskoka, Rosseau and Joseph formed the Muskoka Lakes Association in 1894 in an office on King Street in Toronto. In 1975 M.L.A. membership was 5,280, representing 2,080 households.

"Over the years M.L.A. has been aggressively active on behalf of its increasing membership," said Bryan Vaughan, an Honorary President, one evening when I was talking with him about Muskoka. "The Association has an interest in zoning and other regulations designed to protect property investments. More and better buoying, increased police patrols, improved fire protection and sanitary inspection, all precipitated by M.L.A., have made Muskoka a safer, better place. Renowned business and professional men interested in the lakes find participation a fine investment in personal pleasure as well as a valued public service activity. The roster of M.L.A. officers reads like an international 'who's who.' In 1914 the Association invited U.S. President Woodrow Wilson, owner of Formosa Island, to become a member. President Wilson's letter saying he did not feel he should join because he could not take an active part was auctioned off for $15 in 1915 to raise money for the Red Cross.

"The M.L.A. was instrumental in forming the Ratepayers Association of Medora and Wood. Now we are greatly involved in the ecology of the lakes, teaching water purity and systematically testing for the Ministry of the Environment. As far back as the 1908 annual meeting, the navigation company was being asked to treat sewage from its steamers."

M.L.A. members helped establish the Muskoka Lakes Golf and Country Club on Lake Rosseau near Port Carling, and that Club's excellent docking facilities are the locale of the annual regatta (and, less frequently, the Antique Boat Show). Tilting, somewhat like a medieval joust, is an outstanding regatta event. Two contestants standing in canoes, each armed with a long pole tipped with a kapok-filled bag, attempt to push each other into the water; each canoe has a paddler to manoeuvre and provide ballast. The sailing committee arranges instruction at six different locations on the three lakes.

Retiring after ten years of wholehearted service as Commodore, Robert W. Purves was named the Association's first Honorary Commodore at the 1975 annual meeting. Discussing his life-long interest in Muskoka boats, he told me that early pleasure boats manufactured in Muskoka were copied all over the world. "Contributing to their elegant design and speed potential were the wealthy tourists who spent their summers in Muskoka from the U.S. and abroad. Boats were their toys, and they raced each other, just as some people race horses. When they lost a race, they'd take their boat back to the builder and ask to have adjustments made to improve the speed. Who cared about the expense? They say that's how Minett boats got curved windshields before cars. An international glass magnate figured his boat would go faster with less wind resistance, so they worked out the design. Betty Carstairs, international racing queen, did much of her trial work in Muskoka."

VIII *THE PENINSULA ROAD TO ROSSEAU*

The Peninsula Road, formerly Highway 632, now Muskoka Road 7, branches north off Highway 118 in the westerly limits of Port Carling and runs up the neck of land between Lakes Rosseau and Joseph.

PORT SANDFIELD

About two miles up Muskoka Road (MR7) an iron bridge spans the cut between Lake Rosseau on the east and Lake Joseph on the west. The Reverend A. S. Herring, an English clergyman visiting English emigrants who had come to Muskoka with the aid of St. Paul's Emigration Society, of Clerkenwell, London, was given the honour of opening the cut officially and christening the community with the name of Port Sandfield "in the name of Her Majesty Queen Victoria and of the Dominion of Canada". The name of Port Sandfield had been chosen in honour of J. Sandfield Macdonald, Premier of Ontario from 1867 to 71 and joint premier of United Canada in 1862.

The cut has a long board dock on either side. On the south side at the Lake Joseph end is a small park with picnic table. The Port Sandfield Marina is opposite on that part of Lake Joseph named Cox Bay. This marina innovated a system of keeping boat fenders in place by using nylon cleats, which has proven popular with boat owners in Muskoka and farther afield.

The village shops and post office are on the north side of the bridge. Look for a new township park at Port Sandfield, comprising approximately two-thirds of an acre of land and about 200 feet of frontage on Lake Rosseau.

The Cox Family and Prospect House

A promontory overlooking Lake Rosseau behind the Port Sandfield shops on the east side of the highway was the location of Prospect House—a resort founded by English immigrants in 1884—which played a colourful role in Muskoka history.

Enoch Cox, the founder of Prospect House, was the second son of a timber merchant in Stratford-on-Avon, England. In the early years after his marriage in 1847, Enoch had severe health problems, and was advised to change his occupation from dry-goods shop owner to the outdoor life of a farmer. He then farmed for fourteen years, his family increased to four daughters and two sons, and his health improved, but his farm

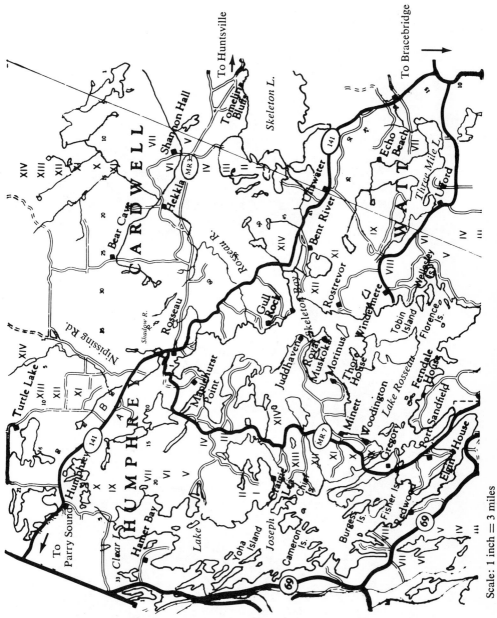

Scale: 1 inch = 3 miles

Photo by J. Bain

The *Sagamo* entering Port Sandfield, c. 1946.

Ontario Archives

The supply boat *Constance* at Port Sandfield, c. 1904.

Courtesy Claude Snider

Regatta at Port Sandfield, c. 1908.

revenue decreased owing to high rent, depression, bad crops and poor weather. Emigrating to Canada was a common topic of conversation, and Enoch caught the fever.

The Cox family sailed from England in March 1871. After a rough, cold crossing, plagued with seasickness, they landed at Portland, Maine, and proceeded by train to Toronto, where the exhausted Mrs. Cox declared she could go no farther. "I'm not going to the backwoods," she is quoted as saying, "to be devoured by wild beasts or savage Indians." The strain of moving out of England and the unpleasant crossing had weakened Enoch also, and it was agreed they would stay in Toronto, at least for a while.

They spent their first night in Toronto at a hotel, but doors were slammed in their faces the next day when they hurried out to find a boarding house. They were astonished to find that to be "just out from England" made them very unpopular. Many Torontonians professed to be heartily sick of English immigrants, their conceit, their English accents and their complaints about things that were different from back home, especially as they had come to Canada to better their condition and nearly always did so.

On the third day of their search, a good-natured Irish woman let them have two rooms. Within a few weeks their landlady decided to leave her drinking husband and give up the boarding house, and the Coxes persuaded her to rent the house to them. The grown-up children had been unsuccessful in finding work in Toronto, but the boarding house would give the girls remunerative work at home.

One of their first boarders was John Rogers, the young Englishman who had been living on Lake Joseph. Through him Enoch Cox arranged to rent for three years a fine small log house with a good-sized clearing on Lake Joseph belonging to a young friend of Rogers who was dying of consumption. Enoch planned to take up some nearby lots for himself before the end of the three years.

Enoch travelled to the Lake Joseph property in May 1871 with his twelve-year-old son, Edward, by train, stagecoach, steamer and rowboat. During that summer their food consisted mainly of salt pork, bread baked by Enoch and all the Muskoka bass they wanted. They spread a mixture of pork fat and carbolic acid on their skins and kept smudge pots blowing smoke around them to discourage the hordes of mosquitoes which gave them no peace whether sleeping, eating or working.

Before returning to Toronto at the end of September, Enoch Cox had located land for himself nearby—at the south end of Lake Joseph (around the corner from today's Elgin House) on a bay to which he gave the name Avon Bay in memory of Stratford-on-Avon, England, the home of his youth. He had carried out the necessary work on the rented property, at times with the help of a hired settler, and had arranged to have five acres chopped and ready for clearing up in the spring, in accordance with his rental agreement.

Enoch and Edward returned to Muskoka each spring as soon as navigation opened. At the termination of the three years' rental agreement, they built a log shanty on their own land and devoted their full time to developing the property. The family soon delighted to see lying along the shore their cleared land, planted in oats which grew so high and green they hid the disfiguring stumps. Mrs. Cox and their daughters kept the boarding house in Toronto and travelled back and forth to Muskoka, both to assist Enoch and to holiday. After the railway reached Gravenhurst in August 1875, the trip was less fatiguing.

When Enoch inherited some money upon the death of his father in England, he purchased the land on the canal between Lake Joseph and Lake Rosseau at Port Sandfield and built a "boarding house" to accommodate 50 guests. The family had decided that soon there would be more money made in Muskoka by boarding summer visitors than by farming, even though the season was short—just the months of July and August. Visitors to Muskoka were becoming more numerous, and there were few hotels to accommodate them (one of which was Summit House at the top of Lake Joseph). Prospect House started out as a plain barn-like structure of two and one-half stories with verandah. Because of its strategic situation at a steamboat stop, visitors began to arrive in July of their first summer, before the facilities were quite organized for them, and continued to arrive to fill up every bedroom as soon as it was ready for occupancy.

The following spring Mrs. Cox moved from Toronto to Muskoka to make her home at Prospect House, which was described by a contemporary observer as a well-run hotel. Its facilities were expanded in the ensuing years to include a ballroom and tennis courts, pleasant verandahs, shady groves for lounging, and bathing houses on the sand beach. By 1888 it had accommodation for 300 guests at $1.75 per day or $9.00 per week, with special season rates for families.

One daughter married John Rogers, and they took up land adjacent to her father's land and had five sons and one daughter. Another Cox daughter married into the Burgess family of Bala. Edward Cox, who ran Prospect House after his father retired, had five daughters and one son. When Prospect House was destroyed by fire on September 15th, 1915 (during World War I), it was not rebuilt, but many descendants and branches of the Cox family live in Muskoka today.

Fanny Cox (1848–c. 1935), using the pseudonym Ann Hathaway, told the story of the Cox family in the book *Muskoka Memories*, published in 1903, although she clothed the people and locations in anonymity. The Cox family by this time had lived in Muskoka for 30 years and seen many changes. The hard-working settlers were benefiting from the yearly influx of pleasure-loving "tourists", who gained in number each year and came as early as May 1st to open their cottages—an endless variety of summer houses ornamented with swinging hammocks, bright-coloured flags and awnings. "Even the sunburnt settlers' children look forward with delight to the time of their arrival," Fanny Cox wrote. "The homes of the settlers were, as a rule, small and roughly furnished with little except children; of the latter the supply was unlimited. . . . many families ranged in number from ten to fifteen."

The Muskoka Express

For those who drive to Muskoka today in peak travel periods when the highways are crowded and hazardous, under repair or being widened, the travelling time might even seem relatively short and uncomplicated if viewed in the light of Fanny Cox's description of train travel about 1903:

> . . . In July, between the hours of ten and eleven in the waiting-room of the Union Station, Toronto . . . watch the rush of passengers through the doors as the stentorian voice of 'Bob' Harrison calls out the 'Muskoka Express'. . . .
>
> Let us follow the crowd downstairs and see the piles of baggage being loaded on the cars—cases of provisions, blankets and bedding, trunks, valises, boilers, tubs, pails, cradles, perambulators, every mortal thing you could think of—all bound for the 'Muskoka Express'. . . .
>
> Large numbers of Americans, too, are buying islands and land here and putting up houses for themselves and families, where they can entertain their friends and spend the summer months in true country fashion. These Americans, so far as I can ascertain, are well liked by our settlers. . . .
>
> It is a pretty sight when the 'Muskoka Express' runs down to the wharf and disgorges herself of her living freight, to see once more the stately 'Medora', dear to the heart of every dweller in Lake Joseph, the 'Nipissing', the 'Islander', the 'Kenozha', all waiting patiently for our advent, besides half a dozen or more private steam yachts. . . .

Supply Boats

A chapter in *Muskoka Memories* is devoted to tales of the early supply boats. The *Constance*, owned by Homer of the village of Rosseau, and the *Mink*, owned by Hanna of Port Carling, ran on Lakes Joseph and Rosseau. During the summer months, the Cox family had two visits a week from each boat at their wharf. After the tourists had departed, the boats came only once a week until the ice froze over the lakes.

These boats carried a full stock of food—soup, meat, vegetables, fruit and cheese—and family needs from corset laces to boots, the stock varying according to the season. The meat department was operated by competent butchers who used large quantities of Muskoka ice to keep the meat fresh. Brisk trading was carried on with growers of fruit and vegetables who came to the boat at various stops to sell their produce.

When the supply boats made their last few trips in the fall, they carried snow-shovels, shoe-packs, moccasins, ice-tongs, skates and all things required for the cold winter.

NORTH FROM PORT SANDFIELD

The Elgin House Road branches off MR 7 on the west a short distance beyond Port Sandfield, travelling one-half mile down the west side of Cox Bay to the highly-respected Elgin House resort.

Elgin House was started in 1898 by dynamic Lambert Love (1855–1947). Born at Love's Corners (now Richmond Hill, Ontario), the fifth son of Robert Love and Mary Ann Fleury, he learned blacksmithing after his family moved to Wellington County; then he moved to Muskoka, subsequently entering his business card in the 1879 *Atlas*:

L . L O V E

BLACKSMITH AND CARRIAGE BUILDER

Buggies, Waggons, Cutters, and Sleighs always
on hand or made to order. Horse Shoeing a
Specialty. All work guaranteed.

Lambert Love and Maggie Isaac were married in May 1879. In 1885 their son, Lambert Elgin, was born, and the family moved to Lake Joseph where Lambert Love worked a shingle and sawmill until he began building Elgin House.

With additions such as East Lodge, West Annex, North Lodge, Shoreview Lodge and a golf course, Elgin House was soon a thriving resort where many guests stayed for the season, a common occurrence in early resort days in Muskoka. When a contingent of new guests was brought to the dock by a navigation company steamer, the transportation used by the great majority of guests, there was a tremendous flurry of activity while the guests were registered and conducted to their rooms and the bellboys transferred the immense stacks of trunks and luggage from the dock by horse and wagon.

Lambert Love was active in the Glen Orchard community and church. His son, Lambert Elgin, never forgot the Sunday church service at which his father rose to confront the visiting minister with the words, "I completely disagree with you," and stalked out of the church. A young boy at the time, Lambert Elgin knew that if he didn't go out with his father and get in the boat he would have a long walk home—sufficient motivation for him to rise also—so, painfully embarrassed, he followed his father out of the church.

In 1908 Lambert Elgin Love married Mabel Dunstan, who died at the birth of their fifth son. One infant son was drowned; one son, Howard, was killed overseas in World War II. Lambert Elgin was handed the business when his father was aged 70. The surviving sons of Lambert Elgin were brought up on the property and took places in the business until they sold it in 1971 to Didace Grisé (pronounced "Deedoss Greesay") and Sons. The Deck Lounge, with an outside terrace for eating and drinking on fine days, is on the waterfront and open to visitors as well as Elgin House guests.

When you stand on the spacious dock of Elgin House today and face south, you will see across the water Glen Home, the resort also built by Lambert Love. After he married a second time (this time a lady considerably younger), he built Glen Home for the two sons born of this union. On the southerly shore of Lake Joseph and close to the Glen Orchard community, Glen Home is reached by turning off Highway 118 at the Appian Way (named by the Loves after the ancient road leading to Rome from the south). Lambert Love died in 1948 at the age of 93, having left two notable landmarks on Lake Joseph. His second wife, Alice, continued to be active in the operation of Glen Home until her death in 1973. The property was sold in 1975 to the Sisters of St. Joseph, Hamilton.

The Hemlock Point Road, just north of the Elgin House Road, leads to Avon Bay where the Cox family had its first property. The bay is today surrounded by summer homes and not fields of waving oats.

The Lake Joseph Community Church is on the west side of MR 7 opposite the Gregory Road. Opened in the summer of 1904 as a Presbyterian Church, it became a United Church following Church Union in 1925, and later a community non-denominational church under the jurisdiction of the United Church of Canada. Popular with summer residents and close to the shore of Lake Joseph opposite Star Island, some of the Sunday morning congregation customarily arrive by boat.

MR 7 crosses the Joseph River over a new bridge about one mile north of the Church. The water flows from Lake Joseph on the west to Lake Rosseau on the east. In 1870 the rock cut at the Lake Joseph end was blasted out to eliminate swift water and allow safe passage to small boats, at the same time equalizing the levels of Lakes Joseph and Rosseau in conjunction with the Port Sandfield cut. In 1897, the channel was enlarged to allow passage of small steamers. The Joseph River was the one sought by the first tourist party from Gravenhurst (John Campbell, James Bain and friends), guided by Thomas M. Robinson in July 1862. By 1866 Campbell and Bain had formed The Muskoka Club, choosing Chaplain's Island in Lake Joseph near the Joseph River as a permanent camp. The Club ceased to exist about 1877 when its total holding of five islands was bought up by John Campbell, divinity graduate from Knox College in Toronto (1867) and Edinburgh University (1868). One of these islands was called Peggy after the Indian Chief Peg-a-ma-gah-bo, who was living there with his family when Campbell and Bain first explored Lake Joseph. Many more details about Campbell, Bain, their friends and their islands are given in D. H. C. Mason's booklet, *The First Islanders*, published in 1957.

The Juddhaven Road now branches off MR 7 to Lake Rosseau resorts on the east, first passing the Minett post office and the large Clevelands House resort which takes dinner reservations, and has nightly entertainment and accommodation for 350 guests, many of whom are from the U.S. Clevelands House dates back to 1869 when Charles Minett named his new Muskoka house after his former residence in England, Cleeve Ville. Because of confusion with the U.S. city of Cleveland, the post office name had to be changed from Clevelands to Minett. The resort remained in the Minett family until 1953. Members of the Minett family entered the boat-building business in Bracebridge and also manufactured fine mahogany toboggans.

The Peninsula Recreation Centre, past the Clevelands House golf course, is the locale of many community activities such as card parties every second Thursday, an annual Hunters' Dance to celebrate the deer-hunting season, the Legion's annual Children's Christmas Party, and February snowmobile safari for residents and visitors followed by pot-luck supper, dancing in the Centre and bonfire on the lake (hopefully an annual affair). The Minett Fire Hall adjoins the Centre, and the Volunteer Fire Department holds its annual dance in October at Clevelands House. The boys play hockey on Port Carling teams which start with Tiny Tykes. Muskoka people put their children on skates at an early age. You're likely to see a chap all of 18-months old tottering about on the ice, but they wait a while before giving him a hockey stick. Look for the Minett Mini-Theatre on summer Sunday nights; Muskoka is attracting many musicians and performers from afar in addition to those born and bred there. Check for the library's current location.

Walt and Beth Ruch live nearby. Walt carves in life size and Beth paints in authentic colours the birds cherished by many purchasers of their works.

The Lakeside Church (Roman Catholic), high above the water on a rocky promontory, has a beautiful view of Lake Rosseau and a large docking area, and is reached by the Morinus Road, which branches to the east from the Juddhaven Road.

The Juddhaven community is at the end of the Juddhaven Road on a point jutting into Lake Rosseau opposite Skeleton Bay, the *entrepot* of the Skeleton River flowing out of Skeleton Lake. Mr. and Mrs. F. E. Judd and eight children came here from Romsey, Hampshire, England, in July 1875, to live in a small log cabin on 200 acres, and started to clear land, build more accommodation and farm. In 1879 Mrs. Judd became postmistress of the Juddhaven post office. She lived until 1919. (Her husband died in 1899.) Various members of the family operated the post office until 1963.

A son, Alfred, and his wife started the resort hotel Ernescliffe as a small operation about 1890, increasing the accommodation from time to time until it reached a capacity for 125 guests in the early 1930s. "Like most of the first resorts, the buildings had four stories with high-ceilinged rooms in order to meet the demand for fresh-air accommodation created by the prevalence of tuberculosis in those times," said W. B. Judd, son of the proprietors. "After a disastrous fire at the Wawa Hotel on the Lake of Bays in August 1923, nobody wanted to occupy rooms located higher than the second storey. That feature and several others, including the Depression, discouraged people from patronizing summer resorts as they had earlier." Alfred Judd died in 1945. It was difficult to operate the resort profitably, and Ernescliffe was sold in 1963.

The Royal Muskoka Island, connected by bridge to the mainland, is in Lake Rosseau near Juddhaven. On this island the Navigation Company built the luxury Royal Muskoka hotel in 1901 as an adjunct to the steamships. Life at the hotel was quite formal; men wore white flannels and blue coats, the early black shoes giving way to fashionable white. Dancing several nights a week attracted the social set from around the lake. There was a short but lovely nine-hole golf course. The Muskoka Lakes Association held its regattas there for some years. A prominent Toronto doctor, who transferred his practice to Muskoka in the summer, used to go up to the Royal Muskoka by boat every evening at 5 o'clock to spend the night, enabling the hotel to claim a resident doctor.

A financial burden from the beginning, it was impossible to operate at a profit, particularly in view of the short summer season, and more so after the Bigwin resort was opened in 1920. After the hotel was destroyed by fire in 1952, the island was divided into cottage lots and is a vacation-home community today.

Professor J. Roy Cockburn told me the Royal Muskoka hotel was not his father's idea but a scheme pressed on him by a group of powerful shareholders. In 1905, four years after it was built, A. P. Cockburn, the founder of the navigation company, quietly died in bed in his Toronto home at the age of 68, having just delivered to the publishers the manuscript for his book, *Political Annals of Canada*.

Returning to Muskoka Road 7, you go around Morgan Bay, past the Maplehurst Road and some lovely views of the top of Lake Rosseau, and meet Highway 141 (formerly Highway 532), the Parry Sound Road, near the village of Rosseau (about 18 miles from the junction of MR 7 and Highway 118).

THE TOP OF THE LAKES

In 1863, two years before A. P. Cockburn moved into the Gravenhurst area and began building the *Wenonah* to provide transportation on Lake Muskoka, the firm of J. & W. Beatty & Co., of Thorold, Ontario, had begun a similar operation in the Parry Sound area on Georgian Bay, part of the Great Lakes waterway, west of the Muskoka Lakes. Subsequent developments in the Parry Sound district contributed to Muskoka's growth.

The Beattys first purchased a sawmill that had been established five years previously on the isolated shore of Parry Sound harbour. Then they built the steamer *Waubano* and sent it on weekly trips to Collingwood, the terminus of the Northern and North Western Railway, to pick up passengers, freight and mail from Toronto. The Beatty men encouraged settlement in the area, unlike many other heads of lumbering firms. They ran a gristmill and established a large wholesale and retail store.

Spurred by the strong and influential recommendation of the Beattys, the government opened up a road 45 miles in length between Parry Sound and Bracebridge, known as the Parry Sound Road, and 76 new locations were issued to settlers on this road in 1867. In the same year a team directed by Surveyor Fitzgerald completed the survey of the Nipissing Road, 67 miles long from the most northern bay of Lake Rosseau to Lake Nipissing, in order to open up the surrounding land for settlement. The Nipissing Road intersected the Parry Sound Road at a point 22 miles east of Parry Sound, about one mile west of the village now named Rosseau. The first 12 miles of the Nipissing Road were cleared and finished by the end of 1867, and settlement advanced rapidly along it.

John D. Beatty held the post of Crown Lands Agent for the Townships of McDougall, Foley and Humphry in the District of Parry Sound, and Cardwell in the District of Muskoka. While it is convenient to refer to these Districts by their present geographical names, they were not electorally formed as such until later.

William Beatty was elected a Member of Provincial Parliament, representing Welland, in 1867—the year of Confederation. He was a militant teetotaler and did everything in his power to ensure that not a drop of liquor could be purchased in Parry Sound. Just across the river, however, a tavern flourished.

By the end of 1872, the Muskoka and Parry Sound Roads were heavily trafficked with supplies being teamed in through Severn Bridge, Washago, Orillia and points south for the winter operations of lumber firms in the Parry Sound and Magnetawan country. Work on the Nipissing Road had progressed slowly, and there still remained 29 miles to construct in order to reach Lake Nipissing. The time had come when it was extremely important to complete this link between Lake Rosseau and the community of settlers who had struggled into Lake Nipissing over the years—without benefit of road, some on foot with their packs on their backs.

Before the winter of 1873 set in, as large a gang of labourers as could be profitably obtained and worked were employed to construct a good winter road on the unopened section of the Nipissing Road, and this plan was carried out for a total expenditure of $7645. This enabled teams and sleighs to reach Rosseau from Lake Nipissing. The railroad did not reach Gravenhurst until 1875, and 15 years passed before the work on the line to North Bay on Lake Nipissing was completed. In the meantime, the Nipissing Road was an important artery.

When A. P. Cockburn had launched his second steamer in 1871, he had christened it the *Nipissing* in recognition of the importance to Muskoka of the Nipissing Road, for during the navigation season the boat would carry to the top of Lake Rosseau the passengers and freight destined for Lake Nipissing when the road was finished as promised, and for intermediary points until that time.

In the midst of this activity at the top of the Muskoka Lakes, an American, William H. Pratt, moved right in and built the first notable Muskoka summer resort on a rocky promontory at the top of Lake Rosseau near the village of Helmsley (later renamed Rosseau). The hotel, named the Rosseau House, was opened in 1870 and had a magnificent view of the lake. The guest charge of $5 per day was about four times the ordinary charge for summer boarding in that era. Pratt had a telegraph office at the hotel, constructed a steamboat wharf for his guests and enlarged and improved the hotel annually with a view to making it the largest and best north of Toronto. Guests came from as far away as England and the southern United States to visit this new oasis in the wilderness. They could reach the Rosseau House either through Gravenhurst and the Muskoka Lakes or from Parry Sound by stagecoach. The stagecoach journey of about 25 miles took at least six hours over rough track, around tree stumps and rock formations, and up and down steep hills. Although far from comfortable, the passengers were invariably thrilled with the scenery and the many delightful views of the lakes along the way.

The few campers and sportsmen who had discovered Muskoka were not at all happy to view this invasion of their wilderness, but the many settlers in Muskoka who had found the farming of the land to be less than advantageous were quick to grasp the significance of this turn of events.

The Rosseau House enjoyed only transitory fame, as it burned in 1883 and was not rebuilt. In the meantime, the Monteith House (then described as "a large and handsome building") had been established at Rosseau, and Fraser's Summit House had been established at Port Cockburn at the top of Lake Joseph.

The 1879 *Atlas* shows that the majority of the lots around the top of Lakes Joseph and Rosseau and on both sides of the Parry Sound Road were occupied by settlers. Several members of the Stoneman family had taken up lots on the east end of Turtle Lake, which is north of the Parry Sound Road, west of the Nipissing Road. Many Stoneman descendants continue to make their livelihood in this vicinity, but, as in other families, some of the young people leave to pursue city careers. Alma E. Stoneman, daughter of the Whitefish Lake Stonemans, was appointed Group Sales Administrative Officer of the Toronto-based

North American Life Assurance Company, in 1973, and that's something for the community at the top of the Muskoka Lakes to celebrate. About 25 years earlier when Alma joined the company, a pretty and competent junior, there wasn't one woman officer, and women in the life insurance business didn't even dream of promotion to the officer level.

Icelanders

Icelanders emigrated to Canada in the years 1873 to 75 because of what seemed a hopeless struggle against poverty at home. The Canadian government had sent agents to advertise the splendid opportunities that awaited settlers in Canada and offered them cheap rates of transportation and homesteads.

The first contingent of 150 Icelanders (one account reads 165 and 230 horses) landed in Quebec in 1873. Instead of being sent to a promised "Icelandic Colony" in Manitoba, they were sent to Kinmount on the Victoria Railway (in the jurisdiction of the Ontario government which had not arranged their emigration), crowded into leaky shanties, and given small plots of land and labour on the railway at 80¢ a day, weather permitting. The situation was so impossible that the majority moved in a body to the Free Grant lands of Muskoka. There also, no suitable arrangements were made for them, and they arrived at the top of Lake Rosseau "in the midst of black flies and mosquitos" to find their way, unaided, to their land over the roughest tracks around the present locations of Rosseau, Bear Cave and Hekla. Hekla is the name of a volcano in Iceland with at least 16 recorded eruptions—an 1873 eruption was one of the main reasons for Icelandic migration.

After the Icelanders had, with pleas for help, made their destitute situation known to Norwegians in Wisconsin, U.S.A., and to other Scandinavian settlements, the Dominion Government took steps to implement its pledge to establish the colony in the West. The Reverend John Taylor, a pioneer missionary, and a group of Icelanders were sent to choose a location in Manitoba. They chose the site that became the village of Gimli, named after the legendary residence of Odin. In September 1875, 268 of the Muskoka Icelanders were conducted by John Taylor at government expense to Gimli, where 1200 other Icelanders soon joined them in a continuing struggle against hardship, floods, illness and misfortune. The few who remained in Muskoka account for some Icelandic names today.

The Shadow River

The Shadow River was one of the area's attractions most often extolled in guidebooks written both by Muskoka people and travel agents in Toronto. The pleasure pursuits of summer visitors have changed so much over the years that the Shadow River is seldom mentioned today. Summer residents may travel all over Lake Rosseau by boat, year after

Shadow River and Rosseau House (Pratt's) sketched by Roper just before the fire of 1883.

year, and be unaware that it exists, because it is only suitable for canoes.

On a bright and warm July morning, armed with a large-scale map, my husband and I rented a canoe at the Rosseau dock. We followed the north shore of Lake Rosseau a short distance and paddled up the first inlet, which is the mouth of the Shadow River. The water in the inlet was shallow, and in places the canoe barely cleared the bottom. After paddling around a few bends, we were delighted with the picture before us. Every detail of sky, trees and surrounding growth was reflected in the water. The river was a long, twisting gallery of pictures: a circular bed of aquatic pickerelweed with every feature of green leaf and purple flowering stalk reflected; tree tops from 50 feet above turned over in the still water, every leaf etched; the white-flowered arrowhead lily, which takes its name from the shape of its exotic leaf; beds of rushes, full of the velvety-brown cat-tail; masses of yellow pond-lilies and white water lilies; ferns ranging in growth from the fragile and feathery variety to the stately Royal. Sitting in the bow of the canoe, I experienced at times an odd dizziness, and a confusion about where reality ended and reflection began.

Our enthusiasm was crowned when we sighted tall Sandhill cranes. The Southern form of the species, these are huge birds for this region, much larger than the Great Blue heron, for instance, and light blue-grey or slate-coloured, with compact body plumage.

This stream was originally known by the settlers as White Oak Creek, but was renamed Shadow River by tourists and guidebooks. Wanton harvesting had by 1890 extinguished the growth of the white oak, its timber much valued by boat-builders; subsequently, Muskoka boat-builders had to import the white oak they required.

Pauline Johnson, the famous Indian poet, visited the Shadow River and wrote a poem in tribute, describing it as

> A stream of tender gladness, of filmy sun . . .
> Midway 'twixt earth and heaven, . . .

Camp Hollyburn

Camp Hollyburn, on a 350-acre lot, just east of the village of Rosseau, has a private lake and frontage on both Lake Rosseau and the Rosseau River. It ordinarily accommodates 80 boys and girls aged 7 to 14, and is operated by Ted and Shirley Yard. Ted Yard was director of the Y.M.C.A. Camp Pine Crest, near Torrance, for 18 years, and is well known for his activities in the Ontario and Canadian Camping Associations.

The June 1974 Kelso Quartet Camp, under the direction of the four musicians of the Orford String Quartet, was held at Camp Hollyburn, an example of noteworthy activities drawn to Muskoka by its camps and resorts. In April 1975, 15 blind C.N.I.B. members from Toronto gathered at Hollyburn to learn how to enjoy cross-country skiing.

ROSSEAU

The village of Rosseau (population about 250), contains a few shops and restaurants and a marina. The Rosseau Community Association sponsors an annual regatta, founded in 1967 as a Centennial project by the late Reverend Joseph S. Ditchburn, and supported by the Rosseau Legion Auxiliary, the Women's Institute and local businesses. The Community Association also sponsors swimming, canoeing and sailing lessons, and holds an annual decorated boat show early in August and winter fun days in the middle of February on Victoria Street in front of the Community Hall.

The Rosseau Memorial Community Hall, well used by all associations, church organizations and the Lions Club, was opened in August 1924, its $12,000 building fund having been raised by public subscription in honour of the fallen in World War I. Fifty years later, in August 1974, the historic plaque commemorating the Rosseau–Nipissing Road was unveiled on the Community Hall grounds. Those attending the ceremony included Mrs. Betsy Merry of Toronto, granddaughter of Vernon B. Wadsworth, who had directed the original survey in 1864.

Inquire about the library service and the scenic Cardwell Road route from Rosseau to Huntsville.

On Highway 141 (formerly Highway 532), south of the steamboat-sized dock where the R.M.S. *Segwun* used to tie up overnight, is the Rosseau School.

Kawandag

The school is located on the property formerly called Kawandag, the summer estate of John Craig and Florence McCrea Eaton, built around 1900. (John Eaton was knighted for services during the First World War.)

Lady Eaton wrote in her autobiography, *Memory's Wall*, that she flew from the Kawandag dock shortly after the war in the pontoon-equipped "crate" belonging to the Bishop–Barker Flying Boat Service from Muskoka to Toronto started by Colonel Billy Bishop, V.C., (John Eaton's niece's husband) and his equally famous flying friend, Colonel Billy Barker. She accepted the ride with Colonel Bishop because she wanted to get to Toronto quickly, and a staff member telephoned Sir John in Toronto to meet her with the car at the Toronto waterfront. After almost two hours in the open cockpit, in those days a "lightning" trip, Lady Eaton was greeted by a most perturbed husband with, "You, a mother of five children, risking your life in a thing like that!" Lady Eaton finished the story by telling that her upset husband's driving up Yonge Street was so erratic that she finally burst out, "I may have been taking a risk when I went in the plane, but that was nothing compared to the danger I am in right now!" and his laughter relieved the tension. Sir John died of pneumonia at a tragically early age in 1922.

The Royal Muskoka Hotel, built in 1901.

Monteith House, Rosseau, c. 1910.

Kawandag in the 1950s.

Lady Eaton was deeply devoted to the study and performance of music, generously supporting such organizations as Toronto's Conservatory of Music, and the Rosseau community benefited from this interest. When she was visited by such virtuosi as harpist Joseph Quintile, she would order her large and powerful steamer out in the early evening with her guests playing enchanting music on the after-deck. Edward Johnson, later Manager of the Metropolitan Opera of New York, once spent a month there seriously preparing for his next season's opera and concert tour. Kawandag had furnishings of great beauty, including some priceless antiques, and each of its 15 bedrooms was decorated in the theme of the name given to it, such as the "Butterfly Room".

From 1947 to 1958 Kawandag was operated as a summer resort by Kawandag Limited, a company whose major shareholder was Maurice Margesson, sports entrepreneur and tennis player. The outstanding tennis courts, installed by Slazengers, the sporting goods firm, accommodated the Muskoka Lakes annual tournament (now held at Clevelands House) and were visited by many prominent tennis players. During this period, you could tie your launch to the spacious dock and order a lunch or dinner, preceded by a champagne cocktail or the drink of your choice in the conservatory overlooking Lake Rosseau.

Then, around 1965, Maurice East, organizer and idea-man, who was controlling operations also at Muskoka Sands Inn and Killarney Mountain Lodge, turned it into a tourist attraction by constructing a palisaded fort and staging a pageant several times a day.

Rosseau school took over the property in the late 1960s. A private school which enrols up to 100 boys, it offers cross-country and down-hill skiing two afternoons a week in winter, a district Outdoor Education Day in September, water sports in summer, and a five-week summer course for upgrading subjects. Inquire about summer painting classes for adults.

The main house of Kawandag was destroyed by fire in January 1973.

Beyond Rosseau School, Highway 141 winds past Rosseau Falls, a Muskoka beauty spot, and the rock cliff face of Skeleton Bay to the southeast, leading to Bracebridge in 28 miles.

The Coate Family

In 1873, Frederick W. Coate had just settled in his new log house about three miles south of Rosseau village. The railroad ended at the Severn River and a stagecoach carried travellers from the Severn to the steamer at Gravenhurst.

Eleven years later, F. W. Coate's eldest son, Charles, married a Toronto girl, Catherine, whose father had been bringing her to visit the Coate family since the time they were first established in Muskoka. The young couple spent their honeymoon in Muskoka, then proceeded to Memphis, Tennessee, where Charles was employed in the cotton

Rosseau Falls.

Ontario Ministry of Industry and Tourism

Ontario Archives

Bala c. 1910, with the *Ahmic* and the *Cherokee*
docked at the C.P.R. Station wharf.

Ontario Ministry of Industry and Tourism

Bala Falls.

Guide Book and Atlas of Muskoka and Parry Sound Districts, 1879

Among the islands on Lake Joseph, a sketch by
Seymour Penson.

exporting business. After eighteen years in Memphis, a city of heat, dust, flies, yellow fever and post-Civil War chaos, they moved to New Orleans with their three children. They usually spent their summers in the house they had built on the Muskoka farm. In their early summers they explored Muskoka by canoe, taking trips to Georgian Bay, Catherine Coate attired in the dress of the 1890s—which covered her from neck to ankle—and a brimmed hat. They were such ardent canoeists and campers they thought nothing of taking a baby with them, although the route was complicated and entailed many portages.

When Charles Coate retired from business in 1922 they returned permanently to Rosseau. He died in 1926 but his widow, Catherine, lived 28 years longer to the age of 92. One of the ministers who conducted her burial service was the Rev. J. S. Ditchburn (1891–1968), the son of Rosseau pioneers who was married to her daughter, Marian Wynne. Ordained at Trinity College, Toronto, after serving overseas in World War I, he served Episcopal churches in New Orleans and Detroit, and was chaplain at the State University of Louisiana for 20 years, employing his special talents as a youth leader. He returned to Muskoka permanently in 1949, was Anglican incumbent at Bala and MacTier, wrote a book, and served on Bala's town council.

In the 1870s and '80s, the Coates, the four Ditchburn brothers and a few settlers of the then distinct "gentry class" joined together for little dinners, whist and loo parties. Photographs show them snowshoeing and riding on the frozen lake in sleighs full of straw pulled by horses. In summer they played tennis and, when swimming, had the convenience of three-sided bathhouses in their bays, typical of the era but now a thing of the past. With so many people cruising around today with binoculars, such a bathhouse would be mighty handy when slipping into the lake for a skinny dip.

IX *BALA*

Highway 69 from Gravenhurst travels along Lake Muskoka's western shore, through Bala, and up the west side of Lake Joseph. It is based on the old Musquosh Road which joined Bala to Gravenhurst in 1872. Starting at the Gravenhurst post office corner and proceeding through West Gravenhurst, you reach the Narrows Road at 4.0 miles, marking the top of Muskoka Bay at the Lighthouse Narrows and the beginning of the wide body of Lake Muskoka.

The Campbell's Landing Marina, about mile 7.2, is one of Muskoka's largest boating facilities. Peter Campbell, born on the property in 1903, made his early living as a boat chauffeur and mechanic for wealthy Americans in Beaumaris, worked as a carpenter at Camp Borden during World War II, and started his marina in 1945. "First I built an ice house, then a boathouse, then a storage shed that could hold six cars. But soon people wanted to leave their boats in the shed instead of cars. That's how it started. Helped by my sons Gary and Raymond, we built an addition nearly every year. We couldn't have afforded to build the whole thing at once as some marinas do. We just built as the demand came, selling some of my land to cover costs." Peter Campbell built cottages in the area and still holds the licence to trap in winter in the bush on the southwest side of Highway 69 across from the Landing. "There's better trapping now, surprisingly, than when I was a boy," he says. He's also happy driving his restored 1913 Minett cruiser. Marjorie Campbell, the woman at his side, enjoys the operation of a summer grocery business, and notes that they installed the first pay telephone in 1956, a great convenience to the community and travellers.

Then Pine, Deer and Pigeon Lakes are on the west side of Highway 69. Beyond these at 9.8 miles is Walkers Point Road (Muskoka Road 30), the entrance to a large, irregularly-shaped peninsula which juts out into Lake Muskoka. The Walkers Point community, in the southeastern section of this peninsula, had received its name by 1879 when four members of the Walker family from Gananoque, Ontario, took up farms there.

WOOD WINDS MUSEUM

The Wood Winds Museum is in the Barlochan area on this peninsula on the same property as the Schell Marina. Telephone Joyce (Mrs. J. W.) Schell to find out when you can visit, or ask a Muskoka Tourist

CNIB

Scale: 1 inch = 4 miles

Information Centre to check. After entering the Walkers Point Road, about 1.9 miles from the beginning of MR 30, turn right at 2.5 miles, then left into the Schell property at 2.8 miles.

The museum collection is housed in an old log farmhouse, a log church dating back to pioneer days (both dismantled on their original locations and reconstructed at the Schell site), and several sheds for machinery and marine exhibits, all near the lake in an old clearing surrounded by "bush", as were all pioneer farms. This particular farm was a free land grant taken up in 1872 by the Parletts, who later moved to Bracebridge where one became mayor.

The Wood Winds collection includes an early map of free grant lands, a pioneer stove, tools, household equipment, a handwoven blanket of intricate design, family photograph albums, an excellent exhibit of Indian handcrafts, and relics recovered by divers from the first steamboat, the *Wenonah*, and from the steamboat *Waome* which met sudden disaster in a storm.

Three items of a bride's trousseau remind us of the Broadley family, the first on the peninsula, who arrived by boat in 1867 long before a road had been cut through the forest. Mrs. Broadley had been brought up in a well-to-do English household and had no training to enable her to cope with a pioneer home. After giving birth to the first child in the community (a girl) and two other children, she was so ill that her husband took her back to England where she died. Mr. Broadley left the three children in England to be brought up by wealthy relatives. When one daughter grew up, she came to Muskoka to visit her father and became engaged to Horace Prowse, son of the Englishman who established the Beaumaris Hotel on Tondern Island near the opposite shore of Lake Muskoka.

Alfred Smith, Joyce Schell's grandfather and the second settler on the peninsula, came in 1868 before this part of Wood township had been surveyed, and he moved several times to find the best land in the Barlochan area. A wealthy English family bought Alfred Smith's first farm from him and moved from England with their servants. They soon left, however, dissatisfied with Muskoka as a substitute for the social and sporting life on an English country estate.

Beaumaris Hotel changed the whole character of this area in the 1890s when it attracted wealthy American and European guests. Before the foreign tourists came, it had seemed to Joyce Schell's grandmother "as if there was no money in the whole of Muskoka." Some of these tourists and others influenced by them bought Lake Muskoka islands and properties on the lakeshore for the construction of large and expensive summer homes. Local farmers acquired small steamboats to carry or tow the building materials, and employment was provided at the construction sites. After building was completed, the servicing and caretaking continued to provide employment. Tanbark discarded from the two tanneries in Bracebridge, for instance, was transported to the islands. Chocolate-brown in colour, it was used for spreading on paths edged with white birch poles.

TORRANCE

Back on Highway 69, drive about three miles past the Walkers Point Road and turn right to go to Torrance. (Torrance was on the highway before 1970 when a bypass was completed.) After passing the Black Lake road, you may turn either left into Torrance or right on to East Bay Road which continues for 2.2 miles, giving access to the peninsula properties on Bala Bay on the west and East Bay on the east.

In Torrance, Queen's Walk Road recalls the 1959 visit of Queen Elizabeth II and her short walk from the main street to the railway line to board her train. The village dock is on Bala Bay farther along Queen's Walk Road. A few cottage resorts and Brandywine Camp Site are in this vicinity .

The story of the first settlers around today's village of Torrance in Wood township was told in *The Early History of Torrance*, a booklet by Mrs. G. R. Jestin, dated December 1938.

The township was named after the Hon. Edmund Burk Wood, Provincial Treasurer of Ontario (1867–71) in J. Sandfield Macdonald's government. In 1867, at the time of Confederation, he was elected to the Canadian House of Commons. He had only one arm and was known by the nickname "Big Thunder" because of his powerful voice and roaring speeches full of references to scripture, poetry and the words of the famous orators before him. At the time of the "Pacific Scandal" over the great railway which was to join British Columbia on the west with the Maritime provinces on the east, E. B. Wood entered loudly into the fray which led to the defeat of Sir John A. Macdonald's government. Subsequently he was appointed Chief Justice of Manitoba in 1874, and held this post until his death at Winnipeg in 1882.

Wood township was opened for settlement in 1869, and Mrs. Jestin tells about three men from Eramosa (a village near Guelph in southern Ontario) who travelled to Muskoka that summer to investigate the government offer of free land. The hardware merchant, William Torrance, with two farmers, Joseph Coulter and George Jestin, took the train to Orillia and then a stagecoach to Gravenhurst. From Gravenhurst the steamer *Wenonah* took them part way up Lake Muskoka and they disembarked on the west shore. The country was rough and rocky, full of lakes and streams, the trees untouched by the lumberman's axe. Old Indian trapping trails through the woods guided them from lake to lake. Two locations were chosen on Lake Muskoka and one on Clear Lake.

Before returning south to Eramosa, Torrance and Coulter stayed long enough that summer to build their own log houses. Jestin's house on Clear Lake was to be built by the only other man the three settlers had found in the area, a French-Canadian lumberman named Jannack, who had a log house on an island later named Bala Park. (The narrows at the south end of Bala Park Island are shown on today's maps as "Jeannette", but local people use the name "Jannack Narrows", which appears to be historically correct.)

The following spring, in 1870, the three men returned to Gravenhurst by wagon with their families and supplies for a year. As the road ended at Gravenhurst, the drivers and teams were sent back to Eramosa, and the settlers and their supplies were transferred to their destination by steamer. When Jestin found that Jannack had disappeared without having even begun construction, the three men and their sons had to build a cabin quickly for the Jestins.

The next year oxen and farming implements were brought in to break up the ground between the stumps of the felled trees. About a dozen more Ontario families and two from England settled on Black Lake, Hardy Lake and East Bay. The older settlers helped the new arrivals to build houses and clear the land, using the oxen in the logging operations.

Jestin gave an acre of cleared land on Lake Muskoka to the community, half to be used for a school and half for a cemetery. A ratepayers' association was formed and responsibility allocated, a school was built and a teacher engaged. In 1875 when the settlers petitioned for a post office, William Torrance was appointed Postmaster and the hamlet took his name. The mail was then brought from Gravenhurst by steamer in the summer and by stagecoach in winter, for by this time the Musquosh Road from Gravenhurst to Port Carling up the west side of Lake Muskoka was well under way.

Around 1878 Olaf Willison came from Sweden and began a settlement around Gullwing Lake and Clear Lake (sometimes called Torrance Lake) which soon included other Swedish families, among them the Strombergs, Walstroms, Fergussons, and Nelsons.

Mrs. Torrance, one of the first three women, died in 1877 giving birth to a boy when no doctor was available. A twelve-year old daughter then took over the mother's job of keeping the house and looking after six other children. Mrs. Coulter was consumptive and did not live long, leaving at least five children. Mrs. Jestin survived to raise her children, but tragedy befell the family of her eldest son, William.

William Jestin married Elizabeth Parker after she had taught for a year at the Torrance school. One day in the summer of 1882, William Jestin returned home in the evening to find his wife, the maid Emma Bailey, the baby and his two other children missing. He called on his neighbours but nobody knew where they had gone and a search was organized. The next morning they found the two children alone on Pewabic Island in Bala Bay. The little girl was fast asleep. Although the boy was wide awake, he was terrified and had not answered the calls of the search party because he thought they were the screams of wild animals. William Jestin learned that his wife had taken the children and the maid to pick huckleberries on the island. Somehow the baby had fallen into the water and his wife and the maid were both drowned attempting to rescue him. Their names are inscribed on the stone which marks William Jestin's grave in Torrance cemetery on the East Bay Road.

Camp Pinecrest on Clear Lake, run by the Toronto West End Y.M.C.A., is indicated by a sign on the left of Highway 69 just before the right-hand turn to Bala.

The Southwood Road (Muskoka Road 13) is also marked nearby. This is a country road running through the centre of Wood township and the Southwood community to Severn Bridge. Fields of undulating rock ridges, like wide ocean waves, border sections of the Southwood Road.

Back in 1870, a surveyor working in Wood township reported that the township was broken and rocky and almost totally unfit for agricultural purposes. The 1879 *Atlas* shows no settlers along its southern and western boundaries and only one in the interior. All the settlers were beside Lake Muskoka on the Musquosh Road (today's Highway 69) and around Torrance.

A summer is not complete for me unless I have travelled the length of the Southwood Road, about 25 miles. One summer evening our family was delighted to come upon a doe and her fawn on the road. They loped ahead of our slowly moving car until we sounded the horn and they jumped off the road into the bush.

The tiny Church of Our Lady, at Southwood, is attached to the West Muskoka Missions, Anglican Church of Canada. Partially built of logs, it is one of the most photographed churches in the whole of Muskoka. A few devoted members keep it decorated and repaired for Sunday services in summer when they are joined by cottagers from Morrison, Muldrew and other nearby lakes. The Harvest Festival, followed by a bountiful lunch on the grounds, is the highlight of the year.

BALA TODAY

According to the Bala District Chamber of Commerce, Bala is Canada's smallest incorporated town, with a population of about 550.

The 1.5-mile approach from the junction of the Southwood Road and Highway 69 is lined with Long Lake cottages on the west and Lake Muskoka cottages on the east. Long Lake is 65 feet deep in the centre and clean. It has 85 cottages on half its shoreline; the other half is privately owned and not yet built upon.

Bala is a lively town in summer with shops featuring the latest in colourful clothes and merchandise. Past several hotels, the Brewers Retail store and the tourist information centre (ask about Georgian College's current summer courses, possibly textiles and leatherwork), you may turn right on to Musquosh Road where the shops and restaurants back on Bala Bay. At the waterfront you may board one of the scheduled boat cruises.

For several years the Ontario Power Boat Association, with the help of local businessmen, has held the Western Ontario Hydroplane Championships on Bala Bay. The weekend-long event in the second half of August includes two dances, a parade, a steak fry, tiny boats streaking across the water at speeds approaching 100 m.p.h., and water ski and kite flying competitions.

On Musquosh Road, the "Kee to Bala" (built in 1941) features dance parties for teenagers, the public Saturday night dance, and little theatre when available. During the Golden Age of the Big Band, the earlier pavilion on the same spot was called "Dunn's—Where All Muskoka Dances". Gerry Dunn recalls that the visiting name bands who played one-night stands at his pavilion included those of Tommy and Jimmy Dorsey, Glen Miller, Les Brown, Cab Calloway, Woody Herman, Count Basie, Duke Ellington and Louis Armstrong. Such headliners, paid from $2,500 up, would attract a capacity crowd of 2,000 with perhaps another 1,000 outside in boats and on the grounds listening to the music through the open windows.

Across the road from the Kee is the Bala Cenotaph in a little park with flower gardens and a long view of the Muskoka River starting out for Georgian Bay. Beside this is a modern cement comfort station, for which Bala is to be complimented; next, more lovely parkland where you can sit on a bench behind a railing and watch Lake Muskoka waters drop into the river while birds flit about happily in the spray.

Cedarhaven Antiques, on the same side of the Musquosh Road as the Kee, is a delightful place to visit; early pine furniture and reproductions are part of the stock. Cedarhaven may be closed in winter; make inquiries. Old-time bottles gleaned from Muskoka lake bottoms are one local specialty. A 1900 Gordon's Gin bottle, for instance, might sell for $7.50.

Trinity Church, a few doors past Cedarhaven, has been attracting many visitors with its "open door" policy. The Rector, Rev. John Watson, lays boards over the pews to display hundreds of pictures of English and Welsh cathedrals and abbeys. Visitors signing the guest book include an amazing number of Britons who go in "to have a nostalgic look at the sights familiar to them and to pick out their birthplaces on the map." The tiny Chapel of the Welsh Saints, most appropriately named as Bala takes its name from Wales, has an altar in memory of R.A.F. Captain Aage Laursen, a Canadian, who lost his life shortly after his 21st birthday in a flying mishap over Wales in late 1940, after having flown 32 missions in the first Wellington Bomber Squadron over Germany and Norway. Look for the crested hooked rug and the petit point pew cushions.

On Highway 69, after you cross the river, are the Bala post office, grocery and hardware stores, Vivienne McDonald's shop specializing in English antiques, a popular bakery and the liquor store.

Bala Memorial Community Centre, built in 1953 under the direction of the Bala Women's Institute and turned over to the town in 1959, is on a side street nearby. The large Annual Antique Show is held there in September during the Cavalcade of Colour.

The $210,000 Bala Area Sports Centre, opened March 1974, with indoor artificial ice rink, is across the road. The basic financing was provided by township debentures for $125,000 and a provincial government grant of $10,000. Lions Club bingos, bake sales and many local fund-raising schemes raised the balance. Inquire if roller-skating is available during the summer months.

Jaspen Park is reached by a left turn to Highway 660 on the south side of the river. A plaque on a small rock in the park area commemorates the 1967 Centennial of Confederation. Benches have been contributed by local merchants and manufacturers. The facilities include a bandstand, drinking fountain, toilets, men's and women's changing houses and an outdoor fireplace. A program of swimming instruction is given at the sand beach, and here you could launch a canoe for a ride on the river.

Stephen Bernard Panting, born 1926 in Bala, had his first experience in surveying "at the end of a chain" down this river when he was in his early teens. After serving in the army for two years, he resumed his education, graduated as an engineer from the University of Toronto in 1952, received his commission as Ontario Land Surveyor in 1953, and became Director, Engineering Services Branch, in the Ministry of Natural Resources. The principal concern of that Branch is the Ministry's construction program as applied to hydraulic dams for fisheries and wildlife management, recreation, and water control. During earlier years with the Ministry, S. B. Panting's work was concerned with control dams on the Muskoka watersheds, particularly fitting for a born and bred Muskoka man, but now that work is the responsibility of local officers of the Ministry.

The bridge over the Muskoka River on Highway 69, with a short approach laid on filled land, was built in 1964, fifty years after Bala's incorporation. Previously all traffic had to follow what is now the Musquosh Road with only a one-lane bridge. There is a plaque describing the Precambrian Shield mounted in front of the blasted rock face in the approach to the Highway 69 bridge. It was unveiled on August 25, 1966.

On the north bank of the river, opposite Jaspen Park, there is more park and recreational land. Rock formations surrounding Bala Falls provide happy clambering for the agile. A peaceful little park contains the historical plaque commemorating the founding of Bala in 1868.

Portage Street is just beyond the park and runs along the north bank of the river. Ontario Hydro has erected a plaque on the side of this street commemorating its early development in Bala. A little farther along the street is the town's public boat launching ramp which gives access to the river below the falls. The street was called "Portage" because small boats are portaged over it from the water above the falls to the river below.

A lane under the railroad bridge opposite Portage Street leads to the large town dock on Bala Bay. A boy pulls boxes of groceries in a wagon down this lane from store to boat. To reach this dock by car, take the right turn off the main street past the liquor store to Superior Propane and turn right.

THE MUSKOKA RIVER

The river which flows out of Bala Bay on the west side of Lake Muskoka over the Bala Falls receives the waters from the lakes and streams in Muskoka and beyond to the headwaters in Algonquin Park, carrying them down to Georgian Bay. Today's maps mark the river as the "Muskoka" because of the anatomy of the watershed, but in early days the name of Muskoka River was reserved for the North and South branches emptying into Lake Muskoka from the north-east, while that part of the river running out of the western shore at the present site of Bala was originally called the Musquosh (or Musquash) River, a name that is often used today. A further complication in name occurs because the river divides into two below Bala at the Moon Chute, and the northerly branch is called the Moon River. Because of this, the river just below Bala Falls is sometimes called the Moon River.

In the 1880s and subsequently, Indians from Gibson Reserve near Bala used to guide fishing parties and canoe trips on the Moon River, a popular spot for sportsmen and canoeing enthusiasts. They could go all the way to Georgian Bay with about 25 portages, some of which were very short. They could then, from what is today called Woods Bay, return to the Muskoka Lakes by way of the Blackstone and Crane Lakes chain to Lake Joseph. In spite of the many hazards of such an expedition and the possibilities of getting lost, families made this trip in the 1880s—often without guides, the mother wearing a dress almost down to the ground and sometimes carrying a small baby in her arms.

The Moon Chute, where the river divides into the Musquosh and Moon, was a dangerous place, but it was flooded in 1938 by a power development at Ragged Rapids on the Musquosh River, about five miles below Bala, with a regulating dam on the Moon.

Nowadays the canoe trippers on the river are mostly young people from Muskoka summer camps. Much of the territory has been built up by cottagers, altering its original wilderness beauty.

Cavalcade of Colour

In early fall, the foliage in Muskoka provides a breathtaking display of colour. In recent years a wide variety of activities and events have taken place between September 15 and October 15, at Bala and other Muskoka communities. Parades, picnics, camera tours, turkey dinners, and dances are among the events held under the aegis of the Cavalcade of Colour. Enquire at tourist information offices about this year's program.

BALA HISTORY

Thomas W. Burgess, the town's founder, disembarked from the *Wenonah* in 1868 about a mile north of Bala Falls at a channel in Lake Muskoka between Sutherland and Bala Bays. A Scot by birth, he was moving to Muskoka from his first Canadian home at Saugeen River, in Bruce County, Ontario. He and his family, using at first a vacant lumber camp as living quarters, located on ten lots in Medora township near his landing point, the channel which became known as the Wallis Cut when it was deepened in 1876 by Joseph Wallis, a sawmill man from Port Carling. The Wallis Cut, incidentally, was further deepened to eight feet in 1925-26 as a navigation aid.

According to the late F. W. Sutton, author of *The Early History of Bala*, Thomas W. Burgess "at once built a sawmill on the Mill Stream to supply building needs and a store to supply surrounding farms," and named his new home Bala because of his recollection of the beautiful Bala Lake section of Wales which he had visited. He had six sons and four daughters, some of whom were born in Muskoka.

Thomas Burgess was appointed Postmaster when the post office was established in 1872, the year the Musquosh Road linked Bala with Gravenhurst. His business interests expanded over the years to include a bakeshop, blacksmith shop and a supply boat. He was Reeve of the United townships of Medora and Wood for several years and acted as an Agent of the Department of Indian Affairs for the Watha Indian Band at the nearby Gibson Reserve after their arrival in 1881. An exponent of the railway, Thomas Burgess died just a few years before the railway reached Bala.

In 1914, when Bala was incorporated as a town, Dr. A. M. Burgess, one of the six sons of Thomas Burgess, became its first mayor. Before that Bala had simply operated under township Council jurisdiction and did not serve a municipal apprenticeship as a village.

Information about the early families of Bala—such as the Guys, Kniftons, Suttons, Jacksons, Greens, Boards, Curries, Mays, Hamills, Clementses, Moores, Spencers, Hurlings, Wilsons, and Huggetts—is given in F. W. Sutton's booklet. A story about his own family, who arrived in 1882, engaged my interest. After making the observation that pioneering was hard on men but harder still on women left so much alone in the bush, early reading having filled their minds with dread of wild animals and wilder Indians, Sutton continues:

> I can imagine my Mother's perturbation when, while alone, an Indian called and asked for the Boss. Mother of course said, he will soon be in; the man seated himself just inside and said he would wait. Hours after, when Dad returned, it transpired the Indian wanted to borrow a gun. What a quandary! Not wishing to make a bad start by offending a native, the gun was lent and the folks went to bed thinking they had seen the last of their gun. Morning came and lo! the gun and a hind quarter of venison were hanging in the porch. A life long champion for the Red Man was won.

Ephraim Browning Sutton, the father of F. W. Sutton, cleared a farm and developed a summer resort, known as Camp Sutton, for use by a group of U.S. Civil War Veterans who had broken away from the famous "Solid Comfort Club" of Beaumaris in search of better fishing grounds. In 1914 he built a brick summer hotel, the Swastika (now Balabay Lodge). From 1886 until his death in August 1917, he was a correspondent for the Bracebridge, Gravenhurst and Orillia papers, which also printed his verse under the nom-de-plume "Muskoka Bard". His only surviving child, F. W. Sutton, was born in Muskoka January 3rd, 1884, three children born in England having died there, "victims to the filthy vaccination system of that time".

NORTH OF BALA

The access road to Acton Island is 4.5 miles north of the archaeological plaque at Bala. The bridge to Acton Island offers a fine view, if you can stop there a minute or so without impeding traffic. The good main road on the island, from which many cottage roads branch, ends at Maddock Marina, 3.8 miles from Highway 69. Across from Maddock Marina, which will provide taxi service if required, is Clovelly Antiques on Bala Park Island, open in summer only. Clovelly Antiques has a room full of antique merchandise for sale and a museum section with parlour, dining room, kitchen and bedroom furnished in the old-fashioned way, where the articles are not for sale.

Bala Park Island is not accessible by road. The Canadian National Railway line runs through the length of this island, however, entering it by bridge over Jannack (or Jeannette) Narrows and leaving by bridge over the Wallis (or Wallace) Cut, from which it continues on to Foot's Bay. Bala Park Island used to have a huge hotel, as illustrated in *Picturesque Views and Maps of the Muskoka Lakes, Canada* (Rolph, Smith & Co., Toronto, 1893), a publication which included timetables and fares for combined railway and steamboat from Detroit, Port Huron, Niagara Falls, Toronto, and Hamilton. Guests could travel all the way by rail after the railway reached the island, but in 1893 they changed at Gravenhurst to Muskoka Lakes steamboat. A. P. Cockburn, the founder of the navigation company, wrote the foreword for *Picturesque Views*, eulogizing Muskoka and using all his persuasive powers to entice visitors.

Medora Lake, on the opposite side of Highway 69, is noted for its 300-acre cranberry marsh, which was the first such operation in Ontario when Orville Johnston began it in 1953. The plants require an elaborate irrigation system and a delicate balance of light, heat and water for a successful growing season. The berries are harvested in October and shipped to the marketers, "Ocean Spray". You may be having a little bit of Muskoka with your Christmas turkey.

On another road off Highway 69 to the right, about a mile north of the Acton Island Road, you can drive along the shore of that part of Lake Muskoka called North Bay, a particularly pleasurable drive in early July when the road is lined with white daisies.

Back on Highway 69 drive north between Ada Lake on the west and Butterfly Lake on the east to Glen Orchard, which derived its name from pioneer families named Orchard. This is the junction point with Highway 118 to Port Carling. Hammond Transportation has a bus service to Bracebridge, Dorset, and Port Carling which you might find useful.

Many area parents involve themselves happily in the progressive planning, education and activities at the central school located in Glen Orchard. The Community Centre, a former school house, is used for Christmas parties, bingo games and other fund-raising activities, Women's Institute meetings, firemen's dances, ratepayers' meetings, card parties and crafts. Visit the "Smithy" display room which, incidentally, was built with salvaged lumber from an old barn. Ted Church, three sons and two nephews (at last count) manufacture a variety of metal products from intricately designed candleholders to circular staircases. The metal is heated in a forge and then turned on an anvil, an art process which is becoming rare.

If you are interested in maple syrup or pine cobblers' benches, coffee tables and desks, look into the Settler's Workshop in Glen Orchard where Jack and Doreen Jennings enjoy using their land and its resources to live as present-day settlers. Fifteen teachers from Wales visited them at Easter 1975 to try snowshoeing and producing maple syrup in the sugar bush.

At the junction point with Highway 118, Highway 69 starts to turn westerly to run along the shore of Lake Joseph, one of the three main Muskoka Lakes, indescribably beautiful and deep, with a deepest sounding of 308 feet in its northerly reaches. Some early cottagers on Lake Joseph moved there because Lakes Muskoka and Rosseau, the location of their first cottages, were becoming too crowded for their taste. They preferred increased travel time to increased people.

Sherwood Inn on Lake Joseph has catered to a renowned clientele from all parts of the globe since it opened over thirty years ago. Inquire about a reservation for the Sunday buffet or for dinner. Milt and Elizabeth Conway recently acquired the Inn. Milt is easily recognized as the former T.V. announcer at the Barrie station; while Elizabeth was a Barrie high school teacher and then travel counsellor for the Provincial Tourist Information Centre at Barrie. (Incidentally, this Information Centre at Barrie has a direct line to Toronto. Look up the number under Governments—Ontario—Industry and Tourism.)

Foot's Bay, on Lake Joseph, with its large concrete government dock, grocery store, post office, boat service centre and cottage colony, is about six miles northwest of the junction of Highways 69 and 118. William Edward Foot came from Ireland with his family in 1871 and soon acquired land beside the bay which was given his name. After moving to Bracebridge, he was active in the Agricultural Society until moving on in 1886 to Manitoba, soon returning to work in Toronto. Subsequently he became Deputy Registrar and Justice of the Peace for more than twenty years at Parry Sound, where he died.

Just beyond the Foot's Bay Road, Highway 69 meets the end of Highway 103, the road opened in 1957 to give access to the Georgian Bay side of Muskoka. If you continue north on Highway 69 for 3.3 miles, you drive out of the District Municipality of Muskoka and into Parry Sound District. Before returning to Muskoka, I should like to describe one point of importance in Parry Sound District, 1.4 miles north of the border on Highway 69, because of the involvement of Muskoka Power Squadrons and Lions Clubs.

The Canadian National Institute for the Blind
Lake Joseph Adjustment Training and Holiday Centre

Built with $350,000 raised by the Lions Clubs of Ontario, the Centre was opened in 1962. It accommodates slightly over one hundred blind or nearly blind guests and is laid out so that a sightless person may move about freely but safely. Different camp periods accommodate different ages from young children to elderly people.

The large swimming area at the beach is surrounded by buoys, and because of the danger of a sightless person swimming under the buoys safety nets hang down into the water from the buoy line. Blind children learn to row and paddle in the buoyed-off area. A nurse is stationed on the beach during all water activities. As an added precaution, the Centre owns a station wagon equipped as an ambulance. In addition, regular search-and-rescue and fire drills are held. The experience will be valuable in life situations elsewhere. Safety railings block off the dangerous sections of the shoreline, and safety gates have been fitted to boat ramps.

Gifts to the Holiday Centre have included a large boathouse, a launch for pleasure touring, a sailboat and a powerful craft for water-skiing. The water-skiing program was inaugurated in 1967 when Bert Wheel, Canadian champion, was called upon to initiate the instruction. The blind have fun and, when they are able to get up on the skis, a great sense of achievement. They ski double with an instructor who gives wake information via his hand on the blind skier's shoulder. Occasionally a blind youth achieves the ultimate thrill of kite flight on water skis. Lake Joseph provides safe, open space, unimpeded by islands, in front of the Centre for these activities. A 20-foot sailboat was presented by the Toronto employees of Allstate Insurance in 1973.

On the shore, handrails connect the buildings, among which are eight resident units, and ramps take the place of stairways. The bedrooms are numbered in braille on the posts opposite each door on the veran-dah railing. Playgrounds for the children have been laid out; a summer-house stands on a high point overlooking Lake Joseph. The murmur of a babbling brook, the perfumes of a scented garden, a nature trail equipped with railing and braille signs all enhance sensory experience. The beauty and vibrant colouring may be enjoyed by those retaining partial sight; picture windows bring the comforting warmth of the sun and the vista of trees and lake into the high-ceilinged lounge. The tuck shop allows children the pleasure of choosing a treat and the experience of paying for it from their own money. Many have handi-caps, severe or comparatively light, in addition to their blindness, and it's particularly heart-warming to see such children move about in this environmental freedom.

A "Day Afloat" held each July since 1965, takes C.N.I.B. children for a cruise on the lake and a picnic at the Island Park in Port Carling. The boats are supplied by members of the Bracebridge and Graven-hurst Power Squadrons; the Bracebridge and Port Carling Lions supply food, treats and gas.

X GIBSON INDIAN RESERVE

bird flies through sky
bird flies down and lands on rocks
and bird is happy
(By Penney Sahanatien, Age 9, Glen Orchard Public School,
November 1974.)

Highway 660, which joins the town of Bala with Highway 103 on the
west, runs through Gibson Indian Reserve. These Indians are descended
from Quebec Iroquois, and the story of why they moved in 1881 to
land in Gibson township, District of Muskoka, would make a great
Canadian movie. There's something for everyone: early Canada, religious controversy, a mob scene, an explosion, a raging fire, Parliament
inactive in the face of outrage, then exodus and pioneer hardships overcome, with the Iroquois as heroes.

GIBSON RESERVE HISTORY

The tale begins in 1717, when a tract of land on the Quebec side of
the Lake of Two Mountains in the Ottawa River was granted to the
Seminary of St. Sulpice, a Canadian branch of the Order of the Sulpicians, of Paris, France. This grant was made to provide a place to
move Indians converted to Christianity in the mission at Sault au
Recollet on the Island of Montreal, because land on that island had
become too valuable for accommodating an Indian Mission. The Seminary was required to pay the costs of moving the Sault au Recollet
Indians to the new land on the Lake of Two Mountains, construct a
church and fort, and give moral and religious instruction to the mission Indians. The buildings at the new location were erected around
a quadrangle and joined by a wall. The Indians built little cabins close
by and the settlement became the village of Oka, subsequently famous
for the cheese made by its monks.

The Sulpicians permitted the head of each Indian family to occupy
and cultivate a small field on condition that the Indian occupants, or
their descendants, would not have right of transfer and that the permission for occupancy might be revoked at any time. All wood needed
for fuel and building might be taken from mission land, and cattle
grazed on common ground adjacent to the village. The Sulpician priests
provided a school for the Indian boys, and sisters taught the girls in
the convent.

Trouble began to brew when the neighbouring hunting grounds became unproductive and the Indians found their plots of ground insufficient to provide food and clothing for their families. Some of the Indians began to take the use of other lands and cut timber for sale. Periodically they were arrested for trespass and committed to prison for these offences, but the Indians stubbornly maintained that the land was theirs and that the Seminary only held it in trust for them.

Protestant missionaries began to visit the Indians at Oka in the early 1870s, introducing them to the Bible and suggesting conversion from Roman Catholicism. Soon about three-quarters of the Oka Indian population—consisting of all the Iroquois with their three chiefs—went over to the Wesleyan Methodist Church. The remaining Indians, mostly Algonquins, remained Roman Catholic.

The Iroquois built a little chapel in the village on ground purchased from an Indian woman whose family had been in possession of it for sixty years. Regular services were held and a Methodist preacher was sent to live with them as a missionary. The Seminary took court action against the three Iroquois chiefs, as trustees of the new congregation, for taking the use of its land for an unauthorized purpose. In December 1875, the court declared that the Seminary was indeed proprietor of the land, according to the terms of the original grant, and it could, therefore, revoke the permission for occupancy.

The counsel for the Indians was not present at the hearing. He was away at the time and claimed the hearing was scheduled without due notice and without his knowledge. If he had been in attendance, he might well have defended them on the following grounds: that freedom of worship was a primary right of all subjects of Her Majesty, Queen Victoria, in every part of the Dominion; that the Seminary was bound by the conditions of the grant to provide religious instruction; that the Iroquois had chosen the instruction of the Methodist denomination (a religious body recognized by the law of the land as fully as the Roman Catholic); and that the Iroquois had undertaken to erect the church at their own expense when the Seminary had failed to honour its obligation to provide the Indians with a place where they could worship in their own religion.

Many of the Iroquois were away hunting the day the court decision was handed down, and a mob of French-Canadians descended on the Methodist chapel and demolished it. With the smashing of the chapel, the dispute became a nation-wide religious controversy, with newspaper coverage, for instance, in the Waterloo *Chronicle*, *South Simcoe News* and Toronto *Globe*. One report said the Indians were told, "Now you see what we can do, it will be your turn next. That's how we'll clean you out, cursed heretics, we are masters now."

The Iroquois chiefs and the Methodist minister restrained the Indians from retaliating, but the situation in Oka deteriorated, until a body of Quebec Provincial Police, armed with warrants for the arrest of 56

Indians for trespass, descended on the village in June 1877, 18 months after the burning of the chapel. Eight arrests were made; the others hastily abandoned Oka. About four o'clock next morning a loud explosion awakened the village and a $50,000 fire broke out, destroying the uninsured Catholic church and other nearby buildings in the quadrangle. The main entrance gate to the quadrangle had been broken through as if by a cannonball, which explained the explosion. It was known that the Indians had had in their possession an old brass culverin which they had sometimes fired off on festive occasions. But the culverin could not be found. The priests accused the Indians of the crime, and the Indians claimed the priests perpetrated it. Outside Oka, it was generally believed that a few Indian hot-heads had acted without the sanction of the main body of Indians.

"Yet all this time," said the Toronto *Globe*, "there is land enough in the Province of Quebec and to spare where game is still to be had and where the soil will yield" to which the Indians could be moved at the expense of the Seminary, the provincial government, and the dominion government. The Methodist church had been urging the dominion government to intervene before the disastrous fire; now further appeals were made. But it was not until 1881 that the Iroquois were finally moved out of Oka. From the possibilities presented, they chose a reserve in Gibson township in the District of Muskoka.

Gibson township was formed in 1880 and named in honour of Thomas Gibson, M.P.P., a man of good judgment whose advice was sought in the Assembly. He represented a Huron county riding in the Legislature of Ontario from 1867 to 1898.

The exodus story is told in *History of Gibson Reserve* (Bracebridge *Gazette*, circa 1952), a booklet by Philip LaForce based on the tales handed down through the Iroquois band and on the observations of his own lifetime, for he was born in 1891 to Gibson pioneers. He says that about 30 families came to Gibson, among whom were those named Commandant, Decaire, Dewasha, Franks, LaForce, Montour, News, Rennie, Rivers, Sahanatien, Stock, Strength, Thompson and White.

A big barge floated the migrating Indians and their freight down the Lake of Two Mountains from the wharf at Oka. At Sainte Anne de Bellevue they transferred to the train that would take them to Gravenhurst. Some families elected to stay in Gravenhurst because winter was approaching. The remainder boarded the steamer for Bala, where a government official gave them the details of the canoe journey down the river to their land. They shot the Cedar Rapids and three more series of rapids without mishap, landing at 3 o'clock in the afternoon of October 31st, 1881.

Predicting it would snow that night, Chief Fleecy Lowi Sahanatien gave immediate orders to put up the tents and gather in a supply of wood. ("Fleecy" referred to the Chief's tightly curled hair, a product of his part-French ancestry.) The ground was so cold that crawling babies could not be put down even in the tents. Mothers cut blankets into strips to wrap around the legs and feet of the children old enough to walk. Had they been one day later on the river they would have met with extreme hardship, for a foot of snow fell that night. Only the men ventured out the next day to shoot a deer for food.

When milder weather returned, the land was inspected, locations were chosen and logs for shanties were cut. By the time the severe winter set in, some were settled in winterized log shanties, others in tents. For food, the Seminary had supplied Chicago salt pork, cornmeal and molasses, "the cheapest lines", but Gibson waters abounded with fish and Gibson forests with deer. Half a dozen large fat carcasses were stripped, the meat was cut in slices and strips, dried and smoked before a strong fire, and put away in boxes for the late winter and early spring when the deer in the forest are lean and the flesh barely edible. The men tanned hides and the women made buckskin moccasins for each member of the family. They had no thread for sewing, but used "babiche", a thread or thong of sinew, gut or rawhide. Candles made from the fat of the Chicago pork provided their only light. They blazed a trail through the woods to Bala and purchased some supplies from J. W. Burgess's store.

In March maple trees were tapped and the heavy run of syrup boiled down, yielding hundreds of pounds of sugar and enough syrup to last a year. The berries and wild apples of the next growing season were sweetened with the maple sugar. In early May, the chief ordered those who had wintered in Gravenhurst to come to Gibson, and bees were formed to clear land and sow crops. The Seminary sent some carpenters from Montreal that summer to build a few houses of hewn timber.

When the corn was well ripened, it was husked and shelled, boiled with hardwood ashes until the chaff came off, then rinsed several times in clear water and dried. The Iroquois used a hand grinder, "ga-ni-ga" in their language, made from a maple log hollowed out to a depth of 16 inches into which the corn was poured, and then pounded and ground with a pole of hard maple four feet long and four inches in diameter, whittled and rounded at both ends with a hand grasp in the centre. The women separated the grinding into flour and corn meal and from these products made a boiled pudding which served as bread, meat pies, wild apple pies, and corn soup.

At first the chief walked back and forth to Bala to get the mail for the post office, called Sahanatien in his honour. Later he bought a horse and the trail was widened enough for a horse and jumper sleigh to get through in winter. Wagons were used later when the government granted money for the road to be widened and for stumps and rocks to be removed.

A small building left by the French carpenters when they moved out was used for a school in 1882. The next year the pioneers formed a bee and built a new school. The Department of Indian Affairs arranged for a succession of teachers and, in 1952, for a new school building which included living quarters for the teacher and his family. In the first log church built by Gibson men, services were conducted by a missionary. The church building was improved, and eventually the schoolteacher became responsible for church services.

In the early days, Mrs. Johanna Sahanatien and Bella Sahanatien (later Mrs. Morris Roberts, who moved to Toronto, but returned to the reserve when widowed) took turns playing the organ for 20 years, followed by two sisters, Lydia and Maggie DeCaire. Then Mrs. Dan Commandant was organist for 50 years and led the singing. On a summer Sunday she would go with the preacher for services at Shawanaga Reserve and Parry Island and then play an evening service at Gibson, an exhausting day "but one quite normal for Rhoda Commandant" (Thora Mills).

The men worked in lumber camps during the winter for board and a wage scale which ranged from $8 to $12 per month. A few years later the scale was increased to $12 and $16. Every spring the Indian men bought livestock with the money earned, and in the summer they cleared and worked the land. The women laboured alongside the men. By 1900, Philip LaForce wrote, every farm family had from 10 to 35 head of cattle, pigs, chickens, and at least one horse, and the community was prospering.

In 1931 a monument was erected in honour of the chiefs of Gibson Reserve to celebrate the golden anniversary of the pioneer arrival. Built of boulders each about the size of a man's head and set in concrete, it has a four-sided, pyramidal shape, with the names of nine chiefs engraved by Jonas Rennie on the granite slab on the monument's face: Lowi Sahanatien, Angus Cooke, Francis Decaire, Napoleon Commandant, Peter Strength, Mitchell News, Albert Commandant, Mitchell Franks, Isaiah Sahanatien. Hundreds of people attended the feast when the monument was dedicated, many from outside the Reserve, including government officials. "Many of the Big Shots were up and seen all what the Indians could do," reported LaForce.

The unique sentence structure used by Philip LaForce in his writing seems to indicate that a group of people living in the backwoods, whose original languages were French and Iroquois, developed a method of expression in English that one would not likely encounter elsewhere. On the other hand, it has been suggested that he deliberately distorted sentences to attract attention, to be different, to establish his image as an Indian columnist. The Ontario Weekly Newspaper Association provided a fitting climax to his career by choosing him the best country correspondent in 1959 (six years before he died) and giving him a great ovation at their annual dinner at the Royal York in Toronto when the award was presented. He wrote about the Gibson pioneers:

All the bee they had made always gave a good chance as prayer meeting after supper. They had God's power those days strong in prayers also in hymns and their luck is coming good in every way. The womans helped their husbands in prayers and in hymns as well. When the French and English was translated to Iroquois Indian language, then nearly every home had the Bible. The wives read every day to the family and say their prayers. It was all in peace living happy every day. Although the hard hardships they went through still had plenty of good courage in their hearts.

William and Mary Kendall

In the Gibson Reserve cemetery are the graves of the Reverend William Kendall (1868–1953) and his wife Mary (1869–1946). Her tombstone is fittingly inscribed, "Many daughters have done virtuously/But thou excellest them all/Prov. 31/29".

William Kendall, an English barrister, had come to Canada in 1904. He married a lovely young Indian widow with two daughters whom he met at a Methodist Mission for the Iroquois near Montreal. Soon after he was received as a Probationer for the Methodist Ministry, and in 1906 was appointed to the Gibson Reserve Mission.

The Kendalls stayed three years at Gibson, and during this time a fine new church was built to replace the original pioneer church. William Kendall was said to have an extraordinary love for God. Mary Kendall knew every man, woman and child on the Reserve, visited them, talked to them, prayed with them and helped them. She could sing the hymns in the Indians' language, occupy a place in the choir and play the organ. During the years in various missions with her husband, she helped many through sickness with her knowledge of healing herbs. She planned building projects, did carpentry and cement work, gardened and drove a car.

When the Kendalls retired from active church work about 1935, they purchased land on which to build a house near the Gibson Reserve, for Mary Kendall wanted to be near the Iroquois, isolated as she was from the tribe in Quebec. It appears that Mr. Kendall was the son of wealthy English landed gentry, but he did not return to his native land to claim his inheritance. Mrs. Kendall died after a stroke in 1946, at the age of 77, and was buried in the Gibson Reserve cemetery. When Mr. Kendall died in his 84th year, he was buried beside her.

GIBSON RESERVE TODAY

The band has 246 members, including men, women and children, only about 90 of whom live on Reserve property. For example, Ken Commandant, a former chief, lives in Bala and is a road supervisor.

"We Indians are not being discriminated against as we were in the past," said Bill Rennie, Band Administrator. "Integration in the schools is making a big difference. The children have been bused to Bala for school since the early 1960s and are not separated any more from the main community. They can and do go to university and get degrees." Bill Rennie's father had sent him to live at a school near London to learn trades. Bill had liked it there, and it worked out well for him. Much of his working life has been spent in the United States where his children were educated.

"My dad, who spoke and wrote English, drew up documents, and acted as interpreter, used to come back here from Ottawa thoroughly disgusted at the type of treatment Indians received when they went to discuss business. They would have to stay down there two or three days to get permission to talk to someone, and when they were able to get in they were never given any real consideration. The difference between those days and now is like the difference between night and day. Now when we say we want to talk to the Deputy Minister, there is no pushing around. The doors are wide open.

"The people themselves took the side of the Indian people; and now there are Indian organizations. A member of our band is on the staff at CORAID (Central Ontario Regional Amalgamated Indian Development Corporation) which represents 15 or 16 Reserves. CORAID advises and assists in economic development and publishes a newspaper for Indians." Bill Rennie is a CORAID director.

The Gibson Reserve Trailer Park, on Webster Lake, is at the junction of Highways 103 and 660.

If advantageous and possible under today's building restrictions, the Reserve could lease 70 building lots, all with 100 feet river frontage and 200 feet depth on the Muskoka River near Highway 103.

Iroquois Cranberry Growers, a business enterprise undertaken by Gibson residents to stimulate their economy, fronts on Highway 103 just north of the Muskoka River. One day in 1965 when he was hunting in thick bush where wild berries grew, Sid Commandant, then chief, conceived the idea of growing the berries commercially. Four years later, after a great deal of preliminary effort, clearing for a cranberry marsh was begun. The first five-year period required an expenditure of $150,000 (from the Reserve and a government cost-sharing program) for developing and planting a suitable area. Orville Johnston, who runs his own marsh on Medora Lake, and Vernon Goldsworthy, known as "Mr. Cranberry" in Wisconsin, have been giving technical assistance.

Inquire about the Gibson park being developed for snowmobiling and other outdoor activities at the site of two experimental "Arctic" houses. These houses are constructed by spraying an inflated polyethylene dome with materials which harden into a weatherproof veneer, completely insulated, and virtually indestructible. Inquire also about the Gibson annual bean supper, customarily held in November at the Community Hall.

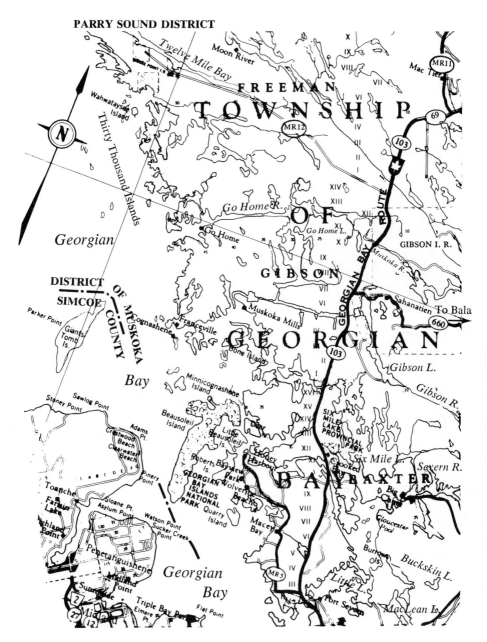

Scale: 1 inch = 4 miles

Gibson Reserve Church.

Geraldine Coombe

Ontario Ministry of Industry and Tourism

Camping on Georgian Bay.

Delawana Inn, Honey Harbour, c. 1930.

Geraldine Coombe

Delawana Inn, 1975.

XI WEST MUSKOKA AND GEORGIAN BAY

The Muskoka township of Georgian Bay was formed January 1st, 1971 to amalgamate for regional government the three former townships of Freeman, Gibson and Baxter, all bordering on Georgian Bay. Since the north–south Highway 103 was opened in 1957, an increasing amount of the Georgian Bay shoreline has been made accessible by new east–west roads. The new municipal offices in Port Severn were officially opened by Ontario Premier William Davis, in July 1974.

GEORGIAN BAY

Georgian Bay has an extremely irregular shoreline and is dotted with 30,000 islands, including those of the Georgian Bay Islands National Park, many of which lie within the District of Muskoka. Exposed both to the prevailing westerly winds of the Great Lakes and to northerly storms, the water is often rough, but the inside channel between the islands and the mainland offers comparative shelter to small boats. Half-hourly marine weather reports and up-to-date charts of the sheltered channels, made first in 1966 by the Canadian Hydrographic Service, have reduced the danger to small boats.

Do not venture out into the Bay without the charts. Buy nautical charts from the Canadian Hydrographic Service (Ottawa) or from Georgian Bay marinas and hardware stores.

Etienne Brûlé was the first white man to see Georgian Bay in 1610. Five years later Samuel de Champlain, founder of Quebec, travelled through Georgian Bay with Huron Indians on his way to Lake Ontario in an expedition against the Iroquois. Champlain referred to it as "Mer Douce" because it was like a sea but had fresh water rather than salt. It was charted in 1822 by Captain Henry W. Bayfield, Royal Navy, and named by him after the newly ascended monarch, George IV.

During the 1812–14 War, American and British forces battled for control of the Bay. The Americans first sought the British at a small post which protected the mouth of the Severn River, an important British trade route used to transport supplies to Mackinac and western trading posts. The Americans had to abandon their attack plan when heavy fog added to the difficulties of finding a passage through uncharted rocks and islands, and provisions ran low during their several days of searching. They sailed away to attack the British post on St. Joseph Island, near Mackinac, and burned it on discovering it had been abandoned. When they moved on to attack Fort Mackinac, they found their guns could not be elevated sufficiently to fire on the Mackinac position above the water. A flanking attack through the woods was repulsed by Indian allies of the British, and the Americans withdrew after an unsuccessful frontal attack. The British were able to retain control of the Bay during subsequent encounters, but fortunately the war ended before it could escalate into a holocaust.

A convenient way for the visitor to get "that Georgian Bay feeling" or perhaps even to catch the Georgian Bay madness that is rampant in the region, is to go over to Midland (about 18 miles from Port Severn) and take the four-hour cruise on the *Midland-Penetang 88.* This cruise runs daily from the last weekend in June through to the first weekend in September (Labour Day weekend), and passes through the islands and along the Georgian Bay shore of West Muskoka. Make a reservation (705-526-6783).

The *Midland-Penetang 88,* a converted 112-foot Fairmile, was used for convoy and patrol duty from June 1943 to May 1945 while based at Halifax, Sydney, and St. John's.

About six miles north of Midland, the boat approaches Beausoleil Island, part of the Georgian Bay Islands National Park which has 55 islands in all and three acres of mainland. Park facilities improve each year as 30 small islands are gradually being equipped with landing docks, fireplaces, and picnic and camp grounds. Landing places have been established, for instance, on Bone Island, at Twelve Mile Bay, and in the Moon River basin.

Beausoleil is five miles long and a mile wide with several small lakes in the centre, contains the Park administrative offices, and has swimming, camping and picnic facilities. Park naturalists conduct a summer program of field trips to give visitors an insight into the interrelationship of climate, water, land forms, plants and animals. Exhibits and a self-guiding nature trail also explain the island's natural features. In the evenings, slides and films are presented in the outdoor theatre.

The Y.M.C.A. has a camp on Beausoleil. A Junior Warden program, designed to inform young people about National Park conservation and recreation, and potential careers within the National and Historic Parks Branch (Indian Affairs and Northern Development), has been introduced on Beausoleil, providing two summer months of work, education and recreation for eight boys and eight girls aged seventeen.

Organized groups who would like programs or walks conducted by a naturalist are invited to contact the Park Naturalist at 705-756-2415. For other pertinent information, write to the Superintendent, Georgian Bay Islands National Park, Box 28, Honey Harbour, Ontario.

As the boat passes Frying Pan Bay at the northern end of Beausoleil, you will see cruisers tied up. Some of these have home bases at various points along the Trent–Severn Waterway. A cruiser-owning friend told me, "Frying Pan Bay is a forming-up place to make the main charge on Georgian Bay. You are well sheltered, the facilities are good and the scenery is nice. The National Parks Commission staff make you feel welcome and are expanding facilities so they can accommodate more cruisers."

Georgian Bay's history is recalled by Brébeuf Lighthouse, a lake freighter guide, named after one of the Jesuit martyrs. The Watcher Islands are described in the cruise guide as "long ago a lookout point for the Huron Indians."

A cottage on Governor Island has a high observation platform reached by an elevator in a rectangular tower. The island was originally a crown grant to Sir John Beverley Robinson, Chief Justice of Ontario from 1829 to 1862 and then first judge of the Court of Error and Appeal.

Georgian Bay islands vary from flat, water-washed rocks, with perhaps one twisted tree pointing southeast, through islands which accommodate one cottage comfortably, to large multi-dwelling islands. All the trees, predominantly pine, bear the unmistakable imprint of the prevailing west wind.

The *Cognashene Cottager* reports the following sign on a vacant island near Go Home Bay:

Trespassers will be forgiven

IF

1. They carefully extinguish their fire
2. They pick up and take with them all garbage
3. They do not disturb the large rattlesnake
   that lives at the base of the pine tree

People who summer on Georgian Bay have learned to live with the possibility of coming upon a massassauga rattlesnake, or they wouldn't have stayed. The massassauga is not normally aggressive, and it usually prefers retreat to attack. Keep a person bitten by a rattler quiet, carrying him if possible, and get him without delay to the nearest hospital or local doctor (familiar with snakebite treatment). The hospitals in Orillia, Bracebridge, Midland, Penetanguishene, and Parry Sound, for instance, are antivenin depots.

Freddy Channel, the village street of the Cognashene cottagers, is identifiable by a large houseboat, the *Vancrofter*, set into the shore. The *Vancrofter*, built about 1885, with room to sleep 25, was towed throughout the islands for Louis O. Breithaupt, of the Breithaupt Tannery in Penetang. She was pinned to the shore in the 1920s and was bought around 1960 by B. Napier Simpson, Jr., because of his interest in preserving a memento of early days when houseboats on the Bay were not uncommon.

Muskoka Mills at the mouth of the Musquosh River, had a population of some 400 in its heyday, when it was a centre of tanbark production. In 1882, when it had used up all the merchantable timber that could be economically moved to it, the mill was dismantled and moved considerably farther north. The settlement became a ghost town and gradually disappeared.

Grandma Whalen first tented on the island that became Whalen's Island (where the cruise boat may stop) in the 1890s, sprinkling lots of salt around the tent as a snake deterrent. Her doctor had recommended that she "get out on one of those islands about 12 miles from town," as she had such serious hay fever and asthma. When the relief she obtained proved gratifying, she built a small cottage. It was quite common for her son to take provisions to her from Penetang by rowboat. Other seekers of relief from hayfever and asthma came along, asking to stay with her, and this was the beginning of the Whalen Island summer resort (destroyed by fire in the fall of 1941), a large percentage of whose clientele were Cincinnati musicians remembered for their impromptu concerts.

Orville Wright, who flew the first powered plane at Kitty Hawk in 1903, came to Cognashene in 1916 and bought Lambert Island, building a cottage on the highest point and an accompanying escalator to haul supplies and luggage up from the shore. It is now a matter of some local regret that a museum was not made of this cottage with its many mechanical gadgets. Fortunately, his 32-foot boat, the *Kitty Hawk*, was discovered in an abandoned boathouse and has been restored. It was a star attraction at the 1976 Toronto International Boat Show.

B. Napier Simpson, Jr., in a *Cognashene Cottager* article, remarks that the Cognashene area was not colonized until some 20 or 30 years after the Muskoka Lakes had become a tourist mecca:

> Few are the cottages known to have been built before 1900.
> . . . The cottage was for summer use only and there was little
> coming and going once the cottage was opened up. Because
> the building was to be used only in hot weather, wide eave
> projections were popular to keep out sun and rain. . . . Most of
> the old-timers have vents high in the gables or in the dormer
> to exhaust the hot air from the roof. . . . To insure a cool in-
> terior, the kitchen was often housed in a separate building
> behind, to keep the wood range out of the main cottage. Food
> was hurriedly moved across the connecting veranda to the
> dining room in the main building. . . .

The local landmark, Blarney Castle, built on the mainland about 1900, is an example of a cottage where the kitchen was built separately, in this instance so that wandering hunters, trappers and loggers in need of food during winter could gain easy access to provisions without disturbing the rest of the house.

Near Blarney Castle is a Samuel de Champlain historical cairn, the southernmost of three marking Champlain's route from the French River.

The tour boat passes close to one cottage, sometimes referred to as a "circle on a rock". Painted grey and with large windows, it is built in a circle around a central fireplace with an outside circular balcony.

Later, I telephoned William Grierson, the Toronto architect, to discuss his design. He said it was a logical extension of the site, a small island with no trees and, therefore, no front or back, presenting views of Georgian Bay in every direction.

When Mr. Grierson planned his own island cottage, on an "emaciated hunk of granite" farther out in more open water, he extended the idea and built a circular cottage around an inner court, decorated with flowers and shrubs, where people could sit outdoors and be protected from the everlasting wind. Building on an island so far out would have been highly impractical before the days of powerful, reliable inboard–outboard motors. Mr. Grierson described how every item for the building had to be ordered, preferably in the fall of the year. Then everything was assembled in Midland during the winter and transported to the building site in April in huge barges. He said that most of the construction labourers were Indian or part-Indian, sometimes with French names, and that many came from King's Bay.

As the boat approaches Go Home Bay, you will see the library and post office of the Madawaska Club. There will probably be a long line-up of young people and children in orange life jackets waiting on the dock to make purchases at the boat's snack bar.

Incorporated in 1898 with more than 1,000 acres of land, the Mada-waska Club's charter allows only University of Toronto graduates to own land. Nevertheless, ways have been found to allow inheriting children who are not U of T graduates the use of their parents' land, and islands which were subsequently added to the original 1,000 acres have been exempted from the ownership restriction.

Although now used as a summer retreat with about 130 cottages, the Club was incorporated primarily to preserve and propagate fish and game and conduct experimental work in forestry, biology and other branches of natural science. In 1912 the Club discontinued its scientific work and demolished its experimental station.

The name "Go Home" seems to have been used by early lumbermen, and originated either with them or earlier fur traders and trappers who considered the landmark the place from which they started for home after isolation in the wilderness. The Indians used the name "Quab-kong" (place where there is iron) referring to iron kettles used in the pot holes on High Rock Island at the entrance to Go Home Bay.

On West Wind Island, in Monument Channel, north of Go Home Bay, is the famous cottage built by Dr. James Metcalfe MacCallum (1860–1943). Born in Richmond Hill, Ontario, young James developed a passion for Georgian Bay when his father, a Methodist minister, was transferred to a Collingwood church which included a mission that ran right up the east coast of Georgian Bay. During his medical career, Dr. MacCallum was associated with the Hospital for Sick Children in Toronto. After he built the West Wind Island cottage about 1911, he used to invite artists (some of whom later formed the Group of

Seven) to stay there. Dr. MacCallum persuaded Tom Thomson to leave commercial art work and devote all his time to painting for one year, guaranteeing his expenses. He did the same for A. Y. Jackson.

After Dr. MacCallum's death, West Wind Island was purchased by Henry R. Jackman, President of the Art Gallery of Ontario from 1959 to 1961, and Mrs. Jackman. The murals in the cottage by Thomson, Lismer and MacDonald, commissioned by Dr. MacCallum, were removed and transported to the National Gallery at Ottawa for display and safe-keeping. There they are known as the MacCallum–Jackman Donations.

In winter when the Bay freezes to a depth of 22 to 30 inches, it is the rendezvous of snowmobilers, but in addition to those who use the machines for sport and pleasure are people such as the France family who live in winter isolation on the eastern shore and depend on snowmobiles to travel back and forth over the ice to town. The community at Franceville was founded by Wilfred and George France and their parents in the 1920s and developed into a summer resort.

HONEY HARBOUR

West from Highway 103 near Port Severn, Muskoka Road 5 (formerly Highway 501), passing a golf course and trailer park at 3/10 mile, reaches Honey Harbour in about 7 miles.

Chartacteristic of Georgian Bay communities, boats owned by islanders and those whose mainland cottages are not accessible by road are tied up by the hundreds in Honey Harbour marinas. Some leave their boats at their cottages, preferring not to store them on the mainland, and use water taxis to go in and out of cottages. The Honey Harbour Boat Works, where Fairmiles were built during World War II for the Canadian Navy, has a car park, taxi service and launching ramp. The Village Marina is farther along the road, and in that direction there is also a public access to the water. Many of the storekeepers, builders and service personnel around the Bay are bilingual French-Canadians.

Delawana Inn at Honey Harbour is a very large resort with a completely new main building, guest cottages and motel-like bedroom units, and it offers a wide variety of entertainment. It is owned by Didace Grisé and Sons who also own Elgin House on Lake Joseph and Aston Villa on Lake Muskoka.

The first Didace Grisé in the region settled at Midland about 1870. He and four sons built the now-defunct Royal Hotel at Honey Harbour around the turn of the century, and they bought the property that became Delawana in 1920. Fred Grisé, one of these sons, married Eda Hartwell, of United Empire Loyalist descent, who arrived in Midland to teach school. Their union was an interesting one because of their differing cultural backgrounds—he from a group traditionally determined to remain French in spite of the transfer of Canada to Britain; she a descendant of those who came to Canada in order to remain British when their fellow Americans were in revolt. In 1949 Fred Grisé handed over Delawana to his son, F. Didace Grisé, who continued the program of steady improvement. A new and larger main lodge to replace the one destroyed by fire in the summer of 1973 was in the final stages of completion in May 1974 when F. Didace Grisé died suddenly from a heart attack at age 59. He had also married a schoolteacher, Marie D'Aoust, and four sons are presently conducting the business.

The shopping facilities in Honey Harbour include a beer and liquor store. Opposite the post office is another large boat launch and car park business. The Exhibit and Information Centre of the Georgian Bay Islands National Park (Department of Indian Affairs and Northern Development) is open Wednesdays and Sundays from 8:30 a.m. to 4:30 p.m. One church has weekly bingo games; movies are shown in another church basement once a week—for children at 7:00 p.m., and for adults at 8:45 p.m.

Honey Harbour has an annual winter carnival about the middle of January which features cross-country skiing and snowshoeing.

Highway 103

North of Port Severn and the Honey Harbour road, a long arm of Gloucester Pool (part of the Severn River) appears on the east, and just above that is the entrance to Six Mile Lake Provincial Park. Both Gloucester Pool and Six Mile Lake have large cottage communities. Estonian-Canadians predominate in one section of Six Mile, resulting in a heightened awareness of the pleasures of sauna baths and the harvesting and preserving of mushrooms. The Ministry of Natural Resources has established a fish sanctuary for stocking Six Mile with lake trout fingerlings and yearlings. A half-mile gorge from Six Mile to the Severn River below the Big Chute is a place of such great beauty that some "Six Milers" think it should be turned into a national monument.

The McDonald River, flowing from the north end of Six Mile Lake through rock formations to Georgian Bay, is soon crossed by Highway 103.

The Gibson River, out of Gibson Lake, flows under the next highway bridge. It reaches Georgian Bay near Muskoka Mills after joining the Muskoka. The Gibson is considered one of the best intermediate grade (or "family trip") rivers by the Voyageurs, a kayak club whose members and their children study animals and birds, identify edible plants for survival training, and enjoy "white water".

The Gibson Reserve Trailer Park, on Webster Lake, is at the junction of Highways 103 and 660, the road which runs east through the Indian Reserve to the town of Bala.

Farther north on the west, Go Home Lake Road is a pleasant route in from Highway 103 to a large boat-parking channel for cottagers, a marina and a post office. Most of the 1,000 cottages on Go Home Lake, many of which have been built since the opening of Highway 103, are accessible only by water.

"One of the nicest one-day trips I've been on in recent years is a circle route through Go Home Lake to Georgian Bay and back again by the River," says one experienced Muskoka canoeist. "You can leave your car at a large parking lot kept by the Ministry of Natural Resources at Go Home Lake." But be warned! There is one open stretch of water in the Bay which is not for the novice canoeist.

If there is a breeze from the north, start your circle by heading into it up Go Home Lake and this saves you heading into it on the much rougher Georgian Bay. Portage at the Fire Ranger station to the Go Home River; about one hour's paddle takes you to Georgian Bay. Head down the Bay, pass the Champlain cairn, turn east into Freddy Channel, pass the Wabena Point store, Portage Island National Park, an open air church, Franceville, Muskoka Mills, and turn up the Musquosh River. The river trip up to the control dam at Go Home Lake is beautiful wilderness, without a cottage, and is considered the best part of the trip. There are two portages plus one walk through on the way up and from the control dam it's an easy paddle in to the dock at Go Home Lake.

The Parry Sound office of the Ministry of Natural Resources will send you small brochures entitled *Gibson and McDonald Canoe Route* and *Moon River Canoe Route*. Ask about any other routes in which you are interested.

At the Muskoka (or Musquosh) River bridge on Highway 103, there is a picnic area on the east side. On the west side of the highway, the Muskoka River now runs through Sandy Gray Lake and Go Home Lake to Go Home Bay, the home of the Madawaska Club.

Sandy Gray Lake was named after a lumberjack in charge of a crew floating logs to Georgian Bay down the Musquosh River in the spring of 1866. While he and his crew were breaking a log jam, Sandy Gray was drowned, along with Henry Hogaboam.

According to the memoirs of David A. Hogaboam, Henry's brother:

> The news of the tragedy travelled to Gravenhurst, where a neighbour of ours, William McNeil, was working. He came straight away, bringing us the news. 22 miles he walked, all night. While we were having breakfast, Mrs. McNeil came in. She could not speak, but kept wringing her hands. My father said, "Mrs. McNeil there is something wrong. Tell it out." All she could say was, "Henry is drowned," and it was enough.
>
> Father got up from the table and walked around to the back of the house. When we got to him he was lying with his face in the mud, poor old man. We managed among us to get him on his feet, and then he said, "Mother, I'll never give up," and

walked into the house quite calmly apparently. Oh, it was pathetic to see him in his resolve not to give in. My parents' hair began to turn grey soon after. It was a hard blow to us all.

Almost immediately after the Hogaboams had received the news of the drowning, Erastus Hanes, from Utterson, David's older brother Charles and his father set out for Bracebridge, where they procured a canoe to paddle and portage to the scene. They found that the rivermen had made a boom downstream and Charles was left to watch and wait when his father and Erastus Hanes went home, thinking it might take some days to find the bodies. During their absence the bodies were recovered and a decision was made by Sandy Gray's father and "friends from the east" to burn Sandy Gray's body "thinking it to be too warm to move him." Charles allowed Henry's body to be burned alongside, and this cremation instead of the traditional burial caused additional grief in the Hogaboam home.

Legend has it that Sandy Gray's spirit is not at rest. Early campers on the Musquosh reported that they were awakened in the dark of night by a mysterious noise and saw a ghostly figure walking nearby, dragging a boom chain.

Hunting and fishing camps were common in isolated parts of Muskoka. One hunter tells of five camps he and friends built at Sandy Gray Falls after they found the deer hunting was good. The first had log walls, four feet in height, a large tent for a roof, the ground for the floor and a sheet iron stove for cooking and heat. The last was a large cedar log cabin with kitchen and a lean-to. Local people recently found their camp on the Moon River had been vandalized and said, "When hunt clubs leave tea, coffee, sugar, etc., in their camp, they do not mind if someone uses these if they are passing by. It is only when everything is thrown out and different things stolen that we wonder what kind of people enjoy destroying something which could mean the difference between life and death to someone who needed a warm, dry place to stay if they were in trouble."

On the east side of Highway 103, north of the Muskoka River, is another development by the Gibson Reserve, the Iroquois Cranberry Growers.

Now you come to Muskoka Road 12, the Twelve Mile Bay Road, running westward from Highway 103. This road, made possible by the construction of Highway 103, opened up the Twelve Mile Bay shoreline and the Wah Wah Taysee (Firefly) Indian Reserve section of the Georgian Bay shoreline, enabling the Ojibway children to transfer to the enlarged MacTier Public School, with high school students going to Parry Sound. A plaque mounted on the north side of the road is inscribed with the name Ma Kah Ga Win Road, which is translated as "Discovery Road", so named by the Ojibway because of what you will discover at the end of the road, opened November 26th, 1966.

The sales of cottage lots in a Crown Land subdivision, made in conjunction with the road development, created the need for a marina. The Federal Department of Indian Affairs provided $100,000 for capital costs and expense of initial operation to the Moose Deer Point Indian Band (which has 125 members) for the construction of a marina, consisting of a store building, slips for 90 boats and winter storage sheds for 80 boats. The marina stays open in winter for snowmobilers. The first marina in Canada solely owned and operated by Indian people, it was officially opened July 25th, 1969, by the Hon. Jean Chrétien, then federal Minister of Indian Affairs and Northern Development.

The Moose Deer Point Marina is at the end of the Twelve Mile Bay Road, and it supplies water taxi and groceries. You can rent a camp or trailer site on a point of land across a small bay, accessible by a fork in the road; some cottages on Georgian Bay and some year-round Indian homes may be reached by a branch off this fork.

Go back down Muskoka Road 12 and take the Galla Lake fork (about 3½ miles before Highway 103). There's lots of room at the lake to back a boat-trailer down for launching. A narrow road circles the lake to give access to cottages and Indian residences. Galla Lake and Lower Galla Lake are joined by Miners Creek to Tadenac Bay on Georgian Bay.

North on Highway 103, on the northwest side of the steel-girdered bridge over the Moon River, there is a spacious picnic area with tables and barbecue.

The Moon Island Park Reserve (currently 15,000 acres in size) near the mouth of the Moon River in the District of Parry Sound is being expanded to about 25,000 acres, and will become a wildlife sanctuary. When development money is available, the park will be equipped with campsites for overnight use, and other amenities for visitors.

About one quarter of all Muskoka land still belongs to the Crown, and much of this is in the township of Georgian Bay.

MacTIER

Muskoka Road 11 (formerly Highway 612) on the west side of Highway 103 leads to MacTier, a village on Stewart Lake. You drive past its Curling Club, the clubhouse of the Canadian Legion Branch 507 with its cut stone block cenotaph "In Memory of Those Who Served their Country", and the MacTier Public School before reaching the MacTier Memorial Community Centre, built in 1956. The Centre contains an artificial ice rink (installed in 1974 with the help of a $10,000 provincial government grant) for hockey, and facilities for wedding receptions, dances, bingo and movies. The food markets, hardware store, post office, liquor and beer stores, all located in one short block on Front Street, serve many cottagers nearby on Lake Joseph and Stewart Lake as well as MacTier's permanent residents. The *Georgian Bay Beacon*, a weekly, is the local paper.

At the end of the business block is the Canadian Pacific Railway with ten through tracks and five for storage and repair. The service required for engines has greatly decreased since the transition from steam to diesel in the 1950s. The roundhouse has been dismantled, the restaurant torn down, the original stationhouse closed, and the railway's smaller operations moved to the former telegraph building. The new bunkhouse next door, made up of 36 prefabricated units with individual rooms, lounge and air conditioning, replaces the railway boarding houses of former days. The houses on Railway Street on the other side of the tracks were built in the days when a much larger payroll was sent to MacTier. The village's population includes many retired railroaders. "I was born and raised in Toronto," one such man said to me as he worked at repairing an assortment of power mowers at the side of his house, "and you can have it."

Turn left at the end of the business block to drive alongside the park with its Centennial Monument and baseball diamond where the MacTier team plays league baseball with teams from Bracebridge, Elmvale, Beaver Creek Correctional Camp, and other communities. Turn right on Maple Street, cross the railway tracks and keep on going to Stewart Lake where an area at the dock has been buoyed off for safe swimming and instruction.

Edward Moore first acquired land around Stewart Lake from the Crown and built a hunting lodge named Buckeye. Although he spent only summers there, he was furious when some of his land was expropriated in 1907 for building the railway, but later, as the community around him changed, he sold some of his remaining land and various lakeside cottages were built. In 1922 he sold Buckeye to a family named Clinch who wanted to accommodate tourists.

Many boys who have sung in Anglican church choirs are familiar with Stewart Lake because Miss Doris Clinch has operated the small resort inherited from her parents as a summer holiday house for these young singers since 1937. St. Simon's, St. James Cathedral, St. Anne's, St. Barnabas, and Grace Churches, all in Toronto, St. Jude's in Oakville, and churches in Muskoka have participated here in choir school, games and watersports.

MacTIER HISTORY

Muskoka Station, the original settlement at the place that became MacTier, was created by the railway. The narrow-gauge track from Toronto to Bolton, built by the Grand Bruce Railway in 1869, was rebuilt to standard gauge in 1882 and extended by the Canadian Pacific Railway to join the transcontinental line at Romford (just east of Sudbury) during the years from 1905 to 1908. Because it was half way between Toronto and Sudbury, Muskoka Station was made a divisional point. Here new crews took over from the crews out of Toronto who stayed overnight and returned to Toronto next day. A roundhouse where steam engines could be taken off for replacement or repairs and a boarding house to accommodate railway men were constructed.

When Hugh Anderson was looking for a place to start a general store in Muskoka, he met at Muskoka Station two friends from the days he had worked as a Grand Trunk conductor. They strongly advised him to start his store at Muskoka Station, and Anderson boarded a work train to buy lumber in Parry Sound. When he asked railway friends in Parry Sound how to get it down to Muskoka Station, one said, "You see that flat car with a winch on it? Pile all you got on there. Tommy is going down to Muskoka Station to get his engine washed out and he will take it down for you."

Next morning, Anderson brushed the snow off his building site and started the 12′ × 16′ store, a rough lumber shell covered with white building paper on the inside and tar paper on the outside. He opened for business November 16th, 1908, ten days after his arrival, having stocked the store with $700-worth of groceries from Toronto and Coldwater.

Soon tiring of having to get his mail from Foot's Bay, Hugh Anderson used his connection with grocery wholesalers in Toronto to get an introduction at the Post Office Department, and convinced it that Muskoka Station should have its own post office; he was appointed Postmaster. Before long, it became apparent that the name was a poor choice when mail bags addressed to Muskoka Wharf and Muskoka Falls came to Muskoka Station and vice versa. When asked to choose a new name, Anderson used the name of A. D. MacTier, the General Superintendent of C.P.R.'s Eastern Division, correctly predicting that this recognition would help to get the community such amenities as nice lawns around the station and recreation grounds.

"In addition to the store business," Hugh Anderson wrote in his memoirs, "I cut a single cord of wood every day at first to keep myself from pulling out. . . . I took on all the feeding of stock that went over the C.P.R. north and south and did this for six years. . . . I fed 1900 remount horses that went overseas in World War I, and it was that job that got me down in health." He sold out to his son-in-law in 1926, and the business is now Boytt's Hardware, on Front Street, operated by Hugh Anderson's grandsons. Across the road is the new post office building opened in 1973.

Charles Robert Clerk (1850–1911), an Anglican priest, also occupies a place in MacTier history. During the construction of the railway, he ministered to the men working on the track and, when Muskoka Station came into existence, he began holding services in the boarding house even before it was finished. Born in London, England, he had emigrated at the age of 20 and worked on a farm near Oakville, Ontario, saving his money to help other family members emigrate to Canada. After six years in Canada, Clerk began study for holy orders and was ordained four years later. While serving at St. James the Less, Toronto, he attended classes for several years in the Trinity College Medical School and acquired knowledge that was useful in emergencies, particularly after his retirement to Freeman township. He farmed in Freeman near MacTier and Foot's Bay, built a log house and a log chapel with a bell on it, and conducted a school for ministry students in the Diocese of Algoma. After his death, the chapel bell was transferred to All Saints' Church in Mac-Tier, built in 1912, and used for many years; now the historic bell is hung over a gate on his grandson's property.

"Clerk carried out a program of baptizing all the children in this area, whether or not affiliated with the Anglican Church," Mrs. A. Spinney of MacTier told me, "simply because he believed all children should be baptized, and he did not care if their families ever darkened the doorstep of his church. These baptismal records have been providing undisputed evidence of date of birth for a surprising number of residents in this community who have no other evidence of their eligibility for government old-age pensions."

FREEMAN TOWNSHIP

Freeman's northern boundary, marking the line between the Districts of Parry Sound and Muskoka, was surveyed in 1865. In 1869 the eastern boundary was surveyed in conjunction with the surveying of Medora township, and in 1880 the southern boundary was surveyed in conjunction with the formation of Gibson township. Freeman's western boundary is, of course, Georgian Bay.

The boundaries having been established, Freeman township was formed in 1881 and named after John Bailey Freeman, Liberal Member of Provincial Parliament for North Norfolk, Ontario, who became government whip in 1883.

The interior surveys of Freeman were carried out in 1895 and 1896 by David Beatty, who found that the township was generally rolling and rocky but well timbered with pine of a good quality, except for a large burnt-over section in the southwest portion. In his report he mentioned a settler named Myers on a 77-acre lot in the southwest (Lot 35, Con. IX) who had a small shanty and a small clearing under crop, all of which Beatty assessed as worth $25. The only other settlers appear to have been Indians named King, Isaac, William and Mekesemonge on Con. VII and VIII.

Beatty believed that about 7,000 acres in the southeastern part of the township would compare favourably with other portions of the District for agricultural purposes, and reported that a fairly good wagon road starting at Foot's Bay had been made into the interior by a lumber company then operating in the township.

Freeman was incorporated as a township municipality October 1st, 1919, with MacTier as a hamlet. The first reeve was a railway conductor, and the first councillors were a railway car inspector, a locomotive fireman, a locomotive engineer and a trainman.

Freeman township was dissolved and amalgamated with the geographical townships of Gibson and Baxter as the township of Georgian Bay, effective January 1st, 1971.

An airport to serve the tourist areas of northern Muskoka and Parry Sound has been proposed for a site just south of the junction of Highways 69 and Muskoka Road 4 in Conger, the unorganized township north of Freeman in the District of Parry Sound. The Canadian National Railways is said to be the major property owner of the site, which was established as an easily-maintained landing strip by a construction company during highway construction.

Healey Lake, reached by a left-hand turn off Highway 69 about three miles north of MacTier, has been the location of annual power boat races in August. Interested people should inquire at Earl's Marina.

XII THE LAKE OF BAYS

HIGHWAY 117

About four miles north of Bracebridge on Highway 11 at High Falls is the junction with the road going east into the Lake of Bays, Highway 117 (formerly 118 East).

The entrance to Springdale Park is one mile east on Highway 117. Two plaques on the pillars convey useful information about Springdale Park and Spiritualism, the left reading:

> These gates were donated by Adam McIntyre as a testimony to his belief in the principle of spiritualism. Springdale Park Association owns and operates this park. It is a spiritualist organization incorporated by letters patent in the Province of Ontario, dated July 21st, 1938. The pillars were donated by the members of Springdale Church.

The plaque on the right pillar reads:

> Spiritualism: The science which seeks for and finds proof of survival of the spirit. A philosophy after so-called death based on the earth life being a training school. A religion fitting souls for immortality. A belief in a life hereafter based on knowledge, not on hope.

William Partridge, a Toronto landscape gardener and Spiritualist, discovered the property that became Springdale Park when he made a 1937 trip into Macaulay township to buy Christmas trees. The Muskoka owners considered it of little value in those depression days because most of the saleable trees had been removed and the soil was sandy, but William Partridge considered it an ideal site for a summer camp with its plentiful springs and mile of frontage on the Muskoka River, North Branch. He consulted with other members of a small group of Toronto Spiritualists, and they formed a non-profit organization to buy the Muskoka property for a religious meeting place. The congregation of Springdale Spiritualist Church in Toronto was organized shortly after the Springdale Park charter was obtained and proved to be the means of promoting interest in the Park.

The original building lots sold for $25. A Lot Owners Association was eventually formed to deal with social activities, repair of roads and the erection of a store and post office to function during July and August. The Park's church seats 100 people, and visitors from all parts of Canada, the United States, and abroad attend services conducted Wednesdays

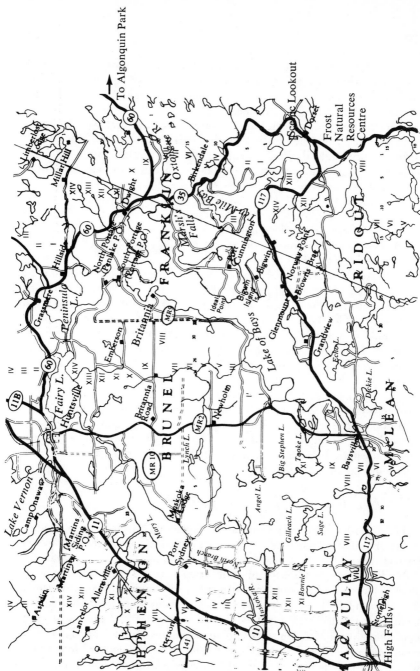

Scale: 1 inch = 4 miles

and Sundays at 7:00 p.m. It would be incorrect to assume, however, that everyone within Springdale Park is a Spiritualist, as many of the present owners of cottages and year-round homes in the now enlarged community are of other religious beliefs.

Other cottages have been built privately over the years on the banks of the Muskoka River, North Branch (which flows out of Mary Lake, through Springdale Park, over High Falls and through Bracebridge to Lake Muskoka), and some tracts of land with river frontage have been developed into cottage communities.

The Bracebridge Golf Club, with pay-as-you-play privilege, is one mile east of Springdale Park on Highway 117. Just past the golfing is a ranch with horses for trail riding.

The Stoneleigh community on Stoneleigh Lake is enlivened by a large camp for young people.

About 10 miles from Highway 11, Richard Karon has a studio in the woods indicated by a sign reading "Oil Paintings". The road to Fairy Falls is indicated by a small green sign on the right, 10.2 miles from Highway 11. Go about 1.6 miles along this road, turn left into a narrow track and follow it to the Muskoka River, South Branch, and Fairy Falls. They are Lilliputian, like something out of *Gulliver's Travels*, or like Niagara in miniature. Iron pegs sunk into the rocks are left over from logging days; several cottages have been built on the riverbank downstream. A pastoral quiet may reign, or children transported from a nearby camp by horse and wagon may be swimming and picnicking like a band of carefree gypsies. The 1879 *Atlas* shows people named Farey occupying that property. As Muskoka waterfalls were often named after the landowners, I assume that Farey Falls turned into Fairy Falls and thus acquired an aptly descriptive name.

Mark Langford and McLean Township

The experiences of early settlers in this part of Muskoka were recalled by Mark Langford when he was 78 years old, an alert and erect man over six feet tall.

Mark's father, Thomas Langford, travelled to Bracebridge in May 1870 to locate land in company with three other men—Messrs. Attridge, Forester and Gilberts. All were from the vicinity of Stratford in the County of Perth, Ontario. At Bracebridge they learned there was good land available in McLean township, and Thomas Langford and his three companions registered their claims to the nearest unlocated lots which were in the middle of a tract of wilderness unbroken even by trails. This didn't discourage the applicants as the government had promised to build a colonization road through McLean immediately—a road which had been surveyed in 1868. Thomas Langford, a cripple as a result of a mill accident, became ill in Bracebridge and was not able to make the journey to see his land before returning home.

In October, Thomas sent his seventeen-year-old son, Mark, to Muskoka with Attridge, Forester and Gilberts to erect dwellings and make preparations for the family to move to their new land in McLean township. They carried blankets and axes with them and in Bracebridge purchased flour, bacon, tea, sugar, tin cups, tin pails, plates, knives and forks. Loading everything on their backs, they set out. Even though strong and accustomed to hard work, they found their loads heavy and cumbersome as they followed a rough road that went east from Bracebridge then north through Macaulay township "as far as Mr. Tookey's place .... about 4½ miles". (James Tookey was reeve of Macaulay township in 1875.) From the end of that road, a five-mile footpath through the location of Thomas Bruce led to the location of William Hussey; the Langford location was another seven miles beyond.

At the end of the first day the four men stayed overnight at the home of settler Bruce, having walked only seven miles. By the end of the second day they had still not reached the locations (although they were within a mile and a quarter) and, as Mark Langford wrote, "worn out and discouraged, we gave up the idea of making a road in here. We built a fire and lay down by it that night. In the morning we held a council and determined to leave McLean. We left the 50 lbs. of flour at the root of a tree and took the back track. . . ."

On the way to Bracebridge they sold their bacon, groceries and dishes to Mrs. Hussey "for a trifle". Mrs. William Hussey was a frail-looking mother of five children, direct from England. Assisted only by her ten-year-old son, she carried all their supplies in from Bracebridge during the first eighteen months she was in McLean Township while her husband was away working in a lumber camp.

Mark Langford and his friends got work in Bracebridge, and Mark wrote to tell his father in Stratford that they just could not make a road to their location fit to move the family over. His father replied that he was determined to move and would get others to make the preparations if Mark could not.

Stung by his father's barbs, Mark returned to McLean township three weeks later with Attridge and Gilberts and dug up the flour, most of which was still fit for use. (The third man, Forester, gave up his location and didn't go back.)

They built a small hut with an open front facing a big rock; thatched the roof and sides with hemlock brush and put a good layer of fine hemlock brush on the ground for beds—a wilderness survival technique which might be useful today. A fire laid against the rock kept the hut warm and was used to bake their cakes and fry their pork. Meals were prepared only after nightfall so that no daylight hour was lost from work. They walked to Bracebridge several times and once returned with a 60-pound grindstone. By Christmas, when they moved back to Bracebridge, the snow was three feet deep, the shanties were almost finished and a fairly good trail was cut through to Mr. Hussey's. Daniel Gammage and his brother, two new settlers doing the same work a mile and a quarter away, had cut a path through to the Langford location.

Thomas Langford, driving his own team and accompanied by a hired team and driver, arrived in Bracebridge in March with the rest of the family after a six-day trip. The teams proved to be useless for moving into the location through four feet of snow, and oxen hired for the purpose were not able to break a road for the teams. The men had to haul by stages—first with one horse pulling a light sled over a footpath they broke from Bracebridge to Tookey's, then by hand-sled from Tookey's to Hussey's. The track beyond Hussey's having been obliterated by new snow since Mark and his companions had come out at Christmas, they broke a new path to the shanties and carried or hauled in by hand-sled what they could.

The snow did not go off that first year until well on in May, and the only crop the Langfords were able to sow and harvest was potatoes. Mark and his younger brother walked to Bracebridge all that summer for their supplies, making the round trip in a day with 60- and 40-pound loads. When the snow came again and the swamps froze, they drove a yoke of steers (received in trade for one horse) to carry their supplies, and the round trip took two days.

McLean township was almost entirely settled by landseekers who arrived in 1871. Mark Langford records that the population, young and old, climbed to forty persons, and a great deal of fine pine was burned as the settlers cleared their land.

In June 1871, W. H. Brown came to McLean. He followed the rough trail to the Langford settlement, where he stayed for a few days while looking over his location on the land adjoining the falls on the Muskoka River, South Branch, at the place now known as Baysville. In return for his commitment to build a sawmill, the government granted him additional land. He went back to his home in Burford (west of Hamilton, Ontario, near Brantford), and returned to McLean in the spring of 1872 with his family to build a shanty and begin clearing the land for the mill.

Also, in the spring of 1872, John Wattie located on isolated land in Brunel township on the shore of the Lake of Bays. As he could reach his land only by way of McLean township and up the river and lake, he arranged with the Langfords to build a boat for him, using a large pine tree close by the river above the falls and some lumber and hardware from Bracebridge. This was the first row-boat on the Lake of Bays and an example of how "later comers" could use the time and talents of the first settlers to ease their way.

In the summer of 1873 the long-promised road to Baysville was finally cut through, and quite a number of settlers moved in that year. Supplies could now be hauled in by team, and the difficult task of hauling in the machinery for the mill was accomplished.

The bridge across the river at Baysville was also built in 1873. Before that time settlers crossed on a cedar raft. In a crossing attempt in the autumn of 1872, a father and son named Spong had been swept over the falls and drowned, and they were the first two buried in the public cemetery at Baysville.

Captain Huckins purchased the little steamer *Wabamik* for the Lake of Bays from A. P. Cockburn, the founder of the Muskoka Lakes Navigation Company, and had it transported with great difficulty over the soft, partially flooded road, in the spring of 1876. The *Wabamik* was used for four years; then Captain Huckins and W. H. Brown built the *Excelsior*, a boat of 50-foot keel.

Mark Langford married when he was 23 and he and his wife had four daughters, a son (Henry) and a happy home with everything they needed to eat—maple syrup, beef, eggs, garden produce, ham, cream and butter. Forest fire swept through the north-west section of McLean on September 1st, 1881, destroying many homes and much of the year's crops. Mark Langford was one who lost his house and barn, but rebuilt and carried on.

The land between Bracebridge and Baysville and around the Lake of Bays—all that land of rock and scrub today—was taken up as farms. Satisfactory crops were produced at first because of the leaf mould, but the land gave out after a few crops had been taken off. Land which had supported pine turned to sand; land where hardwood grew proved to be better. It has been said that because many of the settlers had to go off to the lumber woods to earn money and didn't raise animals, they didn't have manure to fertilize their crops and sustain the land. Mark Langford, for instance, worked as a "scaler" measuring harvested pine logs for the payment of government dues. After the lumbering experience he kept his son Henry at home because he didn't want him working in the rough camp atmosphere.

Mark Langford died on March 21st, 1940, at age 87. When he was getting old and people had stopped farming, Mark worried that all the work had been for nothing. "But it was nothing of the kind," said his daughter, Alberta Langford (1886–1974), when I visited her in 1964. "If those little farms hadn't once been cleared, tourists couldn't have come up here." And when tourists began to arrive in increasing numbers, a series of fine boats was placed on the Lake of Bays by C. O. Shaw, the president of the Anglo-Canadian Leather Company in Huntsville, who also began building famous Bigwin Inn on the Lake of Bays in 1913.

For nearly 50 years, Alberta Langford operated the telegraph station established by her father. Part of this time she also acted as telephone operator for the Lake of Bays and Haliburton Telephone Company before it was absorbed by Bell Telephone. She was church organist for more than 50 years at Bethune United Church and was a charter member of the Baysville Women's Institute.

BAYSVILLE

Enter Baysville on Highway 117 slightly beyond the Fairy Falls road. Muskoka Road 2 starts its northerly run to Huntsville near Baysville's southern entrance, giving access to various small lakes such as Tooke and Menominee.

Baysville is on the southern end of the Lake of Bays where it flows into the Muskoka River, South Branch. A wide concrete dam across the river controls water levels. Below the Baysville dam, the river winds through McLean, Oakley and Draper townships (now wards) and over Muskoka Falls into Muskoka township. It empties into the North Branch of the Muskoka River beyond Bracebridge.

During its lumbering peak, Baysville had as many as seven hotels and was the lumbermen's headquarters because timber cut in the Lake of Bays district was generally floated through Baysville. The logs were channelled into a timber slide beside the dam. The Baysville dam, site of W. H. Brown's 1872 sawmill, is today surrounded by a park in which is located a Historic Sites plaque telling that McLean township was surveyed in 1862 by Robert T. Burns, Provincial Land Surveyor, and opened for settlement in 1868 under the Free Grants and Homesteads Act.

An "Explorers" marker in the same park just above the dam contains a record of official expeditions into Muskoka from 1819 to 1837.

When the steamship was the means of carrying the freight and passengers to points around the Lake of Bays, Baysville was the southern terminal, and remaining from those days are two large and high docks, one on each side of the river, near the Highway 117 bridge.

Close to the southern dock is the village park founded in honour of Canada's Centennial in 1967, and cared for by the Baysville Horticultural Society. A fence of Muskoka stone and wrought iron was subsequently constructed as a memorial to Miss Helen Kippax, a summer resident for many years and a widely-known landscape architect. A second park has been designated across the highway for the location of a cenotaph honouring those who served in the two World Wars. The cenotaph is to incorporate the stones from the first Baysville gristmill operated by Bill Gammage in 1877.

Turn right at the Baysville southern entrance for the Community Centre, which houses a skating rink, dancing area, Public Library one evening per week, and such activities as the Annual Flower Show in August. A township dock is on the river behind this building. The nearby Curling Club, started in 1955, has an active program and entertains visiting rinks from outside Muskoka for such events as the Bigwin Bonspiel. Follow the road along the river past the baseball diamond and municipal office to the cemetery; turn left to reach the main street for grocery stores, car and boat servicing and Lincoln Lodge. Lincoln Lodge has developed into a popular eating place, "The Best Place by a Dam Site", by the late Robert Menzies, McLean township councillor, past president of the Baysville Horticultural Society, and active member of the Baysville Lions Club.

The Croft, a shop close to Centennial Park, has been building up its specialties for over 10 years, emphasizing Canadian books and hand-crafts, including Indian and Eskimo. Not far from The Croft, two metal workers manufacture brassware, mostly reproductions of antique pieces.

Over the Highway 117 bridge, turn left for a coin laundry, a family-owned store open seven days a week during July and August which sells drug sundries, meat, fish and vegetables, and two marinas.

The annual regatta is held early in August.

A noteworthy Baysville son is Earle VanClieaf, a graduate of Brace-bridge High School, who became president of the Sangamo Company, Canada, and later vice-president, Power Equipment Division, of the Sangamo Electric Company of Springfield, Illinois.

Across the Highway 117 bridge in Baysville, a road bearing to the southeast leads to Heeney Lake and Heeney Creek (the original name appears to have been Hay).

A little farther along Highway 117, a road to the east runs to Dickie Lake, named after the first settlers on its shoreline, Mr. and Mrs. Moses J. Dickie, who had moved there from southern Ontario. Originally from Scotland, members of the Dickie family had emigrated to South Caro-lina, then—as United Empire Loyalists—to New Brunswick, and later to Ontario around Brantford, Paris and Burford.

Echo Lake, three miles northeast of Baysville, is on the same road. According to the 1879 *Atlas*, it was named because of "seven places where first-class echoes are heard". One can enjoy a hike through the woods by following an old logging trail from Baysville to Echo Lake. Indeed, many small lakes around the Lake of Bays present a variety of recreational opportunities for those who like to travel off the main high-way to savour nature's delights, perhaps to canoe, cycle, bird-watch or sketch.

Highway 117 has been described as the highway of artists. At least five craft establishments are within the next few miles, including The Log Cabin, across from Bigwin Island, a colourful store full of treasures from Canada and abroad, owned and operated by Eva Sheil, world traveller; and Langford Canoe, a mile farther, noted for its quality canoes which are sold all over Canada and abroad.

BIGWIN

After passing Grandview Lake, Highway 117 turns towards the Lake of Bays shore at the mainland parking and docking facility for the 600-acre Bigwin Island (19 miles from the junction of Highways 11 and 117).

C. O. Shaw, president of the Anglo-Canadian Leather Company in Huntsville, began building Bigwin Inn on the island in 1913. The mam-moth and exquisite fireplaces were built by a Huntsville man, James McFarlane. After delays resulting from World War I, Bigwin Inn was finally opened in 1920 and became one of North America's top summer resorts.

Bigwin Inn, opened 1920.

The village of Dorset.

"Bigwin Inn had character, thanks to C. O. Shaw," wrote Samuel Forsythe, who started out as an assistant manager and registered the first guest. "When a male guest entered the Bigwin Inn rotunda for the first time he automatically removed his hat as he would were he entering the Cologne Cathedral."

The hotel accommodated between three and four hundred guests and employed a staff of two hundred. Shaw's navigation company steamers brought the guests and their trunks. For entertainment, Shaw hired famous musicians at great expense. The hotel had elegant table service, and large conventions were held there. An accountant said that Shaw paid for Bigwin in its first seven years of operation.

Shaw died in 1942, and in 1947 the first of a series of new owners took over Bigwin; its glory faded by degrees. In 1950 it was still considered the biggest and most expensive of Muskoka summer hotels, there was a dance band in the dance hall every night, and a jazz trio from New York played in the bar. A chamber trio of piano, cello and violin played in the tea shop or on the deck in the afternoons and accompanied soloists at the Sunday evening concerts organized by the musician who played the Hammond organ in the dining room at dinner. The pianist was Mario Bernardi who became conductor of Ottawa's National Arts Centre Orchestra and the cellist was Donald Whitton, now first cellist with the N.A.C. Orchestra.

Bigisle Enterprises Limited acquired ownership in 1969 and converted a three-storey 150-room wing of the hotel into condominium suites for sale as summer residences or as retirement homes. A second building is being converted to town houses, the golf course is being rebuilt, and a 3,000-foot air strip has been installed for private and charter planes. An interesting feature that remains from earlier days is the series of roofed and pillared cement walkways and steps built by German prisoners during World War I.

The 1879 *Atlas* states that the Indians used to do all their trading on the island with John Bigwin, an Indian who exchanged furs for provisions, that it was named Bigwin's Island, and that "an Indian Chief's daughter and several other Indians are buried on the island." Chief John Bigwin was an honoured guest at Huntsville's Golden Jubilee in 1936 and, although old and almost blind, led his band in a war dance on the town hall steps. He died in July 1940 at the age of 101.

The WaWa Hotel which stood at Norway Point from 1907 to 1923 was owned by the Canadian Railway News Company. C. O. Shaw, who later built Bigwin across on the island, had a share in the supervision of its development. Muskoka's greatest tragedy, the WaWa Hotel burned to the ground in 35 minutes early Sunday morning, August 19th, 1923, after a dance, and 11 perished; three were guests, and the others were hotel employees who were sleeping in the tower, the only part of the large hotel more than two storeys high. Seven people were seriously injured. Most of the guests were able to escape with ease, leaving their belongings behind, partially because the electric lights continued to function through the first 20 minutes of the fire.

THE LAKE OF BAYS

After you leave Bigwin, heading for Dorset, Highway 117 affords various opportunities to see parts of the Lake of Bays, the name given by Alexander Murray when he explored the Muskoka Lakes in 1853 for the Geological Survey of Canada. Murray made no mention of trading posts or traders, but when Alexander Shirreff had travelled through this lake during his 1829 expedition from the Ottawa River to Georgian Bay, he wrote that the lake—then known as Trading Lake—appeared to have been a principal station of the traders as there were deserted vestiges of several substantial posts. Lieutenant Henry Briscoe called it Lake Baptiste on the map of his 1826 exploration; David Thompson called it Forked Lake in 1837 when he passed through it on his way to the Ottawa River.

With an estimated 350 miles of shoreline because of its many bays, islands said to number 100, and an elevation of 1034 feet, the lake is about 10 miles at its widest (interrupted by the Port Cunnington peninsula which reaches down the lake almost to Bigwin Island), $11\frac{1}{2}$ miles long and, in places, 260 feet deep.

One wonders what lives in those 260-feet depths. Pioneer Mark Langford's son, Henry, spoke about seeing a monster in the Lake of Bays on a number of occasions. When people refused to take him seriously, he made a joke of it and would tell exaggerated stories about finding a huge swath cut into the woods by the monster when it had risen out of the lake. After Henry's early death (he was found one Sunday morning helpless in his overturned car and died as a result of his injuries), the Lake of Bays monster lived on. On various occasions, six men spotted "the thing" riding the waves and sporting about in the lake, but each man was alone at the time, and thus unable to substantiate his claim. Then it was fortuitously sighted by two men when together, and they received expert opinion that what they had seen could be a monster sturgeon, a creature whose existence has been verified. Two men and two women, all members of a long-established Lake of Bays family, subsequently signed the following statement: "On Sunday, July 26th, 1959, at approximately 9:25 a.m. in Lake of Bays north of Lloyd Green's, I sighted what was believed to be a very large fish approximately 10′ to 12′ in length. We watched the object for about 12 minutes. The object moved across the lake from Thomas' point toward Prices' point. The object was observed through binoculars."

The Lake of Bays Association has a membership of about 1400, representing approximately 25% of all Lake of Bays cottagers, and the extent of their support of local merchants and tradesmen has a large influence on the area's economy. Three past presidents have been appointed honorary members in recognition of their services: Harley Neilson, on year book; John Govan, on water sampling; and Harry Wright, on township planning board.

Leslie M. Frost Natural Resources Centre

This Centre, encompassing 55,000 acres of Crown and provincial reserve lands with dozens of lakes and streams, is about seven miles south of Dorset off Highway 35. Mr. Frost, an active naturalist and historian, was Premier of Ontario from May 1949 to November 1961. The Centre, with its picnic areas and two hiking trails, may be used by the public and outdoor-oriented groups. Events to celebrate National Forest Week in May include guided hikes, axe and chain-saw demonstrations, boat trips on Lake St. Nora to give prospective property owners tips on choosing and managing land, a fur exhibit, and a forest fire control and water bombing display.

The buildings of the former Ontario Forest Technical School, constructed between 1944 and 1949, are the hub of the new Centre. O.F.T.S., generally called "the Ranger School", qualified forestry technicians and conservation officers for the Ontario government and the forestry industry until the qualifying courses were transferred to the Community College System (1968). Some school groups live in for a week's wilderness experience.

DORSET

Just before Dorset, Highway 35 (based on the old Bobcaygeon Road) comes up through Haliburton on the east to meet Highway 117, and the road we are travelling continues on towards Dwight as Highway 35.

As Highway 35 bypasses Dorset (approximately 17 miles from Baysville), turn left off the highway to visit this village. A popular port-of-call for small boats in summer, little Dorset is nestled into a background of mountain greenery. A new post office, a snack bar, a general store and a boat-servicing establishment are clustered near the entrance to the bridge which spans the narrows. On a warm summer day the bridge, just wide enough for one-way traffic, may be decorated with young people preparing to jump or dive into the water below.

On the other side of the bridge a gift shop sits beside the dock which once accommodated the old steamers. Beyond this is Robinson's General Store which offers modernized grocery shopping side by side with a display of bear, caribou, Arctic wolf, and lynx pelts or rugs stretched on the ceiling, all reminiscent of a fur-trading post. Polar bear skins are difficult to acquire because of heavy competitive bidding at fur markets by Japan and other countries, but Robinson's may have one on display, or perhaps a grizzly bear rug valued at more than $3000. Their antique iron pots and crocks are not for sale, but you may be interested in a papoose board with embroidered pouch for carrying baby on your back. Across the parking lot from Robinson's Store is a newer building which contains the bank and liquor store.

Logging operations in the late 1800s sparked Dorset's early growth until it had three general stores, several hotels, and churches which were the centre of community life. An ambitious scheme was implemented by one lumbering firm, Gilmore Bros., to send logs all the way to Trenton on the east end of Lake Ontario. Their logs were assembled on the Oxtongue River and floated 20 miles or more to the Lake of Bays, then towed to a spectacular overland slide one-half mile long near Dorset. Carried first by an endless chain into the slide and floated uphill on water forced into it by powerful pumps, the logs were then lifted by another endless chain over a huge dam into higher waters draining into Raven Lake. From there it was downstream to Trenton, much too far, as it developed, to make this a paying proposition, and the route was abandoned.

Proceeding on the Dorset road past the shopping centre, Community Centre and Public Library, turn right at Highway 35 for the Highway Park on a body of water (unofficially called Trading Lake) into which the Hollow River flows down from Haliburton's Kawagama Lake.

The Dorset regatta is held in July, and snowmobile races, with a full schedule for stock snowmobiles, are held in the middle of February.

Head for the fire tower by making a left turn at Highway 35 from the Dorset road. Within less than a quarter mile, you will see the Scenic Lookout roadsign. Turn left and follow the road up the hill, leaving your car at either the lower or upper parking lot. The base of the fire tower is on the upper level. (Well-maintained outdoor conveniences are also on this level.) Tables, barbecues and drinking water are provided for picnickers.

The 100-foot metal tower was opened to the public in 1967, Canada's Centennial year. You may climb the stairs with railings on both sides at your own risk; children must be accompanied by an adult. From the glass-enclosed top cabin of the tower, 465 feet above the water level, you get a 310-square mile panoramic view of the Lake of Bays and many small lakes. It's worth hours of travel to see this view of Canada's incomparable Muskoka scenery.

On your way to Dwight, you will find another picnic area on the lakeshore about 6.7 miles past the tower, and two miles beyond this a road to the left leads down a large peninsula to Port Cunnington. The peninsula divides the Dorset side of the Lake of Bays from the Dwight side, reaching so far down into the lake that at the end of the road through Port Cunnington you see Bigwin Island across a narrow channel of water. In addition to the usual cottage communities, there are several resorts around the tip of the peninsula at Port Cunnington and Port Ideal.

At the Highway 35 bridge crossing the Oxtongue River about nine miles past the tower, you may fish or walk on the rocks by Marsh's Falls. Below the falls a canoe, rowboat or outboard motor can take you the two miles to the Oxtongue's well-buoyed mouth on Dwight Bay. Lieutenant Briscoe regarded the Oxtongue River as a continuation of the Muskoka. In 1826 he ascended the Muskoka River to the Lake of Bays, crossed it "in a N. N. E. direction 9 miles . . . and left it by a continuation of the River we had been ascending."

Captain G. F. Marsh owned three 100-acre lots surrounding the falls in Franklin township, according to the 1879 *Atlas*, and an adjoining 100 acres was owned by Richard Marsh. Lots were also owned by G. F. Marsh and A. Marsh in neighbouring Brunel township.

Captain Marsh, who died in 1901 (one source says 1905), had started an early boat service on the Lake of Bays; added to it by buying Captain Alfred Denton's interest in boats running out of Huntsville. He was influential in securing construction of the Portage Railway on the neck of land between the Lake of Bays and Peninsula Lake, thus linking the two lakes for freight and passenger service. In all, this linked the Lake of Bays with the railway centre of Huntsville and the whole chain of Peninsula, Mary, Fairy, and Vernon Lakes. While the Hoodstown rapids and dam prevented passage from Vernon Lake into Fox and Buck Lakes, small boats could be carried over the short portage to Fox Lake, or goods could be portaged from one boat on Vernon to another boat on Fox.

Algonquin Park

A short distance past the bridge over the Oxtongue River, at the junction of Highways 35 and 60, a right turn will take you out of Muskoka and head you towards Algonquin Provincial Park. The park serves an important function for Muskoka by protecting its headwaters.

DWIGHT

The Dwight roadsign is 1.8 miles past Marsh's Falls, and about 11 miles from Dorset. There are several grocery stores and a laundromat on Highway 35/60, while the residential and resort part of Dwight is down beside the lake. Turn left off Highway 35/60 to Dwight Bay Road and proceed one block past the post office and municipal office to the waterfront, where a large dock, a public boat ramp and a narrow sand beach are washed by the waters of the Lake of Bays.

The lakeshore road to the left—a dead end—passes lodges and tall pines and provides access to the cottages lining a short strip of the shore.

If you turn right instead of left at Dwight Bay, you will see more cottages and lodges and will cross the small bridge over the stream known locally as the Boyne, where Orangemen have been known to gather on July 12th for the ceremony of "crossing the Boyne". This road eventually divides; the left fork follows the shore of the Lake of Bays to service cottage properties, while the right fork (an earlier road to Huntsville) meets the road to South Portage. At this junction, a right turn will take you back to Highway 35/60, and a left turn down the west side of the Lake of Bays. Write to the Dwight Business Association for information about the annual St. Patrick's Winter Weekend.

Dwight was named for Harvey Prentice Dwight (1828–1912), President of the Great Northwestern Telegraph Company, who in 1863 made up a party (probably of four men) to travel up the Muskoka River, South Branch, by canoe. Indians hired at the village of Rama guided them. Dwight induced various influential U.S. and Canadian sportsmen to accompany him in the subsequent years of his exploration—trips primarily undertaken for hunting and fishing—to see for themselves the country of which he had spoken so enthusiastically. "In the course of two or three years we found our way as far as Trading Lake or Lake of Bays and the country was most magnificently wooded and this lake was full of beautiful islands," Dwight recorded. At this time he did not find a single settler or lumberman on the Lake of Bays.

While William Hanna was living with his mother in a little shanty at South Falls (Muskoka Falls), Dwight hired him on a number of occasions to guide for him. This was the William Hanna who became a leading merchant in Port Carling and whose name is borne by Port Carling's Hanna Memorial Park.

Dwight and his companions also employed as guides the early settlers at the top of the Lake of Bays, among whom were Frank and Dick Blackwell, Edmund and Archie Gouldie, and Tom Salmon. After Edmund James Gouldie, a trapper and trader, had opened a store and was providing accommodation for hunters and travellers, Dwight wanted to put in a telegraph office in connection with the expansion policy of the Great Northwestern and for the convenience of himself and his influential friends from Toronto, Hamilton, Montreal and New York. They had established headquarters for the Dwight–Wyman Sporting Club on nearby Long Lake in 1868 or 1869. The Club's first cabin was built of logs 20 to 50 feet long and had a canopied hearth, open on three sides, large enough to roast a deer carcass on a spit.

The name of Dwight was chosen to identify the post office and telegraph office, in recognition of Dwight's friendship to the community. He had provided cash in return for work and guiding and had presented one guide with a horse, possibly the first horse in the area. He remembered the community children at Christmas by sending parcels of food, toys and clothing. He gave an organ to a pioneer church and provided good books for a circulating library.

H. P. Dwight was referred to as "The Father of Canadian Telegraphy" in the newspapers at the time of his retirement from the active management of the Great Northwestern Telegraph Company in 1903. While in charge of the distribution of telegraph operators in the trouble zones during the Fenian raids, he had rendered important services which enabled the government to act knowledgeably and promptly. The Fenian Brotherhood, the American branch of the Irish Revolutionary Brotherhood founded in Dublin in 1858, was intent on invading Britain's North American colonies (which became Canada by 1867 Confederation) to hold and use as a base of operations against Britain. When armed Fenians began to gather at border points in March 1866, Canada called for volunteers for defence and 14,000 men responded. By 1871, when Fenianism was doomed to failure, Canada had more than 30,000 men under arms, but in the meantime Canada had been kept in a chronic state of alarm by Fenian forays and resentment had been high against the United States for allowing raids to be made from her territory.

Dwight also received public acknowledgment in parliament from the Minister of Militia for similar services performed during the Northwest Rebellion of 1885.

Although not a teetotaler, Dwight was against a liquor licence for the village when it was discussed in 1906. "It is bad enough in large towns where there is a police force to keep order, but infinitely worse in a backwoods town frequented by idle lumbermen and sometimes other disreputable characters. Let it once be known that you have a liquor shop, and the reputation of Dwight as a sober, respectable village will be sure to suffer. One drunken spree in a season will injure the reputation of the place as a summer resort beyond recovery." Dwight didn't get the liquor store then and still hasn't one.

When James Dickson, Provincial Land Surveyor, stayed at the Dwight Temperance House about 1885, he recorded meeting a number of "hardy and bronzed" settlers who had come to meet the boat, get their weekly mail and make a few purchases at the store. From the Dwight House verandah he had a magnificent view down the bay of well-fenced fields of waving grain, comfortable farmhouses and good barns. The view today is quite different, for the shores are heavily wooded and dotted with docks and cottages, many of which are hidden by the trees.

Dickson was on his way to camp in what is now Algonquin Park, and subsequently wrote *Camping in the Muskoka Region*, although the Lake of Bays is the only part of the District of Muskoka as it is constituted today that he writes about. In his account, he describes passing "little churches and unpretentious schoolhouses, each with its quota of strong, hardy, and in many cases barefooted, boys and girls, presided over by the neatly-dressed and courteous lady teacher." He speaks about "thriving and well-stocked farms, with good dwellings and capacious barns . . . well-fenced clearings of waving grain and new-mown hay . . . everything denoting the success and approaching independence of the hardy backwoodsman who only a few years ago penetrated these wilds, with, in many cases, only his axe and hands, to hew out for himself a home in the unbroken and then almost unknown wilderness."

Then Dickson adds, "How is it that our towns and cities are so crowded with the poor and starving, with their cry of no work? Out here there are thousands of farm lots . . . free for the taking," where with no rent, high taxes or high-priced fuel a man can grow potatoes and other vegetables and keep a cow, pig and hens—so many of the necessities of life.

Charlie Thompson, a well-known resident of Dwight who has designed and constructed some of the best cottages in the area, spent an evening telling me stories about earlier days. Two 100-acre farms near Dwight had been in his family since the 1870s.

> After my great uncle had taken the first hay off his property, he and a friend started out to walk south to find work. By the time they reached Gravenhurst, Uncle's heels were so blistered they went into a hotel where the proprietor gave them salt and hot water to soothe their feet. Then they continued on their way and worked long enough "at the front" to get enough money to buy a cow each which they had to lead all the way back. That was how Uncle got his first cow and got started.
>
> Very few made ends meet. They survived but did not progress. My Uncle Wellington did very well, but he was a hard worker, and his wife was a hard worker. They worked from daylight to dark. But unless you did that you didn't make it. Because you couldn't.

During Charlie Thompson's childhood in Muskoka, as far as he knew, shoes were only for the rich. His mother, with 12 children and stepchildren to care for, made footwear for them out of old coats and felt hats and underwear out of ladies' stockings discarded because the feet were worn out. When he was seven years old and desperately anxious to help his mother, he was chopping and stacking firewood for the long, cold winter ahead. Surprisingly, his mother was still in good health at the age of 93.

"I came back to Muskoka in 1930 when I was 20 and my wife, Dorothy, was 18," Charlie reminisced. He continued:

> I had been a seed salesman in Toronto, but the depression had ruined the business. We had no money, but we lived in a shack and I worked around the farms of relatives and their friends while I waited for the farm I was going to inherit, handed down from my grandfather. It had been leased for a three-year period, for very little rent, to coincide with the time I would reach 21. . . .
>
> I was never in bed past 5:30 a.m., and I had all the barn chores and my breakfast over by 8 o'clock, and then I worked right through until dark with a few breaks for food, and mostly long after dark, sometimes for my uncle. . . .
>
> In the winter of 1931 I went to work on the highway being put through Algonquin Park. The pay was $10.00 per month

and your bed and food, and I got $10.00 extra because I had a team of horses by that time. That was good pay. Some similar jobs only paid $5.00 per month. I used to walk home every Saturday night after work and supper, starting about 7:30 or 8 o'clock from Canoe Lake, and starting back for the camp about 4 o'clock Sunday afternoon. It was about 19 miles to the farm, but I was a young fellow and I ran most of the way. It was often very cold. I remember one time thinking it must be mighty cold and being aware of the crackling and snapping and popping all around and everything else so still. Later I learned that it was minus 62 degrees Fahrenheit. The camp foreman had been telephoned and told not to let any of the men go home, but I'd already left. . . .

My uncle tried to talk me into taking over his farm and giving up mine which he described as a heap of rock, but I kept it for its shoreline. When I was badly hurt in an accident with my team in 1947 and it looked as though I might never recover, I was offered $2 a foot for the lakeshore, but I wouldn't take it. Uncle said, "You'll never do better."

Charlie Thompson only sold pieces of shoreline when he had nowhere else to turn for money. By 1969 the selling price had reached $6 per foot, and since then it has risen astronomically.

*   *   *   *

To complete a tour of the Lake of Bays, drive past Dwight on Highway 35/60 for two miles and turn left to South Portage. From South Portage Muskoka Road 9 goes down the western side of the Lake of Bays to the Britannia Hotel. Britannia has a golf course with professional, all-weather tennis courts, dancing and evening entertainment, and the Lake of Bays Sailing Club's annual regatta in early August. Open all year, with winter skiing and curling, it has a new 70-room addition.

Muskoka Road 9 continues past Britannia to Muskoka Road 2; a left turn here takes you back to Baysville, about 15 miles from South Portage.

XIII *SKELETON LAKE AND MARY LAKE*

Highway 141 (formerly 532) intersects with Highway 11 about 12 miles north of the Highway 118 exit from Bracebridge. Going west from Highway 11, Highway 141 passes through Utterson.

Centennial Acres, beyond Utterson, was officially opened in June 1972, "to provide a natural environment for rest, recreation, research and leisure learning" according to the terms of its charter. The general public are welcome to attend conferences and lectures at Centennial Acres' Global Conference Centre, where distinguished speakers may be heard on such topics as "Toward a more humane society", "Communicating in the global community", "Education for leisure", and "The Future in Canada". For more information about programs, and accommodation and membership, write to Box 960, Bracebridge.

At Beatrice Climatological Station, off Muskoka Road 4 a few miles south of the intersection with Highway 141, members of the Hollingsworth family, aided at times by obliging neighbours, have made official weather observations since 1871, recording high and low temperatures, precipitation (rain or snow), and wind velocity for each 12-hour period. A monthly compilation is forwarded to the Atmospheric Environment Service at Toronto and transferred to tapes for easy referral and permanent storage.

Dinosaur Land, opened in August 1965, is west of the intersection with Highway 141 on Muskoka Road 4, as it comes up from Beatrice and continues towards Windermere. (Admission fees: 50¢ for children; $1 for students; $1.50 for adults; subject to change.) Displayed throughout the grounds are authentic life-sized models of prehistoric animals built by the late Bill Kanerva, whose father built similar models for Calgary. The largest model represents an original expenditure of $11,000, while others range in cost from $3,000 to $5,000. Two films are shown at regular intervals in the 70-seat movie theatre, one a serious educational film showing paleontologists discovering fossils estimated at 100,000,000 years old and reconstructing the animals, the other a lighter Walt Disney film entitled *A World is Born*.

Another attraction is a Mesolithic Community of some 7,000 years ago with human-sized models at their daily tasks. Artist Bob Cunningham, working with the owners, spent seven months sculpting the figures and constructing the village. Picnic tables are scattered throughout the property (take insecticide, necessary here as elsewhere); and a picnic area on high rocks, shaded by tamaracks, with a barbecue pit, overlooks Three-Mile Lake a half mile or so distant.

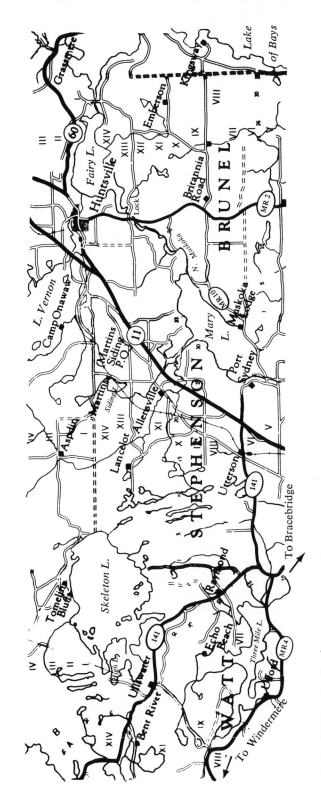

Scale: 1 inch = 3 miles

Owner Harold Prebble, a second-generation Muskokan, also operates a popular Go-Kart track next door to Dinosaur Land for drivers at least 12 years old.

SKELETON LAKE

Go north on Highway 141 (formerly 532) past Utterson to Raymond, where Ann (Mrs. Heinz) Niederhauser established the Raymond Cross-Country Ski School in 1975. Training goes on all year; when there is no snow, dedicated skiers practise with "roller skis" on pavement. Heinz Niederhauser coaches for the Canadian Ski Association. Seek out the Raymond Skokies to learn about successful winter carnival Run-a-Bed racing.

The main road into Skeleton Lake, 920 feet above sea level, is off Highway 141 past Raymond, and leads to the long-established Wilson's Lodge where the early cottage community, which included a noticeable number of Toronto secondary school teachers, used to congregate for the Saturday evening square dance. Nearby is one of the area's outstanding topographical features, a cliff 250 feet high, locally called Devil's Face. Cottagers extol the beauties of Skeleton Lake's islands and deep, crystal clear water.

In the Ullswater vicinity, look for the Ministry of Natural Resources park and fish hatchery and another interesting landmark, High Lake, a small lake more than 60 feet higher than Skeleton with an outlet falling into it.

Skeleton received its name, according to Bert Shea in *History of the Sheas and Birth of a Township* (c. 1970), when surveyors working on the north shore of the lake found on the rocks human skeletons which, they judged, had lain there for several years. Nearby settlers were intrigued by this mystery and questioned an Indian chief who revealed that he and his people had camped one winter on that site. The lake was usually full of trout and nearby swamps were usually the yarding place for deer, but whatever took place that winter the camp was facing starvation and had to move. Some members were already weak, and one 14-year-old boy was unable to move and would have to be left, but his mother, a young widow, refused to leave her son to die alone. The deathly silence of winter settled on them, the story goes, as the voices of her people faded in the distance. The fire burned out, the cold crept in, and they died together. The lake, thus named, became a lasting memorial to a mother's devotion to her helpless son.

PORT SYDNEY AND MARY LAKE

On the east side of Highway 11 opposite the Highway 141 intersection, Muskoka Road 10 leads to Mary Lake. After passing Stephenson Cemetery on the north side, this road turns right (south) in about a mile to take you through Port Sydney.

Reminiscent of an English seaside resort, lodges, stores, post office and Community Hall (opened July 1, 1925) face the water. Various entertainments are held at the hall by such groups as the Stephenson Lions, and the popular Cavalcade of Colour dinner there in September is usually attended by 1,000. The outstanding beach and picnic area has conveniently placed benches for resting and enjoying the view. Go well south of the government dock for the best swimming. Here a firm sandy bottom slopes gently down until the water is deep. On a hot summer day the refreshing clear water of Mary Lake is a memorable delight.

In addition to the many cottages on Mary Lake, the Muskoka River and nearby small lakes, there is a substantial cottage community on a side street in Port Sydney close to the beach area. The local yacht club is active, and numerous sailboats race round the buoys and islands.

A mixed-doubles canoe race co-sponsored by the Port Sydney Chamber of Commerce and the Huntsville Branch of the Royal Canadian Legion is a highlight of the summer season. The 15-mile course is from Huntsville to Port Sydney with low winning time of about $2\frac{1}{2}$ hours.

Accommodation in Port Sydney and around Mary Lake is offered by a number of hotels and lodges, some of which remain open in winter for skiing and snowmobiling. The snowmobile has opened up areas that are inaccessible muskegs during the summer. You can take a snowmobile safari from Mary Lake to Oxtongue Lake, about 27 miles, and at times you can get guided 125-mile trail tours at Port Sydney.

The annual Port Sydney winter carnival, held in the second half of February, includes snowmobile races, trail safaris, cookouts and a Saturday evening dance party in the Community Hall. For a program write to the Port Sydney Resort Association, Port Sydney, Ontario.

The Muskoka Loppet, held since 1970 in the first week of January, is Ontario's largest cross-country skiing event. It starts at Hidden Valley on Peninsula Lake and ends in a course through the Mary Lake islands to Port Sydney. Sponsored by the Muskoka Winter Association and Jordan Wines, the activities include a free polka dance at the Port Sydney Community Hall on the Saturday prior to race day, "a natural family gathering for one of Canada's most exciting skiing events."

Christ Church, the Anglican mother church in northern Muskoka, stands on a hill beside the lake south of the picnic grounds. It celebrated its 100th anniversary in August 1973. One of the three oldest Muskoka churches still in use today, it was built with hand-finished lumber and square blacksmith nails on land given by A. Sydney Smith. You enter the churchyard and cemetery through a lych gate (traditionally provided to rest a bier while awaiting the arrival of the clergyman) dedicated to the memory of Sydney Smith. Posted on the picturesque gate are the words:

> This is God's acre
> Sacred to HIM
> Sacred to the Departed
> Whose Bodies rest here

The church is ordinarily open for visitors, and you will see the greeting which begins, "Friend, there is a welcome in this Church for thee." The Lord's Prayer, Commandments and Nicene Creed were engraved and gilded on wood panels in the chancel by the Rev. C. R. Clerk, appointed to the Mary Lake Mission and Christ Church in 1890. During his two-year incumbency, he completed the east end of the Christ Church interior and hand-carved the beautiful panels.

You might be fortunate enough to hear the Christ Church carillon pealing out majestically during your visit. Luther's *A Mighty Fortress is Our God* is particularly impressive in this environment.

The maintenance of Christ Church has sometimes provided a focal point for activities within the summer community. The Muskoka news section of a 1907 Toronto newspaper, for instance, reports a successful musicale held on a cottager's verandah in aid of Christ Church renovations. One of a series of musicales, the program was made up of vocal and instrumental selections rendered by the ladies.

When you leave Christ Church and proceed along the main road through the rest of the village, now predominantly a cottage community, you will come to the bridge over the river. Just below the bridge, on the road which proceeds in a wide semicircle through the outskirts of the village and back to Highway 11, is a second picnic ground with a barbecue, referred to locally as Indian Landing.

Turn left and cross the bridge, continue to bear left, and you will come out at the parking area for the Scenic Falls picnic site on the rock ridge beside the dam. On a warm day in summer the laughter of excited children will greet you from the natural rock slide across the ridge in the water below the dam. Cries of "Just once more! Please, just once more," fill the air when a parent tries to drag off a child, even if he has been sliding for hours.

Children, usually clad in orange life jackets, teenagers and a few energetic adults climb up the rocks, wade through the water to the top of the slide and plummet down to the pool below. All will be visibly wearing out the seats of their pants with repeated slides. Wear old bathing suits substantial enough to prevent embarrassment; some children wear several sets of old camping shorts. A sign warning about a possible undertow is ignored in favourable weather; it would be foolish to use the slide at a time of high water. Large groups of boys from several nearby camps, having a "day away" on the cook's day off, sometimes swell the visiting population.

The music of the carillon, ringing out clearly in the peace on the other side of the river, may barely be heard above the sounds of falling water and youthful exuberance. As evening approaches and the swimmers depart, the shores of a pool below the falls are quietly lined with fishermen practising the gentle art of casting.

The Port Sydney dam is part of the system for conserving the watershed, fish and forest between Algonquin Park and Georgian Bay, all

The *Gem* on Mary Lake, 1898.

Cruising northerly out of Mary River Lock.

now the responsibility of the Ontario Ministry of Natural Resources. The rock ridge beside the falls was worn smooth by water flowing over it for thousands of years before the dam construction channelled the water into a narrower fall.

Port Sydney History

Port Sydney is located in Stephenson township, where David Hogaboam was the first reeve. Hogaboam and his family had come to Muskoka in 1862 from Winchester, Ontario, a community north of the St. Lawrence River between Ottawa and Cornwall. He and his son Charles had carried seed potatoes on their shoulders from Washago, crossing the river at Bracebridge on a fallen pine tree. In the spring of 1865 his isolated family at home ran completely out of food while they anxiously awaited the return of father and older sons from work on the Parry Sound road. David Junior and Eliza Jane ate maple buds and their mother cried and prayed. In 1865–66 the Hogaboams helped build the first steamboat, the *Wenonah*, in Gravenhurst. When Henry, an older son, drowned at Sandy Gray Lake while driving logs in June 1866, the previous hardships the family had suffered paled into insignificance.

After Stephenson township was opened for location under the Free Grants and Homesteads Act of 1868, a few new settlers arrived, followed by a number of others in 1869, many of whom were brought from England by the steamship *Prussian* on three successive voyages. On reaching the river, the earliest of these immigrants were met by John McAlphine, a bachelor straight from Scotland, thought to have been the first man of the Port Sydney community. He would come across the river below Mary Lake in his dug-out log canoe, the *Man-Killer*, and paddle them back to his one-room shanty, often keeping them as guests for the night. McAlphine is credited with making the first dam on the site when he drove stakes around a large pine tree which had fallen across the water and banked the structure with mud and stones.

The new arrivals soon furnished themselves with canoes similar to McAlphine's by cutting down trees, shaping them and hollowing out the centre. The women, as well as the men, learned to manage them efficiently. Men of the Hanes family, who had settled at Utterson several miles west of Mary Lake, would make a log canoe to order for $10 and were available to assist the new arrivals to build their log cabins, according to stories by early settlers collected and printed in 1927 by the Port Sydney Women's Institute.

Logs cut to the required lengths were laid on each other to make the four walls of the first cabins, a door was cut and the roof put on. A primitive "cob-roof" was made by laying logs across the walls and covering them with clap-boards. A good tree was cut into lengths and split into clap-boards, which were smoothed with a draw-knife, the shavings saved and used for mattresses. Tables and stools were made out of split logs.

At that time the land was covered with the original dense forest. Great sheets of rough, dry moss, three inches thick, were peeled off the trees, taken home in bags, pounded into the chinks of the log cabins and plastered over with clay from the river bed. This made the walls absolutely tight, and no wind or cold could penetrate. It was often the children's duty to gather the moss.

With no nettings or screens, the settlers were at the mercy of clouds of black flies and mosquitoes. They had never had such tormentors before and were absolutely unprepared for them. Smudge fires to lay a smoke-screen were set around the cabins but proved of little value. Bitten so badly about the face and neck that it became impossible to turn their heads, the settlers had to turn their whole bodies if they wanted to look around. Bites became infected, adding to the suffering. But fortunately, as time went on, the settlers seemed to develop an immunity to the stings and were less and less bothered.

A humorous story in illustration of the mosquito plague concerns an early farmer who was ploughing his back acreage one day. At noon he tied his team of horses to a tree while he went home for lunch. When he arrived back there were no horses to be seen—just four large mosquitoes playing horseshoes for the harness.

A grindstone for sharpening axes and utensils was an important asset in any pioneer community, and the one in the Port Sydney area was supplied by Ernest Smith. When Mr. Smith arrived in Toronto from England, he learned from John A. Donaldson, the Dominion Agent, about the land in Stephenson township, and proceeded to Bracebridge and took the stage to Utterson. Most new Mary Lake settlers walked from Utterson, but Ernest Smith was one of the few who had enough money to pay the stage driver extra to take his baggage—two trunks, a camping outfit, a cast-iron bake-kettle weighing fifteen pounds and the grindstone—all the way to the lake.

All from far and near went to sharpen their tools on Ernest Smith's grindstone, a well-remembered kindness because the owner of a grind-stone did not always give his neighbours access to it.

McAlphine built the first sawmill. All the settlers gathered to raise it, and they celebrated after with a social gathering and dance, according to the custom. Later McAlphine sold his mill and land to A. Sydney Smith (1846–1925), whose rise to prominence prompted the settlers in 1874 to name the community Port Sydney. It was not incorporated as a village until 1934.

The McInnis family arrived with small children in November 1871 to occupy a 14′ × 16′ shanty built by pre-arrangement. Three feet of snow lay on the ground, and their land was miles from Port Sydney. Many a morning, it is told, the mother's hair was frozen to the pillow in the bitter cold of that first winter. She went nine months without even seeing another woman, a not uncommon occurrence as women with young families away off in the bush were unable to leave them while men who went off to work in lumber camps were spared this terrible isolation. The nine-year-old McInnis boy walked the round trip of 16 miles to Port Sydney for supplies and mail every two weeks, often through deep snow.

At this time, when a man's wage was as low as 50¢ per day, the price of tea was from $1 to $1.75 per pound. Bread was baked in large bake-kettles with tight-fitting covers, and later in stone ovens—delicious bread far surpassing in flavour the bread baked in modern ovens, according to reminiscences.

"Grandma Brown" was the only nurse in Stephenson township for many a year and was considered as good as any doctor. When roads were poor and doctors hard to get, she often walked ten miles or more to a sick bed.

A school was organized about four years after the first settlers arrived. Held in a shed originally built by Ernest Smith to house some oats over the winter, it consisted of four posts with a roof on them boarded up to a height of about five feet, above which it was open. The open part let in light and air but also a driving rain which would wash the work from the pupils' slates and force them to take shelter on the opposite side. The pupils sat on blocks of wood at a long desk formed by a plank sloping from the wall with a little edge on it to keep the slates from slipping off. They used any books they happened to have at home, which were usually old-country readers and arithmetics. An educated woman from England who lived nearby with her husband first undertook to instruct the children for three months during the summer.

Port Sydney did not escape the forest fires which raced through the District periodically, doing great damage and consuming houses, barns and crops. One serious fire was experienced in 1879, and the devastating fire of 1881 nearly wiped out the village. The settlers loaded their most valuable possessions into their canoes, boats and rafts and went out into the lake for many hours.

The weather had its vagaries also. One son of a pioneer family that arrived in 1869 recalled a bad storm which swept over Mary Lake. "It cut a narrow path across the waters throwing them on either side as a gigantic plough would. It passed through the woods on the opposite side, cutting a swath before it. When it had subsided this path resembled a government road just after the trees had been felled."

Mr. and Mrs. James Jenner, among the first arrivals, came over from England on the *Prussian* and loaned McAlphine $80 to buy the first saw for his mill. The "Clyffe House" resort which they began near Port Sydney is one of the few resorts that has been operated by the same family for over 100 years. "Grandmother started the tourist business with a small guest house after visiting friends had encouraged her with their admiration of the scenery," I was told. Clyffe House was the name of Mrs. Jenner's English home. Seven of her eight children left for the west to ranch. The remaining son, Robert Jenner (1878–1949), and his wife Agnes took over the operation of the business in 1907. He was very enterprising and enlarged the operation with a number of buildings. Huge vegetable gardens were kept in those days and there was lots of help, including four Jenner children who all went to university and worked at Clyffe House while not in school. "The tourist business was still good in the 1920s and 30s," one of Robert Jenner's daughters told me. "Not having cars, guests came by train, stayed for the summer and provided their own entertainment. Now we are gradually converting to apartments and cottages." Inquire at Clyffe House about the annual exhibition of watercolours.

Navigation

When the roads north of the line between Utterson and Port Sydney were little more than blazed trails, freight and food for people and cattle were often brought by stage to Mary Lake and taken in canoes up the lake and river and into Fairy, Vernon and Peninsula Lakes for the early settlers in these areas. Mary Lake is at a lower altitude than Fairy Lake, and a falls at the north end of the Mary River (Muskoka River, North Branch) obstructed navigation.

In June 1873 a contract was let by the Ontario Department of Agriculture and Public Works to a John Carroll to construct a lock on the Mary River at the place known as Fetterley's (Hiram Fetterley settled on this land about 1863) and now known as The Locks. Mr. Carroll's contract provided for the payment of $16,900 to clear the ground, acquire the timber and construct a wooden lock. The original falls were left as a mill site, and a channel was dug to accommodate the lock. The total expenditure on this construction to December 31st, 1877, amounted to $29,209.74, according to the 1877 Departmental report.

Concurrently, plans for building a steamer at Port Sydney were implemented by the company running the stages, Messrs. Denton and Smiley; and in June 1877, on Mary Lake, was launched the 60-ton steamer *Northern*, a side-wheeler which could run in four feet of water and carry 200 passengers (although some accounts say 400 passengers). The *Northern*, an 80' vessel of 24' beam, was built for $7,000. Captain Denton was the master.

Steamers then linked Mary Lake with the Hoodstown rapids which are located on a stream connecting Lake Vernon with the Fox and Buck Lake chain.

Before starting out to visit the Mary River Lock from Port Sydney, a pleasant car trip, make a note of your mileage at the Port Sydney bridge. Travelling northeast by the shore of Mary Lake on Muskoka Road 10, you pass the property of the Muskoka Baptist Conference at approximately 5.8 miles. Turn left on to Muskoka Road 2 at 7.8 miles. The parking lot for the lock is at 10.0 miles, but stop first at the roadside park ¼ mile short of this for a view of the river.

A park and picnic area surrounds the lock, as is customary in Ontario, and it is operated by the Ministry of Natural Resources. The gates, which weigh several tons, are opened and closed manually by the lock-master, and the valves that control the flow of water into the lock are also hand-operated enabling the lockmaster to regulate the water flow according to the number and weight of boats locked in. As many as 30 craft may be packed into the lock, which measures 70′ × 18′ and has a drop of 14 feet. It's a pleasant spot to swim (but not in the lock) and to walk down the river on a well-worn path.

XIV HUNTSVILLE

MADILL CHURCH

About two miles south of Huntsville and 17 miles north of the Highway 118 Bracebridge exit, a historic marker sign on Highway 11 points out the road on the west leading to the Madill Church. The log church, completed in 1873, and its cemetery are popular with artists and photographers. Two unusual headstones of sheet iron with glass windows, the earlier dated 1880, attract the attention of those interested in methods of inscription. Captain George Hunt, the founder of Huntsville, was buried here in 1882.

The Ontario Archaeological and Historic Sites Board has erected an informative plaque on the site.

HUNTSVILLE TODAY

Turn right off Highway 11 on Muskoka Road 3 to enter Huntsville and stop at the Chamber of Commerce building on your right to pick up folders, the summer *Vacation Guide* with its listing of monthly activities, and to ask for any information you may require, such as directions to the Dyer Memorial or local golf courses.

Situated 80 miles south of North Bay, the next important centre, Huntsville with its population of 3,500 is sustained in large part by the lumbering and tourist industries and the regional offices of Ontario Hydro, Provincial Police, Department of Highways, Ministry of Natural Resources, and Algonquin Forestry Authority. Ontario's Agriculture and Food office, maintained since 1912, offers guidance and attempts to solve problems in farm operations ranging from crop improvements to livestock breeding. An important addition to the economy has been the Kleenex tissue plant built in Chaffey ward (formerly township) near Huntsville by Kimberly–Clark of Canada who predicted in 1969 that the production of 100 tons of tissue daily would employ more than 90 skilled persons at the plant, and that their earnings would bring about $650,000 to the community, in addition to the other money generated by the industry. Domtar Construction Materials has also chosen to locate in the Huntsville area, and its new plant will open in 1976.

Proceeding along Main Street towards the heart of Huntsville, you will drive along Hunter's Bay, on Lake Vernon, and see the Canadian National Railways Station, log storage area and lumber mill. The green and flowered parkette overlooking the tracks was the Centennial garden project of Huntsville's Horticultural Society.

As you approach Centre Street, the town theatre and post office are on your left. On your right, past the Empire Hotel, one of a chain of four north country hotels, Eaton's has a large department store at the corner of West Street, supplementing the many independent shops of Huntsville which stock clothes and equipment for town and country. The liquor store is one block back of Eaton's on Minerva Street. Nearby on Main Street are the Public Library, Municipal Building, and the office of the *Forester*, Huntsville's weekly newspaper which appeared first in November 1877.

The lane to the town dock on the Muskoka River is opposite Brunel Street, just before the bridge which used to swing to let the steamers through. Consult the timetable at the dock for the *Miss White Pines* cruises. Over the bridge, to your left, are a supermarket and the Brewers Retail. The Huntsville District Memorial Hospital on Mill Street is reached by Church Street, just over the bridge on your right. Originally a cottage hospital built in 1949 by the Canadian Red Cross, it has been expanded several times to meet the needs of residents and visitors.

As the Muskoka River which bisects Huntsville runs north and south, the part of Huntsville which contains the Empire Hotel, Eaton's and the Municipal Building is the west side of the river; whereas the hospital is on the east side of the river. This can be confusing if you are spending any time in Huntsville and seeking out locations, especially as Main Street East is on the West side of the river because the street is divided numerically by Centre Street.

Entertainments in Huntsville include the August carnival on the Royal Canadian Legion grounds, the Fall Fair in September at the new Agricultural grounds on Muskoka Road 2 West (Ravenscliffe Road), Cavalcade of Colour, and all the winter carnival events which start off early in December with Skokie's Ball.

The Huntsville to Port Sydney Couples (or mixed-doubles) Canoe race, jointly sponsored by the Huntsville Legion and the Port Sydney Chamber of Commerce, takes place annually in mid-July. About 15 miles, with low winning time of $2\frac{1}{2}$ hours, the contest is watched by spectators in boats, on lakeshore and river bank, and at the Brunel (Mary River) lock where the participants portage.

Club 55, for senior citizens—whether or not Club members, is in the Town Hall basement, attractively converted with a 1975 $15,426 New Horizons grant. The entrance is on street level, and there is a wheelchair ramp.

The Muskoka District Band, made up of 30 to 40 players from different Muskoka communities, is directed by Dr. Lynn Sargeant, of Huntsville. The presentations by this band and several groups of musicians within it, including a 14-piece dance band, greatly enhance many Muskoka events.

Florence B. Murray, Professor emeritus, Faculty of Library Science, University of Toronto, was born in Huntsville, where she attended school to Grade XII. After graduation from the U of T in English and History, she studied at the Ontario Library School, and held a Carnegie Scholarship at the University of Michigan where she obtained a Master of Arts degree in Library Science. Her work at the Toronto Public Library was especially concerned with rare books and manuscripts, and for 20 years Miss Murray collected books on Muskoka and Haliburton, searching for information in the libraries of Canada, the United States, and Great Britain. This interest resulted in *Muskoka and Haliburton 1615–1875*, published by the Champlain Society for the Government of Ontario and the University of Toronto Press (1963), an invaluable and stimulating reference book for Muskoka residents, history students and writers.

The Huntsville Public Library on Main Street will show you the library copy kept in the Muskoka reference collection. Ask also about other local books, including Ruby Henley's *Are All the Children In?*; *Reflections: Muskoka and Lake of Bays of Yesteryear* by Sidney G. Avery, who has served as Huntsville mayor, Chamber of Commerce president, and in Rotary, Masonic, and winter sports promotion; and the Centennial Souvenir booklet *Old Home Week* published by the Royal Canadian Legion, Huntsville Branch 232. The latter two publications are illustrated with historical photographs.

To reach Huntsville Memorial Park, go to Brunel Street, drive up the hill and proceed a few blocks to Park Drive on your left and the entrance to Memorial Park. In the park there is tourist camping, the Pioneer Village and Museum, and, from a lookout maintained by the Lions Club, a marvellous view of Fairy and Vernon Lakes. Also in the park, the Huntsville Memorial Community Centre has an arena with artificial ice all year to accommodate a summer hockey school as well as winter hockey. Boards cover the ice for summer lacrosse games. Inquire about a summer skating school (figures, free skating and dance) sponsored by the Huntsville Recreation Commission.

The Muskoka Pioneer Village and Museum in Memorial Park is open daily during the summer from 10:00 a.m. to 5:00 p.m. Check fall weekend hours. (Admission is $1.25 for adults, 25¢ for children 12 years and under, and $3 maximum for a family.) Inquire about demonstration times for old-fashioned baking and preserving, carding and spinning, candle making, and pottery. Staff members and volunteers wear authentic costumes. An auxiliary group, Friends of Pioneer Village, was formed in 1970 to gather historical material, aid the Museum in acquiring antiques, and organize volunteers.

The Rotary Club of Huntsville purchased the 33-acre site for the Museum in 1966 and began assembling old buildings with, whenever possible, their original decorations and furniture to represent a community of the period from 1869 to 1910. Included are three early log dwellings, an 1880 house, an 1895 schoolhouse, a general store, a barn and a sawmill.

Colonization road from Utterson to Port Sydney, sketched by
George Harlow White in 1871.

A scene in Muskoka Pioneer Village, Huntsville.

Section of 800 cross-country skiers racing from Hidden Valley to Port Sydney in the
January 1976 Muskoka Loppet (sponsored by Muskoka Winter Association, Box
1239, Huntsville, and Jordan Wines; individual and team awards are presented).

School, Muskoka Pioneer Village.

The interior of a settler's shanty near Huntsville,
sketched by George Harlow White in 1871.

G. L. Hunt's log house, 1875, sketched by
George Harlow White.

A museum building was erected in 1967 by the Rotarians as a Centennial project, aided by the Centennial grants of the townships of Cardwell, Chaffey and Franklin, and grants from the provincial and federal governments. This building became the new home of a collection of pioneer artifacts started in the old Huntsville public school in 1958. In the basement, a replica of a trapper's cabin has been built.

The Georgian College Summer School of the Arts (with its headquarters in Barrie) offers a variety of courses at the Huntsville High School on Brunel Street in subjects such as batik, writing, modern dance, hatha yoga, ceramics, painting and sketching, jewellery, theatre arts and upholstery. Myrna Cook, who customarily teaches loom weaving, operates the Loom Shop on Highway 11, south of Huntsville, where she also gives lessons and does custom weaving. Summer school canoeing, golf, sailing and tennis are, naturally, taught outdoors.

Beyond the high school, Brunel Street soon becomes Muskoka Road 2, and will take you to the lock and park on the river between Fairy and Mary Lakes and from there through Brunel Ward to Baysville on the Lake of Bays.

Arrowhead Provincial Park, four miles north of Huntsville off Highway 11, has 1,880 acres of forested hills and valleys, Arrowhead Lake, a smaller lake called Mayflower Lake (stocked annually with brook trout) and parts of the Little East and Big East Rivers. Its facilities include beach, swimming and picnic areas with fireplaces for daily visitors, and campgrounds for the overnighters. The park is open for winter camping (ploughed campsites, piles of firewood and heated washrooms), skating, ice fishing, snowshoeing and snowmobiling, with miles of groomed scenic trails. The camper under canvas on a winter's night needs to have a Coleman stove, lantern, catalytic heater and arctic sleeping bag. Even then he might think longingly in the middle of the night of the warmth of the washroom building.

During the summer, evening shows are held Tuesday and Saturday at dusk. Conducted hikes start at 10 a.m. on Wednesdays and Sundays from the sub-office on Mayflower Lake. Check all details at the park office and inquire for dates of art shows and other activities.

Kinsmen Beach, $2\frac{1}{2}$ miles from Huntsville on Vernon Lake, provides a safe sand beach, swimming, picnic tables, outdoor fireplace, and a concession that sells snacks and treats. Take the Ravenscliffe Road to the Kimberly–Clark plant, turn left and drive down to the lake. No dogs are permitted here.

HUNTSVILLE HISTORY

At the end of August 1865, a four-man tourist party in canoes started up the north branch of the Muskoka River from Bracebridge to Mary Lake, proceeding from there to Fairy Lake and through the river to Lake Vernon. Their diary, "Up the Muskoka and down the Trent", was printed in the Toronto *Globe*, October 4th, 1865. It does not mention any inhabitants on the river at the present site of Huntsville, but it gives the following information about settlement on Vernon Lake:

> This is a round-shaped lake, with several large bays, lying within two miles of Fairy Lake, and nearly north of it. Here we met with the first settlement after leaving Brace Bridge, there being about a dozen clearings and log houses or shanties along the southern and eastern shores. The best farm and buildings are owned by an Indian who has reared a large family upon his farm, and appears to be getting along finely. Most of the shanties are surrounded with clearings of but one or two acres planted in potatoes and corn for use in the Fall, while trapping or trading for furs, and their owners cannot therefore be called settlers.

William Cann is said to have built the first little shanty on the bank of the river in 1860. He used it each fall when he came up from Orillia to hunt and fish. After Chaffey township was surveyed in 1869 by Walter Beatty, Provincial Land Surveyor, William Cann located land, built the first Huntsville hotel and was elected Treasurer when the Village of Huntsville was incorporated in 1886. He eventually left the District because of financial difficulties following unprofitable investments, and it is said he died in Kentucky where he had been working in the cotton fields. Cann Street on the east side of the river reminds us of him.

Huntsville was named after Captain Hunt who first travelled to the area in the fall of 1868 to consider the advisability of moving to Muskoka. Born on the Isle of Corfu in the Mediterranean, where his father served as a British officer, he followed his father into the army, ending his military career in the province of Quebec after organizing a militia unit. Four of his young children died in an epidemic of "black" diptheria while he was in Quebec. After retiring from the army, lack of economic opportunity drove him to consider taking up life on free grant land. He decided to move to Muskoka and arrived with his wife and remaining children—three daughters—in May 1869. (Four more children were born in Huntsville.)

Captain Hunt chose land in the first concession of the township of Chaffey on the east side of the river, built his log cabin and immediately began pressing the government to extend the colonization road the last three miles to his settlement. He was eventually appointed to superintend the work on the road which became the main street of Huntsville. This road continued in an easterly direction to serve settlers on Peninsula Lake in the location that became Hillside.

An educated man, Captain Hunt assisted incoming settlers by writing important letters for them. A devout Presbyterian, he held the first Sunday School as soon as his cabin was completed. He organized the first school when there were only a dozen families settled; opened the first retail store to sell tea, tobacco, flour and pork; was appointed the first Postmaster; pressed to have a doctor brought to the community; and had already become interested in the fight to have the railway routed through Huntsville when he died of typhoid fever in 1882, at the age of 52.

The battle for the railway continued for several years, and finally in 1884 the government reversed its previous decision to route it through Hoodstown and Parry Sound and consented to the route through Huntsville. The railway arrived in 1885.

In the deeds of all property he sold, Captain Hunt, an ardent teetotaler, is said to have inserted a liquor clause:

> In the event of any liquor being sold, bartered, traded or consumed on said lands, during the lifetime of any of the grandchildren of Queen Victoria or within twenty-one years after the death of any of the grandchildren of Queen Victoria, this indenture will become null and void and said lands shall be returned to the estate of George Hunt.

Captain Hunt's present heirs say that, to their knowledge, no one has ever been able to produce a deed containing this clause. The story has been repeated, however, so that there is a commonly held belief that the reason the main part of Huntsville developed on the west and hilly side of the river, rather than on the east and flatter side where Captain Hunt held his land, was because of this clause which business establishments would not want in their deeds. Some supporting evidence may be found in the following advertisement in an August 1872 issue of the *Free Grant Gazette*:

> Building lots at Huntsville. For sale cheap to parties intending to build and improve immediately. Purchasers will be bound not to sell liquors on the property. Shoemaker, Church, Post Office and private day school in the village.
> Apply to Geo. Hunt, Huntsville
>
> A good blacksmith wanted, a teetotaler and Protestant preferred.

The Hunt heirs incline to the view, however, that Huntsville developed on the west side of the river partially because of the land sales of Allan Shay, and later because the railway ran along the shore of Hunter's Bay and turned away from Huntsville before it reached the river.

Allan Shay came to the District of Muskoka in May 1863 with his wife and small baby, travelling by wagon with his wife's family, the Hanes, from Chesterville in Dundas County. There were thirteen members of the family in the expedition, and they came well equipped for pioneer life with quantities of food, sheep, cows and chickens. The trip to Muskoka took six weeks.

The Hanes settled near Utterson in Stephenson township, and the Shays settled about three miles beyond them in an isolated section. The Shays built a log cabin, a "root house" in which to store vegetables, venison, fish and salt pork, and a shed to house their animals, which included a team of oxen.

The young Mrs. Shay first became aware of neighbours who lived about a mile away when she looked out of her cabin one day and thought she saw an animal in the woods, but as the creature came closer she saw it was a young girl with a potato sack for a dress. She seemed like a wild creature and ran away when Mrs. Shay first attempted to approach her, but after several more such appearances she was persuaded to come to the house.

The girl's father, a seafaring captain, was away on a trip the following winter when Mrs. Shay discovered that his wife had pneumonia. Because Mrs. Shay had nothing with which to treat the sick woman, she walked to Bracebridge and back (about 30 miles) while two feet of snow fell and then nursed her neighbour back to health.

In 1869 Allan Shay moved his family to Huntsville, about nine miles farther north. James F. Hanes, his father-in-law, was by this time occupying 100 acres running from Hunter's Bay back along the west side of the winding river. Allan Shay bought an adjoining 100 acres after the government reclaimed it from squatters who had failed to do the required building, clearing, etc.

Before moving his family up, Shay had built an eight-room, two-storey log house on what is now the corner of Centre and Main Street, and this was the first substantial house in Huntsville. As soon as people began to arrive, he had his land surveyed into building lots and began to sell them. He named the street which bisected his property Centre Street, and a number of cross streets were named after members of his family—Duncan, Cora, Florence, Lorne and Minerva. He soon acquired a farm one-half mile outside the village. With the help of his sons and hired hands, it soon became a large operation, using twelve horses.

Mrs. Shay was often called in cases of medical emergency. Once a child had a penny (the old-type penny, much larger than today's 25¢-piece) stuck in her throat. After turning the child upside down, Mrs. Shay stuck her finger down the throat, dislodged the penny and drew it out. The doctor had also been sent for; when he arrived later, he said, "If I had known you were here, Mrs. Shay, I could have saved myself a trip."

After his wife's death in 1910, Allan Shay left Huntsville to live with a sister in Sault Ste. Marie, where he remained until his death 22 years later.

Huntsville was incorporated as a village in 1886 when there were about 400 residents. The railway is credited with bringing about an upswing in the economy of the pioneer settlement by providing shipping facilities for the export of local white pine. Six saw mills were soon established which, in addition to the existing machine shops, foundries, gristmill, woollen mill, cheese factory, and the steamboats, gave employment to the villagers. Then about 1890, a tannery was established and large quantities of hemlock bark, used in the tanning process, were purchased from nearby settlers. A hospital was established by Dr. J .W. Hart, and much of its revenue was derived from the sale to lumbermen of yearly hospital tickets for $5.00. When a lumberman had an accident or took ill, he would be brought into the hospital and cared for "under his ticket".

A rapid increase in population brought about Huntsville's elevation to the status of a town in 1900. Huntsville had suffered severe loss by fire in 1894, but this led to its remodelling and modernization, and substantial brick buildings replaced the many stores and offices destroyed on Main Street. Spurred on by the need to protect a growing tourist industry from the risk of typhoid fever (which had killed Captain Hunt), Huntsville installed a municipal water supply and filtration plant.

Schoolteachers, doctors and lawyers provided leadership in community affairs and they received great support from C. O. Shaw when he came to Huntsville as head of the tannery. Mr. Shaw was an able cornetist and Mrs. Shaw an accomplished vocalist. They organized a building called "The Stable", a place where the horses were stabled downstairs while their owners were entertained upstairs in a large music room.

Mr. Shaw conceived the idea of a band when he observed Italian members of the community (who had been brought over from Italy by his company) meeting on the riverbank each Sunday to sing and play their musical instruments. The result was the 75-piece band of the Anglo-Canadian Leather Company, which won competitions and received many invitations from outside Huntsville. Mr. Shaw imported musicians when necessary, and the band was a wonderful diversion for the men who worked with him.

Rev. Robert Norton Hill

When Captain George Hunt superintended the work on the road through Huntsville and beyond, the latter part of the work was on the beginnings of the present Highway 35/60 towards the community of Hillside, where the Rev. Robert Norton Hill had first arrived in July of 1867, the month and year of Confederation.

The Rev. Hill, a Methodist minister in Schomberg, Ontario, had become interested in moving to Muskoka when talking to Thomas McMurray, editor of the *Northern Advocate*, at a conference in Toronto. The conference had decided on a union of Wesleyans and Methodists. This union resulted in surplus ministers, of which Hill was one. With four sons and two daughters to provide for, Hill determined to go to a

The Anglo-Canadian Band at Huntsville
Bandstand.

The *Empress Victoria* at Huntsville wharf, c. 1897.

Sailing on Fairy Lake.

new part of the country where he could locate enough land for each son to have a farm.

Hill drove by horse from Shomberg to Bradford, took the train to Belle Ewart and travelled by boat through Lakes Simcoe and Couchiching to Washago, where he hired an Indian guide. They canoed down the Severn River to Georgian Bay, up the Moon River to Lake Muskoka and up the Muskoka River to South Falls, where he called on Thomas McMurray. The guide then returned to Washago. McMurray showed Hill the land where the Muskoka Airport is today, but Hill thought the soil light and sandy and wanted to see more of Muskoka before making a decision. He walked to Bracebridge to make further inquiries, proceeded to the Hogaboams, stayed overnight and was driven to the Madill home at Allensville, the end of the government road. Madill told him about Vernon Lake, a few miles farther on, where several families had settled.

At Vernon Lake the next day, he met the Fetterleys, Bildsons and Hanes on the south end, and Mr. Bildson took him by canoe down the river to Fairy Lake where they spent two days and Hill chose 800 acres. He returned to Bracebridge to register the land under squatters' rights, as this was before the time of the Free Grant Act.

That night in Bracebridge, Hill had a dream that the land he was looking for was beside a lake with a point jutting out in the water and an island beside it. He returned to Ira Fetterley's on Vernon Lake and told him his dream and his doubts about the land chosen. Fetterley told him about the lake east of Fairy Lake (Peninsula Lake) and drew a map of it. When he drew the peninsula and recalled there was an island beside it (today called Hills Island), Hill asked Fetterley to take him there by canoe. Hill examined the soil and was satisfied with it, and the two men chopped down some trees to indicate to other people that the land was claimed. Hill made a map, returned to Bracebridge, cancelled his first claim and registered the new one, and returned to Schomberg.

In the following spring of 1868, Hill returned to Muskoka with his wife and two oldest sons, aged 17 and 15 years. At Fetterley's seven men joined them and travelled with the Hills to their land to build a cabin for the boys to live in alone that summer. In four days the cabin was finished, using windows and a door brought from Schomberg. Then Rev. Hill and his wife departed, with some misgivings, leaving the boys to clear the land and face the perils of the wilderness. The boys chopped all through the summer, living on bread, butter, salt pork and venison supplied by the Hanes, and returned to Schomberg in the fall.

In the spring of 1869 the family moved up to Muskoka. Three of the boys and their father spent nine days travelling from Schomberg to Vernon Lake with two teams of oxen drawing two wagons, and nine cows following a cowbell tied to the first wagon. They left the wagons at Vernon Lake, and after swimming the cattle across the river (shallower in those days before the lock was installed on the Mary River), drove them through the woods to Hillside, the father going before to blaze trees to mark the trail which later became Highway 35/60. Then the Rev. Hill returned to Schomberg to bring his wife, two daughters and youngest son by train, boat, stage and wagon to Vernon Lake. In the meantime his three sons cleared the brush and logs from the river between Fairy and Peninsula Lakes so they could move their belongings the last nine miles by boat. It was the end of June 1869 by the time the family got settled in their new home.

The fallow chopped the year before was burned over and planted with corn between the stumps to provide feed for the cattle. The cattle survived the winter by feeding on the top branches of the newly-felled trees, supplemented by a feed of corn stalks each night. The following summer the Hills built stabling for the cattle and more accommodation for the family.

In 1869 Sinclair township was opened for settlement, and the land around Hillside was all taken within the next few years. A school house was built, and the first teacher was a daughter of a pioneer family. Church services and Sunday school were held for almost 20 years in the schoolhouse. Many Sunday mornings the Rev. Hill and one son would paddle a log canoe to Huntsville to hold services in Captain George Hunt's home, returning for Hillside Sunday school in the afternoon and church service in the evening. He married the young people, baptized the children and conducted the funeral services.

The settlers built the Hillside church (now the United Church) in 1892 three years before the Rev. Hill died. The centre portion of the memorial window names Rev. Robert Norton Hill and the right portion Leonard Hill, whose generous contribution made the church possible. The left portion is a memorial to other pioneer families: Brown, Emberson, Evans, Fleming, Fraser, Francy, Green, Hill, Hodgeson, Lang, Lassiter, McDonald, Thompson and Walker. Rev. Hill's 1880 house is now in Huntsville's Pioneer Village. Hillside's United Church Women welcome visitors to their Pancake Frolics on some Thursdays in summer.

Cruising the Lakes

During the zenith of the steamship era around 1900, as many as 10 passenger and freight boats plied the waters around Huntsville, some towing logs to the local sawmills from dumping grounds around the lakes. A steamboat could go as far as the Hoodstown rapids at the Fox Lake end of Vernon Lake. In the opposite direction, it could steam past the swinging highway bridge to Fairy Lake and then east to Peninsula Lake through the canal dredged in 1886–88 from the river between Fairy and Peninsula Lakes and pile-driven along some stretches to prevent bank erosion. Small steamers could go south to Mary Lake through the Mary River Lock, under construction from 1873 to 1877.

Captain A. N. Hogue, who had sailed for over 50 years on Great

Lakes and ocean-going ships before retiring to the easier summertime runs out of Huntsville, reminisced to me in 1954 about the *Algonquin*, the second vessel by that name and the last of the heavy freight and passenger ships out of Huntsville. As the heavy ship's gangway was in the bow, Captain Hogue had only to put her nose against the dock for loading and unloading. "If the weather was rough and the *Algonquin* bumped hard, a dock might take off into the bush and I'd have to wait and see if it was coming back out again," the Captain joked. At one place they threw the mail bag off as they went by and the postmistress threw back the bag of outgoing mail on their return trip, all without stopping. "With quite a few feet of water between us, she had to be good," said the Captain. He also happily recalled a hitch-hiking dog which would board the *Algonquin* at North Portage on Peninsula Lake, ride to Huntsville, get off the boat when they docked and go uptown. But when the ten-minute warning whistle was blown on the boat the first creature to come down the walk to the wharf would be that dog, ready to go home.

In 1954, Captain Hogue was master and wheelsman of the M.S. *Iroquois II*, a sturdy twin-screw launch which seated 100 passengers. The *Iroquois II* made an excursion twice daily from the Huntsville docks (the Huntsville bridge swung open for it) through Fairy and Peninsula Lakes to North Portage, where the passengers went for a ride on the Portage Railway.

In the narrow, winding canal between Fairy and Peninsula Lakes, Captain Hogue recalled an earlier day when a big steamer belonging to the owner of a palatial summer home came around the bend, heading for the *Algonquin* leaving no room to pass. The Captain saved the day by taking the *Algonquin* up the bank. Then a great argument ensued about who did or did not sound a whistle.

After passing many resorts and the Penlake Golf Club on the end of the peninsula where the Hills settled and from which the lake gets its name, we landed near the south-east extremity of Peninsula Lake at North Portage. Here we transferred to the Portage Railway (since dismantled). Probably the smallest commercially operated railway in the world with a length of 1⅛ miles, it received its charter in 1900 and the Ontario Government granted $25,000 towards its construction. It provided an important transportation link between freight and passenger steamers on the Lake of Bays and Peninsula Lake because a navigable water route between the two lakes was impractical on account of the difference in their altitudes. Peninsula Lake is approximately 931 feet above sea level, while the Lake of Bays is 1,034.

The track was narrow gauge (42 inches) and the railway owned two small locomotives of the type used in mines, two passenger cars (originally Toronto horse-drawn streetcars), two boxcars and two flatcars. The engine was filled with water at a tank at the Lake of Bays terminal once every round trip. In addition to its scheduled runs, the train would

Ontario Archives

The *Algonquin II* in the canal between Fairy and
Peninsula Lakes, passing a stack of steamer fuel.

Ontario Ministry of Industry and Tourism

Portage Railway at Lake of Bays terminal, in the 1930s.

make a special trip to carry the boats and kits of canoeing and camping parties across the portage.

This little railway provided people with a lot of fun. Officially named the *Portage Flyer*, it travelled about 15 miles per hour. It was sometimes referred to as the "Lake of Bays Express" and other people called it the "Hot Tamale" because of the occasional fire started by a spark from the engine landing in dry bush. The train stopped running in 1958, the locomotives were sold and shipped out of the District and the tracks were pulled up in 1964. A steam engine and much of the track are now in an amusement park in St. Thomas, Ontario, where both are kept busy entertaining children and steam buffs.

Much of the Fairy and Peninsula Lakes scenery can be admired while travelling by car. Take Muskoka Road 3 north from Huntsville and turn right very shortly on Highway 60 which takes you along the north shore of Fairy Lake. Within two miles, a picnic area on an elevation on the north side of the road gives a good view of Fairy Lake.

Muskoka Road 23, off the south side of Highway 60, crosses the canal between Fairy and Peninsula Lakes on a high old iron bridge designed to allow steamers to pass under it. Signs will direct you to the 18-hole Strathcona Golf Club, a pleasant place to stop for snacks even if you don't want to play. Follow Muskoka Road 23 about six miles past farms and through forest along the Peninsula shore to the old steamboat dock at North Portage, and a connecting road will take you to South Portage and the Lake of Bays.

HIDDEN VALLEY

In 1967 there were about a dozen cottages in Hidden Valley, about six miles east of Huntsville on Highway 60, but the intervening years have seen dozens more vacation and permanent homes of eye-catching, expensive design—from Swiss chalets with open balconies on two levels to tall, angular white brick structures with huge expanses of glass—on such streets as Chalet Crescent and Slalom Drive. The Beach Club is for members only. A 1500-foot chairlift takes skiers to the top of Peninsula Peak on the north shore of Peninsula Lake. The observation tower overlooks 2500 square miles of lakes, hills and forests. Check each year to make sure the Highlands Ski Club is open to daily skiers if you are not a member or staying at the resort.

The Muskoka Loppet is a cross-country skiing race which takes off from Hidden Valley on a Sunday early in January, continues across Peninsula Lake, and ends 30 kilometres (19 miles) later at Port Sydney. It is believed to be Canada's largest single-day skiing event, attracting 800 contestants in 1976. The first three men completed the course in just under two hours, although the winning time has been 10 or 15 minutes less when weather conditions were better. The sections include:

men's élite, ladies' 30 kilometres, junior men 21 and under, men 22 to 44, and men 45 and over. Some events are also held in the 7.5 kilometre distance. At the refreshment stop, the 1976 participants were served a total of 60 gallons of blackberry soup (a mixture of hot tea and berry concentrate with sugar), 250 oranges (cut in sixths), and 35 pounds of chocolate pieces. The racers don't stop; they take from an extended hand and charge on.

MUSKOKA ROAD 8 (FORMERLY HIGHWAY 514)

Follow Highway 60 for about seven miles northeast of Huntsville to reach Muskoka Road 8, a particularly beautiful road when the leaves have changed in the fall.

The road to Walker's Lake comes up shortly on the west. This lake is only about one mile across, but the water is as deep as 52 feet. Robert Walker, a coal miner intending to go to Pennsylvania to work in the mines, sailed from England in 1876 with his wife and six sons, having left three daughters in England. On shipboard he met people who told such glowing tales of Muskoka that he changed his plans and decided to go to Muskoka. The Walkers bought an ox and a wagon in Gravenhurst and advanced slowly northward over the 40 miles to their 200 lakeside acres. They built a cabin, cleared land to raise vegetables, and soon constructed a sawmill and gristmill on a waterfall dropping out of their lake. In 1928 their descendants decided to go into the resort business and built Royal Oak Lodge. Recently a development company, Walker's Lake Estates, subdivided the property around the lake for cottages.

Solitaire Lake is well known because of Limberlost Lodge, established in 1921 by Gordon Hill, a member of the pioneer Hill family. Limberlost Road branches east off Muskoka Road 8 about five miles north of Walker's Lake Road. A network of skiing, hiking and riding trails connect many small lakes with Solitaire.

At Limberlost, in about 1960, I talked with the elderly Dr. Reazin who was living with his wife in a cabin on the Limberlost property. His father had been a School Inspector in Victoria County from about 1870 and had later performed the same role in Muskoka. In 1892, while a young medical student, Dr. Reazin taught the school which operated for summer sessions only near Limberlost at Miller Hill, a place highly recommended to visitors today for its beautiful view. He kept a little tent on the Limberlost point, and after school when the weather was good he would get into his birchbark canoe and paddle all over the lakes.

When asked for a story about the old days, he chose to tell me of the visitor who came to Huntsville from an outlying settlement, stopped a man on the street and asked him a long stuttered question. The Huntsville man happened to be a stutterer too, and he started, "W-w-w-well y-y-y-y-you c-c-c-could g-go", and the visitor laid into him and they had "the biggest fight that was ever pulled off in Huntsville." A few years later Dr. Reazin was on his way to visit his father's property on Doe Lake in the Parry Sound District and engaged a livery service man at the railway station in Sprucedale to drive him out. He stuttered, and on the way Dr. Reazin was talking to him about it from the medical point of view and told him about the Huntsville visitor who had the fight. The driver laughed and said, "I w-w-was the d-damn f-fool."

Dr. Reazin's career as a medical missionary took him to the Northwest Territories and the Yukon, where he also prospected and traded in furs. He eventually came back south and, after a graduate course in medicine, entered private practice in Toronto and was appointed Medical Officer for the Transportation Commission. Upon retirement he accepted an appointment from Limberlost as resident physician, living on Limberlost property until his death at age 94 in March 1963.

Back on Muskoka Road 8 near Brooks Mills Road, stop at Mizpah Pioneer Cemetery. A plaque by the cemetery hill reads in part: "Here lie some of the stout-hearted pioneers of this community who carved their homes and their lands from the forest. . . . Therefore was the place called MIZPAH for he said, "The Lord watch between me and thee when we are absent one from another" . . . ." A large wooden cross marks the grave of an unknown Indian buried by settlers "with a blanket for a shroud". The community church built in 1884 was once adjacent to the cemetery. Later it was rebuilt as a school and now stands as a home nearby at the Limberlost corner.

Bella Lake is reached by the township road running west off Muskoka Road 8 about nine miles above Highway 60.

Drive past Billie Bear Lodge and the cottages by the lake to the Antioch Conservation Area, some 228 acres including 3,000 feet of beach and shore property and the Antioch Bog at the west end of Bella Lake. The Conservation Area gets its name from the first post office in Sinclair Township located at the west end of the sand beach on Bella Lake and named Antioch by Muskoka pioneers after the biblical Antioch where Barnabas and Saul of Tarsus went to preach the gospel, "and the disciples were called Christians first in Antioch".

The founding of Antioch Conservation Area is a remarkable story of selflessness and philanthropy worth recording. In early September 1967, S. M. Thompson, a summer resident of Bella Lake for 30 years, negotiated the purchase of the property from Marion Hill, of Limberlost, and with ten neighbours, he petitioned the Lieutenant-Governor for a charter in the name of The Mabel Hart Brook and Marion Hill Memorial Foundation.

Mabel (Billie) Hart, born in 1887 in a log cabin on Bella Lake, married, at age 17, a man who had come up from the United States to holiday on Bella Lake at the little resort they subsequently operated and renamed Camp Billie Bear. Billie, a beautiful and vivacious brun-

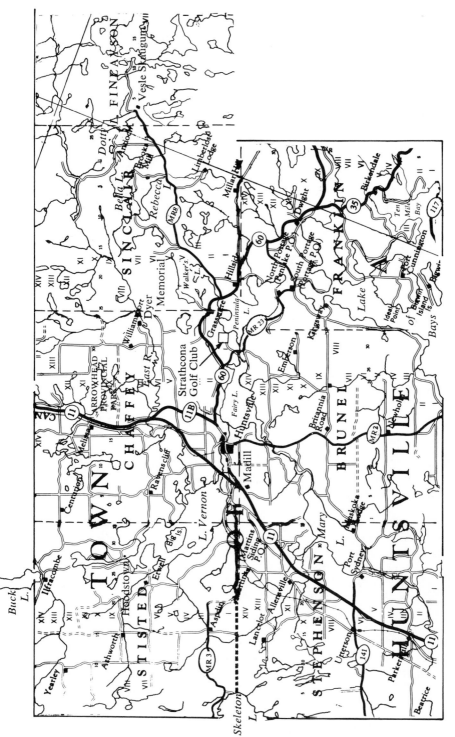

Scale: 1 inch = 4 miles

ette, was equally at home in New York City drawing rooms with her husband and in the wilderness with gun and canoe. She later married Edgar Brook, of Brook's Mill, after the death of her first husband. (The plaque marking Mizpah Cemetery was erected in her memory.)

Marion Hill (née Higgins) had come from London, Ontario, to holiday at Limberlost and married the owner, Gordon Hill. A zealous conservationist, she sold the property on Bella Lake only on condition that it be retained in its wilderness state, and the purchase price of $60,000 was paid by people who gained nothing but the establishment of the Conservation Area. The new owners say, "In these days when natural forests are rapidly disappearing and shoreline and beach are rapidly being developed, a place where one can walk over bush trails or along a quiet beach without conflict with, or trespass on, private property is an invaluable privilege." Until their indebtedness is discharged, they don't have the money to pay for a caretaker and must themselves do all maintenance work.

The beach at the Conservation Area is the locale of August canoe and swimming races and the September corn and wiener roast held annually by the Bella-Rebecca Cottagers Association. "We are privileged", said its president, "to enjoy a heritage of incomparable beauty. Let us firmly resolve that nothing we do shall ever mar what we ourselves have not created, nor be faulted by those who will follow us for being derelict in our duty to preserve absolutely what nature has bestowed upon us."

Vesle Skaugum is farther along Muskoka Road 8 at Interlaken between Oxbow and Dotty Lakes. This World War II rest camp was the first haven of refuge for Norwegians who had escaped to Canada to join the Norwegian Air Force. Here they took basic training, which included a 21-mile ski race with full military equipment and was the forerunner of today's Muskoka Loppet. These Norwegians are also credited with stimulating local interest in ski jumping through their expertise.

Vesle Skaugum (meaning home or clearing in the woods, and named in honour of the Norwegian home of Crown Prince Olav and Crown Princess Martha) was built before Little Norway at Muskoka Airport, and when the early trainees were graduated they marched all the way to Toronto with full equipment, doing the 160 miles in eight days, according to Dennis Stone of the Muskoka Tourist Association. After Little Norway was built at Muskoka Airport, Vesle Skaugum graduates went there for their flying training.

Vesle Skaugum's log buildings are reminiscent of those built in Norway. The Norwegian crest, a lion with a broadaxe surmounted by a crown, decorates the doorway of the main building. Today, on the lawn outside, stands a grey granite monument in memory of the members of the Royal Norwegian Air Force who gave their lives. It bears the inscription:

As screams of eagles
Linger in the Air so
Shall their names ring
Across the seas, a mes-
sage of liberty to the
Hills of Home

The Parkdale Kiwanis Club, Toronto, has been operating Vesle Skaugum since the war to provide subsidized or free holidays each camp period for some 200 boys or girls, aged 7 to 14, whose parents need assistance.

Muskoka Road 8 then leads into isolated lake areas settled by some intrepid cottagers, and to a corridor of wilderness territory where I have picnicked and swum with an explorer's delight. Previously part of Haliburton County (Finlayson township), this administratively isolated corridor separated Muskoka from Algonquin Park until January 1st, 1971, when it was brought into Muskoka with the formation of Regional Government.

Dyer Memorial

The Dyer Memorial is on Williamsport Road, seven miles northeast of Huntsville via Highway 11 and the Harp Lake Road. From its parking lot, broad steps constructed of lightly tinted pre-cast concrete lead up the hill to the 42-foot column. The column was built by Detroit corporation lawyer Clifton G. Dyer, who died in 1959, in memory of his wife, Betsy Browne Dyer (1884–1956), and is inscribed: "As a permanent tribute to her for the never failing aid, encouragement and inspiration which she contributed to their married career, and as a final resting place for their ashes. An affectionate, loyal and understanding wife is life's greatest gift." The ashes of both Mrs. and Mr. Dyer are in two copper urns at the top of the column.

A local stonemason, Herb McKenney, constructed the column of Muskoka stone on a 20-foot square base in the centre of a 4200-square foot terrace. Construction costs, including the 10-acre botanical garden with many species of North American plants, amounted to more than $100,000. Estate funds provide for a caretaker.

Rolling lawns, flower beds and tree-lined walks strewn with pine needles surround the memorial column. Aquatic plants grow in reflecting pools, supplied from a series of springs, and streams ornamented with little brown bridges drift down through several levels. Tree plantations and Muskoka rock provide a background, and it is hoped eventually that nature trails will traverse 450 acres. Looking out from the face of the monument, one sees the mountainous ridge on the far side of the East River valley.

The Dyers spent their 1916 honeymoon on a canoe trip in Algonquin Park, returning to Muskoka on their 20th anniversary to tent on the

East River near the site of the present memorial. In 1940 they built a cottage on the bank of the river, and visited there each summer, and some winters. By providing this memorial, Mr. Dyer has introduced the beauty of this backwoods country to many who would otherwise have no purpose in wandering in the East River Valley.

A number of men who settled in this vicinity in the 1870s worked in lumbering in the days of the big pines, an important factor in the support of the Muskoka economy. The logs were driven to Vernon Lake and Huntsville on the Big East, a river so circuitous that one camp often sufficed for two nights while the intervening day was spent driving the logs around a U-turn in the river and back to the camping spot.

XV STISTED

F. M. DELAFOSSE, AN "ENGLISH BLOOD"

After the District of Muskoka was opened for settlement, a few ingenious men seized the opportunity to pay the expenses of developing their land by setting themselves up as teachers of land husbandry or dairy farming. They enrolled young men from Great Britain as students on the premise that these young men would take up free land grants and settle on them when they had learned all about backwoods work.

The story of one of these farming apprentices is related in the book *English Bloods* by Roger Vardon (pseudonym for Frederick Montague Delafosse), who left Liverpool, England, for Quebec in May 1878. He was then 18 years old and weighed 100 pounds.

Frederick Delafosse had been born in Bengal, India, in 1860, where his father was a Captain of Artillery. Captain Delafosse, in poor health, returned with his family to England when Frederick was seven, and died soon afterwards. Within a few years the mother also died, and Frederick's uncle became his guardian.

When the uncle received letters from a retired army officer in Muskoka offering to take Frederick as a farm pupil for three years at a fee of £100 per annum, he decided to enroll his ward. He was leaving for India and anxious to make some lasting arrangements about Frederick. As the boy's academic record had not been brilliant, the uncle reasoned he would not be able to pass Army examinations, but his great enthusiasm for cricket and other sport might have fitted him for roughing it in the colonies. Muskoka seemed like a happy solution to the uncle, and his ward was stunned by the speed with which his future was arranged. If Frederick had had it to do over, he certainly would have rejected the whole wretched plan. His mature reflections pointed to the conclusion that the same money and effort spent introducing him to some other method of earning a living would have been much more productive.

Frederick's ocean voyage from Liverpool to Quebec was pleasant and uneventful, except that some Canadians on board denounced the scheme to which Frederick was committed as barefaced robbery, and would have found him other means of employment had he been free. One of his fellow passengers kindly showed him the historic city of Quebec and saw that he was safely on the train for Toronto.

Alone in a Toronto hotel, Frederick immediately became the target of a confidence man who fleeced him out of $5.00. On the train to Gravenhurst, he handed over another $5.00 to a woeful man to buy medicine for his horses which suffered from a mysterious complaint.

When this same man tried to get more money from him to help his sick wife, Frederick, now running short of money, began to realize he was being taken and made up his mind to turn a deaf ear to any further supplications. Fortunately, the next person to approach Frederick on the train proved to be a fatherly Muskoka man, Mr. Wardle, who listened to the reason for Frederick's trip with astonishment but offered to help him reach his backwoods destination.

Frederick took the steamer from Gravenhurst to Bracebridge and felt that no scenery could be more wonderful. On all sides was primeval wilderness with the exception of a few small cottages and immense booms of logs tied to the shore. He was excited and pleased with the herons, loons, ferns and waterplants, and felt that he had indeed come to a sportsman's paradise.

On arrival at Bracebridge, Frederick discovered that his luggage had been left at Gravenhurst, the train terminal, and also that he had somehow lost his baggage checks. Little did he foresee that three months would elapse before he would get possession of his clothes.

Bracebridge had about 1200 inhabitants and was filled with rivermen attached to the different drives. Intending to stay the night, Frederick registered at one of the hotels, but he became increasingly uncomfortable after dinner as the centre of attention of the rough crowd of men in the hotel sitting-room. He was jibed at unmercifully for his genteel appearance and his contract with Captain Martin, about which he had been indiscreet enough to tell them. He, in turn, found their rude talk objectionable and their tobacco chewing and spitting positively unbearable, and he left to find Mr. Wardle's log house on the main road. On the way he floundered in and out of mudholes in the growing darkness while black flies and mosquitoes attacked him in clouds.

Before dawn, Frederick started out with Wardle and his older son and their ox-wagon. The spring run-off was at its height, and the journey on corduroy roads through swamp and over rocks was painfully rough, with much time spent in prying the wheels of the wagon out of the mud. They reached Utterson, about 15 miles from Bracebridge, at 8 o'clock in the morning and continued north, the clearings growing ever scarcer. After an unbroken stretch of forest that continued for miles, they reached the Stisted Road, a rough track going north and south through the centre of Stisted township. At 5 o'clock in the afternoon Frederick parted company with the Wardles, as the property where Wardle was taking his son to settle was now in a different direction.

Alone in the wilds for the first time, Frederick was fearful of the unknown forest beasts; since he had started for Muskoka he had been besieged with exaggerated tales about these dangerous creatures. The sudden diabolical cry of a screech-owl about a foot above his head nearly drove him to the end of his sanity. After six miles with only a blazed trail to follow, up hill and down into the declivities of swamp and stream, and covered with slime from falling off slippery tree trunks meant to bridge the worst spots, he finally saw through the trees two small log shanties in a clearing beside Buck Lake.

The door was opened to his knock by Mrs. Martin and inside, sitting at the table having their evening meal, were Captain Martin and three students (Melius, Barrett and Harkins), two of whom had also come straight from English schools. Captain Martin told Frederick that the house he had been building for them all had burnt down about a month earlier when it had caught fire while some brushwood was being burned. Most of the household linen and equipment had been lost in the fire, and they had only the barest necessities.

Exhausted as he was by his journey, Frederick was soon awakened from his sleep that night by the relentless attack of the mosquitoes. In the middle of the night the students, who slept in the second shanty, dunked themselves in the lake to escape the mosquitoes and spent the rest of the night huddled around a smudge fire, dozing and scratching.

Frederick soon learned that, in addition to sharing in the "Spring Work", as the youngest member of the household he was expected to carry all the water up the steep hill from the lake, to bring in the wood for the stove, to help wash the dishes and to take messages to the neighbours. The spring work had the planting of the crops as its objective, but first land had to be prepared. Underbrushing and chopping had been started on only three acres, but Captain Martin looked forward optimistically to the time when his land would be waving in grain and stocked with cattle.

Frederick set to work wearing white shirt, stiff collar, patent leather boots and knickerbockers (borrowed from Captain Martin) with the other four inexperienced males in the Martin household. The surrounding settlers found both their attire and their efforts at clearing the land cause for great hilarity. After a few weeks the work was still going so badly that the Captain decided to have a bee and sent Frederick forth with Harkins to ask the neighbours to come with their teams. Their travels took nearly three days, and they had a good opportunity to see poverty and wretchedness among their less fortunate neighbours, some of whom had known much better days. They had a close brush with a bear on the way through the woods, but this was a mere nothing compared to the danger of the "hodags" of which Frederick apprised Harkins —" they climb trees and watch for you and jump on your shoulders and strangle you." (Mr. Wardle had warned him about "hodags".) The boys soon discovered that, around the neighbourhood, they were referred to as the "English Bloods".

By the unwritten law of the woods, all those invited to the logging bee came—about 20 men and 5 teams—and many of the wives came also to help with the food. Captain Martin's gentle ways with his oxen greatly astonished his neighbours, and they attempted to show him what harsh expletives and a good biff with the gad would accomplish. Martin retired from the scene after the hook of his logging chain caught in his trousers and he was dragged over logs and stumps before the oxen could be stopped. The settler who took his place gave the students much better instruction.

The day ended with a merry supper at a table made of long boards placed on improvised trestles, and Delafosse added:

> Nobody as yet knew the exact condition under which we had arrived in the district, and the general impression seemed to be that we had either separately or collectively committed some enormity in the Old Country which had necessitated our departure from its shores. I surmised this from the confidential way in which an inquisitive individual leaned over during dinner and whispered raucously in my ear, "Say, sonny, you ain't old enough to have robbed a bank or anything like that but what in hell did you do to be sent up here?" I replied that I had come in order to make a living. This was altogether too much for him; . . . he gave a gasp, invoked the name of the Almighty, and went on with his dinner.

The log piles were subsequently burned. After the crops were planted in the clearing, the boys attempted to erect fences to keep out marauding cattle. The alfalfa did not come up, probably due to lack of soil. Some turnips grew, but constant alertness both night and day was required to keep the neighbours' cattle out of the crop, especially once the beasts discovered they merely had to lean against the fence to knock down enough to get through.

The men of the Martin household arranged a memorable pilgrimage into Huntsville, 15 miles via the Buck River and Fox Lake, to celebrate Dominion Day, July 1st. All the youth from the surrounding countryside had arrayed themselves as splendidly as possible and swarmed into Huntsville. The cricket match, played in a newly stumped field with boulders and snags everywhere, turned out to have much different rules from those enforced on the playing fields of Eton, but the Martin men soon learned that bloodshed would result from making any issues.

In the summer nights when sleep was impossible because of the mosquitoes, the boys sometimes went out on the lake to still-hunt for deer, a practice illegal then as it is now. A lighted candle fastened on the front of the canoe would lure the curious deer down to the water, and sometimes the boys would shoot a deer to vary their interminable diet of fat pork. On several occasions the boys and their guns ended up in the water with an overturned canoe, and once they were reported and Captain Martin was fined.

The end of summer saw a reduction in the mosquito menace, and the sleep of the students was less disturbed by nearby cowbells at night that brought them jumping out of bed to protect the turnips. But even that winter, peace at night was not to be theirs. Late in October, Captain Martin sent Frederick and Barrett to Bracebridge to take delivery of some cattle he had ordered, although he had no barn in which to house them over the winter. He said that cows were hardy animals and could very well live in the woods near the shanty.

The boys drove two cows, two steers, a yearling heifer, five ewes and a ram the 33 miles from Bracebridge to Captain Martin's. It took them $2\frac{1}{2}$ days to get home, most of the time being spent in an undignified chase of the animals through woods and swamp and backwards over the roads. At night, of course, the boys were forced to seek shelter with the nearest settler, and this did little to relieve their agony.

That first winter was a terrible one, for they had to endure the cold housed as they were in the two shanties. If the fire went out in the stove, everything froze—water, butter, meat, cheeks, ears, noses. The nights were fiercely cold, often as low as $-40°$F. The unfortunate beasts that Captain Martin had acquired tramped round and round the shanty all through the night seeking warmth and shelter. The few that survived the winter were never healthy again. But the Martin household was rich and comfortable compared with many others.

Captain Martin looked forward to the day when a colony would flourish with his house as the parent of it all. The raising bee for Captain Martin's new house took place the following summer. Frederick and the others had rafted the cut lumber up from the mill at Huntsville. Each unwieldy raft had to be paddled through the large Lake Vernon and the lumber hauled across the Hoodstown portage, with the help of the oxen; thence through Fox Lake and the narrow river, on which there was another portage; all this taking five or six days. Delafosse's account continued:

> We used to meet shantymen many a time on these trips and got to be friendly with them. We found them to be fine fellows and willing to take all the enjoyment they could out of life. Men of wonderful strength and vigour they were, capable of performing marvels on the logs. In trying to emulate their feats in spinning them over and over in the water and in riding them down the rivers we got many a ducking. They used to invite us sometimes to take dinner with them on their rafts and regaled us with all sorts of tall stories as to the wonders they could accomplish.

The bricks for the chimney were paddled up from Huntsville and carried on their backs across the portages. Some of the furniture, which included a grand piano, was hauled by ox-team in the winter and some was rafted up.

Soon after Captain Martin's house, barn, and stable were completed, he organized the building of a church and a rectory, and arranged for an incumbent.

Although realizing very early in their apprenticeship that no fortunes were to be made in the backwoods of Muskoka, the students liked the country so much they decided to go ahead with the program, build their own shanties and settle on their own land. A contract was given to a settler to clear two acres of land for each of them, fence the clearing and make it ready for a crop, all for $16 an acre. Barrett and Melius went to their own little house at the end of their first year, but they continued to join in much of the work at Captain Martin's.

Pell, a later student, was an enthusiastic hunter and fisherman who liked the country so well that he wrote for two of his sisters to come and keep house for him, and they built a comfortable house on a farm adjoining Frederick's. Such people had private means or they could not possibly have lived in the style to which they were accustomed. They did, however, make an important contribution to the community by bringing money at a time when it was desperately needed.

Delafosse writes affectionately of three English families, among the earliest to arrive and settle in the area, one of whom had six sons who also farmed. Honest, hospitable and kind, they "gave a distinct tone to the neighbourhood and helped in more ways than one to raise the ideals of the community." Delafosse expresses unbounded admiration for those honest and industrious settlers who had come to Muskoka to make homes for themselves and escape from the servitude of their former existence.

Captain Martin left the Muskoka District a few years after his adventures with the "English Bloods", according to Delafosse, as his lots did not contain enough good land to make it possible to farm successfully. His house and barn eventually disappeared, and the wilderness grew back over most of the clearing.

Delafosse had already come a long way from Bengal, India, via Wellington College in England, to the Muskoka backwoods, but he did not stay on his Muskoka land. He moved to Toronto in the early 1880s and occupied the position of Secretary to the Provost Body of Trinity College for some years. In 1910, after a period of retirement in Lakefield, Delafosse began a new career at age 50 as the first Public Librarian of Peterborough, Ontario, a position he held with distinction for 36 years until his retirement in January 1946.

Ilfracombe

In *English Bloods*, Delafosse tells us that the village, Ilfracombe, that had grown up at the foot of their lake (Buck Lake) had a church and a sawmill, two stores, a bridge built over the river by the government and a post office promised. The 1879 *Guide Book and Atlas* describes it as a new settlement "which has progressed with amazing rapidity since the first commencement of farming work in 1877, . . . composed of gentlemen of good position and means from England, . . . [and with] large clearings," and that the Anglican church was to be built with funds procured from England.

In 1886 it was described in a Muskoka guidebook as the centre of an English colony of high county standing and much cultivation.

A trip taken today to Ilfracombe reveals a different type of village than the one Delafosse saw developing. There is some farming in the surrounding countryside and one or two large farms nearby, but most of the country is inhabited by summer cottagers rather than year-round residents. A charming picnic ground and beach on Buck Lake is situated in the village, and a rustic sign decorated with a coat of arms announces that this is "The Hamlet of Ilfracombe, Founded circ. 1870." It was named after Ilfracombe, England, now the largest resort in North Devon, with fine coastal scenery and beaches backed by wooded hills.

The winding river on which Delafosse travelled on his way to Huntsville flows down to Fox Lake, surrounded today by summer homes. At the foot of Fox Lake is the Hoodstown community.

Hoodstown

Hoodstown figured prominently in the early history of that part of Muskoka because it was thought that the railway would run through it and make it an important distribution centre. The early name of Port Vernon had been changed to Hoodstown in honour of Captain Charles Hood, the presiding genius, who had come from Toronto and erected the grist and saw mills. Delafosse tells us that the village grew to contain three stores, two churches, the mill, a hotel and at least 14 houses. But when the railway was routed instead through Huntsville (1885), Hoodstown slowly declined. Today the name is mostly used to identify the dam which, although small, is an important link in water-level control. The rapids below the dam are narrow and turbulent, and the path of the canoe portage through the woods is still well trod by the young people of the District's summer camps. Many a fire has been lit at the campsite on the Vernon Lake side. (Vernon Lake is said to have been named by John S. Dennis on an 1860–61 survey after Vernon B. Wadsworth, a young pupil in the party.)

STISTED TOWNSHIP

Stisted township, which contains Ilfracombe and Hoodstown, was named after H. W. Stisted, Administrator of Ontario, 1867–68. The first Council was organized in 1874, and by the year 1885 nearly every lot in Stisted's $8\frac{1}{4} \times 9$ mile area had settlers. At the peak of its settlement Stisted had a population of 1,500 and crops of grain, hay, turnips and other vegetables. Logging operations were carried on from the year 1881 when magnificent pines growing to a height of 140 feet were harvested, many of them being 4 feet in diameter, stump high, while some were more than 6 feet. As the tops of the trees where the branches began were left in the woods as useless, the logs taken out were nearly all free of knots.

Ontario Ministry of Industry and Tourism

The Dyer Memorial.

Marjorie Demaine

The Henry Demaine family in 1880.

The Stisted Fall Fair, an annual event since 1885, is held in September at the Stisted Township Hall near Ashworth. Hundreds of visitors join the community for the exhibits in the Hall, program on the grounds, contests and lucky draws.

The Demaine Family

Henry Demaine, of Utley, Yorkshire, England, brought his wife, Mary Ann and six children (Mary Elizabeth 16, Ada Annie 11, William Henry 9, Joseph 7, James Ernest 5, Susan Eorline 3) to Stisted township in the spring of 1880.

A cabinet and pattern maker, Henry had read advertisements in the *Manchester Guardian* which led him to believe that Muskoka's climate was the best in the world, and that game and wild fruit abounded and a great opportunity for farming existed. His imagination was fired, and he decided there would be lots of scope for plying his trade in this new country. The family's ocean voyage to Canada exemplifies the transatlantic journey experienced by immigrants of that period.

On the day of their departure from England, the family was carried by tender to board the *Polynesian* in the river at Liverpool at 10 a.m. on an early April Saturday. The ship, manned by a crew of 70, was built of wood, covered and strengthened with steel throughout. Her exterior dimensions were about 500′ × 80′ with a depth of 50 feet from top deck to keel. She had three masts, one smoke stack, two compound engines driving the propellor at her stern and an average speed of 100 knots in 24 hours. The 800 to 900 passengers were of different nationalities— Swiss, German, French, English, Irish—and nearly all were emigrating to the promised land of America.

Mary Ann Demaine and the six children had four bunks in tiers of two in one small windowless room in third-class quarters three decks below. Henry Demaine slept in a hammock in a separate apartment which accommodated 150 men.

The *Polynesian*, nicknamed the "Rolling Polly" because of her continuous rolling and pitching, passed out to sea at high tide that evening to begin the 21-day voyage. The children escaped the nauseating air in their quarters as soon as possible the next morning to breathe in deep draughts of the pure, fresh air on deck and were overcome by a feeling of desolation. England was nowhere in sight and the ship was alone on a great expanse of rolling, tumbling water.

The Atlantic rollers tossed the Rolling Polly about like a piece of cork, and her bow would sometimes rise to a dizzy height of twenty feet. For the first few days the majority of the passengers were violently sea-sick and in despair, and the crew also was in despair with the resultant scrubbing and cleaning. When this passed, the passengers became more cheerful and gathered in social groups.

For breakfast, the steerage passengers were served porridge, bread, marmalade, tea and condensed milk. Dinner consisted of meat, potatoes, vegetables, bread, tea and condensed milk; supper of bread, buns, jam, sea biscuits, syrup, coffee and condensed milk. Fish once a week and an occasional plum pudding provided the only variety to this menu.

One day about 60 "Home Boys", ranging in age from seven to ten years, were assembled on deck to sing songs and hymns. Abandoned or orphaned, they had been rescued from the streets of London and other cities by the Dr. Bernardo Homes and were going to Canada to be distributed to different homes, some in Muskoka. Some Bernardo children became cherished members of new families; others were exploited and enslaved.

That night the breaking ice pounded against the ship's side, and Rolling Polly trembled as she once more made headway. She weaved her way through the ice floes the next morning, entered the mouth of the St. Lawrence and headed for the port of Quebec, where the Demaines disembarked. They were all soon aboard the train through Montreal to Toronto, then changed trains for Gravenhurst and embarked there on the steamboat to Bracebridge.

Mrs. Demaine and the children boarded for two weeks in Bracebridge while Henry Demaine went on an exploratory trip to Stisted township, where he bought for £50 (about $250) an uncleared 100 acres which had changed hands several times. During this period Mrs. Demaine decided she did not like the country and begged her husband to return to England, but there was no turning back. They loaded into a lumber wagon driven by a Muskoka man, Nehemiah Hanes, and travelled 30 miles on the first day over rocks, hills and through mudholes.

"On each side of the narrow road rose the thick forest, interspersed with small clearings with log cabins and log barns. What a long distance seemed to divide those clearings," William Demaine later wrote in his account of their migration. "Darkness found us still a long way from the end of the journey. Frogs croaked and whistled; the wagon bumped and bumped."

They stopped overnight at the hotel in the small village of Aspdin, six miles from their destination, and next day proceeded to the homes at Ashworth (the first settler, Stanley Ashworth, had arrived May 1874) where they were to stay until they could get their own house built. The boys enjoyed the new country and, much as their parents lamented it, were pleased with their freedom from "Bobbies", churches, Sunday school and day school. But William Demaine remembers that even as a nine-year-old boy he was more than a little bewildered at the primitive homes of the settlers and the scarcity of food. This hardly seemed like the "land of milk and honey" they had envisioned.

During the next six weeks Henry Demaine erected an 18' × 24' frame house with the help of nine-year-old William. He went on to build some of the early houses in Huntsville and the school at Hoodstown (Stisted No. 7) which was later moved to Ashworth.

Marjorie Demaine

The house built by W. H. Demaine in 1907.

Marjorie Demaine

Winners of the log sending (rolling) contest, Stisted Fair,
1941: Harold Hines, Will Hines (teamster) and Wilson Spiers.

Marjorie Demaine

Stanley Ashworth store and original Ashworth Post Office, built
in the 1890s.

In October 1889, 9½ years after starting out from England, Mrs. Demaine died at the age of 49. Henry Demaine later remarried and to this union a son was born, giving him in all three daughters and four sons. All of these married and had children, and Henry Demaine's numerous descendants are scattered throughout Ontario and in such widespread places as British Columbia, California and Ohio.

Marjorie Demaine, a daughter of William Demaine, lives today at Sherwood Lodge, Etwell (10 miles from Huntsville on Lake Vernon). She has been writing the area's local news for Muskoka newspapers for a number of years, is a collector of old photographs and an enthusiastic historian who shares her knowledge and papers generously. She receives hundreds of visitors each year, among whom are prominent descendants of early pioneers, to view the carpet she has hooked for a flight of stairs on the risers of which she has pictured episodes from the early days of her family's life in Muskoka.

St. Mary's Church, Aspdin

Muskoka Road 3 on the westerly side of Highway 11, opposite the Huntsville southern entrance, is a surprisingly good short cut to Rosseau, points west, and Parry Sound. It passes remnants of clearings and log cabins and, between Aspdin and Rosseau, has clear views of Skeleton Lake, especially when the leaves have fallen.

Aspdin derives its name from a family which occupied at least seven lots in the neighbourhood. Summer Saturdays at Aspdin Community Centre, about seven miles from Highway 11, see barter sales (at 10 a.m. and 2 p.m.), pot luck suppers and dances. Bingo games and euchre parties are scheduled on other evenings.

The spire of St. Mary's Church will direct you to its location. Its history is recounted in a leaflet entitled, *An Account of St. Mary's Church Aspdin, Muskoka, Ontario (Diocese of Algoma)* available from the Society of St. John the Evangelist, Bracebridge, Ontario, or inside the church. It is usually open through summer and autumn but not in winter when the snow is piled deep around the building and not enough visitors are expected to warrant clearing the paths.

The foundation of St. Mary's Church, the first stone church in Muskoka, was laid on Wednesday, September 30th, 1885. It replaced an earlier Anglican church, completed December 1878, built of logs by members of the early community. Before that, in memory of a small boy who died early in 1874, a private log chapel had been built by his brothers, the sons of William Crompton, one of the first settlers in Aspdin who had been a licensed lay reader in Birmingham and Manchester, England, and was ordained a priest in Canada, 1879.

At the latter end of the year 1884, the leaflet explains,

> an unknown lady in England offered to provide funds to the extent of £600 sterling, on condition that a stone Church should

be erected of plain and substantial kind, and that coloured Stoles and Frontals according to the seasons be used, the Eastward Position taken by the Priest, Vases, Candlesticks and Cross be on the re-table, but Vestments not to be used except by special request of the congregation, and with the written consent of the Bishop for the time being.

The names of church officials and every communicant "as well as copies of Church Times, Church Bells and Guardian from England, Globe, Mail, from Toronto, Free Grant Gazette, Muskoka Herald from Bracebridge" were sealed in a glass bottle which was built into the wall; and each child of the Sunday School brought a stone from his own home and placed it in the wall.

A stone font for St. Mary's Church was purchased with £11 sterling collected at a mission address given on June 21st, 1885 by the Reverend William Crompton at St. Augustine's Church, Kilburn, London, England; the pulpit, prayer desks, lectern and faldstool from funds given by the congregation of St. Mary's Church, Hulme, Manchester. Brass candlesticks and an alabaster cross were presented by Major-General Steward, of Prince's Gate, London, England; the bell by Mr. Crompton's wife and children. A noble folio Bible and prayer book came to St. Mary's Church, Aspdin, through Brightstone Church in England. In 1887 the anonymous donor in England gave a further £100 for a tower and spire.

For what reason did the donor choose to remain anonymous? Perhaps because of the Sermon on the Mount, wherein Christ said, "Take heed that ye do not your alms before men, to be seen of them: otherwise ye have no reward of your Father which is in heaven. . . . do not sound a trumpet. . . . let not thy left hand know what thy right hand doeth. . . ." Of necessity in this case, a thoroughly discreet lawyer must have known what his client was doing. But then, shortly after sending the £100 for the tower and spire, she made a pilgrimage to the Holy Land. One evening, while camping beside the Sea of Galilee, she went out for a stroll and was never seen or heard of again. While some may have learned the identity of this generous woman, her name has never been disclosed and her desire for anonymity has been respected.

Yearley

The name originates from the pioneer Yearley family, shown on the Stisted township map in the 1879 *Guide Book and Atlas* as occupying three lots in the northern extremity.

In 1973 approximately 98 acres were sold to the provincial government by William J. Yearley. At the time of transfer, the property had a four-bedroom house and extensive trout ponds, developed by Mr. Yearley with machines he used in his road construction business. Adjacent to 1900 acres assembled by the province for parkland, the Yearley property is rented by the Muskoka Board of Education for environmental studies, residential experience and teacher professional development programs.

Take Muskoka Road 3 (opposite the Huntsville southern entrance) to Aspdin. Follow "Yearley" signs north from Aspdin. The distance from the junction of Highway 11 and Muskoka Road 3 is 18 miles.

CONCISE BIBLIOGRAPHY

Among the many literary sources consulted in writing this book are the following:

Allan, Ted, and Gordon, Sydney, *The Scalpel, The Sword: The Story of Dr. Norman Bethune.* McClelland and Stewart, Toronto, 1952

Armstrong, G. H., *The Origin and Meaning of Place Names in Canada.* Macmillan, Toronto, 1930

Barry, James P., *Georgian Bay, the Sixth Great Lake.* Clarke, Irwin, Toronto, 1968

Craig, Gerald M. (ed.), *Lord Durham's Report.* McClelland and Stewart, Toronto, 1963

Cumberland, Frederick Barlow (ed.), *The Northern Lakes of Canada.* Hunter, Rose & Co., Toronto, c. 1886

Dickson, James, *Camping in the Muskoka Region.* Toronto, 1886. Reprinted by the Ontario Department of Lands and Forests, 1960

Eaton, Flora McCrea, *Memory's Wall.* Clarke, Irwin, Toronto, 1956

Hamilton, W. E., *Guide Book & Atlas of Muskoka and Parry Sound Districts; Maps by Jno. Rogers, Sketches by S. Penson.* H. R. Page, Toronto, 1879

Hathaway, Ann (Fanny Cox), *Muskoka Memories: Sketches from Real Life.* William Briggs, Toronto, 1904

Hunter, A. F., *A History of Simcoe County.* Historical Committee of Simcoe County, Barrie, 1948

Lower, J. A., *Canada: An Outline History.* McGraw-Hill Ryerson, Toronto, 1973

Macdonald, Norman, *Canada: Immigration and Colonization 1841–1903.* Macmillan, Toronto, 1966

McMurray, Thomas, *The Free Grant Lands of Canada, from Practical Experience of Bush Farming in the Free Grant Districts of Muskoka and Parry Sound.* Northern Advocate, Bracebridge, 1871

Murray, Florence B. (ed.), *Muskoka and Haliburton 1615–1875, A Collection of Documents.* Champlain Society and University of Toronto Press, Toronto, 1963

Porter, Cecil (ed.), *The Light of Other Days* (a sketch of the history of Gravenhurst). Haynes, Cobourg, Ont., 1967

Stevens, G. R., *Canadian National Railways, Volume I.* Clarke, Irwin, Toronto, 1960

Vardon, Roger (F. M. Delafosse), *English Bloods.* Graphic, Ottawa, 1930

REGIONAL BOOKLETS AND PAPERS

Bain, Dr. James Watson, Collected Papers (unpublished)

Cognashene Cottagers' Association, *Cognashene Cottager.* 1967, 1968, 1969, 1970, 1971

Cope, Leila M., *A History of the Village of Port Carling.* Herald-Gazette Press, Bracebridge, 1956

Davis, Mayme, *Early Days in Morrison Township,* read before the Severn Bridge Women's Institute, March 7, 1929

Demaine, W. H., *Stories of Early Muskoka Days.* Herald-Gazette Press, Bracebridge, 1971

Drury, Ernest C., *The Story of Simcoe County.* Simcoe County Council, 1960

Jestin, Mrs. G. R., *The Early History of Torrance.* 1938

LaForce, Philip, *History of Gibson Reserve.* Gazette, Bracebridge, c. 1954

Linney, Harry, Collection of Muskoka Papers, University of Toronto Archives, Toronto

Mason, D. H. C., *Muskoka: The First Islanders.* Herald-Gazette Press, Bracebridge, 1957

Port Sydney Women's Institute, *Pioneer Days in Port Sydney, Muskoka.* Papers collected c. 1927

Rice, Harmon E., *Brief Centennial History of Huntsville.* Forester Press, Huntsville, 1964

Robinson, P. J. (ed.), *Madawaska Club, Go-Home Bay,* 1898–1923. Reprinted by the Madawaska Club, Toronto, 1972

Shea, Bert, *History of the Sheas and Birth of a Township.* College Press, Peterborough, c. 1969

Sutton, Frederick William, *Early History of Bala.* Herald-Gazette Press, Bracebridge, c. 1970

Thomas, Redmond, *Reminiscences.* Herald-Gazette Press, Bracebridge, 1969

SELECTIVE INDEX OF NAMES AND PLACES

ACTON ISLAND, 146
Ada Lake, 147
Adams, Captain, 100, 110
Aiken, Gordon and Marie, 61
Aitken, Mary Elizabeth, 112
Aitken, Thomas, 111–2
Algonquin, 216–7
Algonquin Park, 3, 187
Allen, Mr. and Mrs. George, 88
Anderson, Gillie, 26
Anderson, Hugh, 171
Angus, Myron, 78
Antioch Conservation Area, 220, 222
Antique Show, 143
Arrowhead Provincial Park, 208
Ashworth, 243–5
Aspdin, 234, 236
Aston Fairways, 89
Austin, Geo. C., 57
Avery, Sidney G., 205

BADDELEY, F. H., 11
Bailey, Alexander, 55, 74, 99
Bailey, Emma, 140
Bailey, George, 57, 74, 106
Bailey, Irvin "Ace", 80
Bailey, J. T., 21
Bailey, Michael, 99
Bain, James, 52–5, 123
Bala, 134, 136, 141–6
Bala Memorial Community Centre, 143
Bala Trinity Church, 142
Barker, Col. Billy, 131
Barkway, 34–6
Barkway Lake (or Spring Lake), 36
Bartleman, James Karl, 98
Baxter township, 160
Bayfield, Capt. Henry Wolsey, 9, 160
Baysville, 178, 179–81
Bear Cave, 128
Beardmore Bros., 75
Beatrice Climatological Station, 192
Beatty, David, 172
Beatty, John D., 125–6
Beatty, Walter, 209
Beatty William, 125–6
Beaumaris, 89, 91, 136, 138, 146
Beausoleil Island, 161
Beaver Creek Correctional Camp, 67
Bell, John S., 23
Bell, Robert, 12–4, 69
Bell's Line, 12, 15, 69
Bella Lake, 220
Bella–Rebecca Cottagers Association, 222

Bernardi, Mario, 183
Bernardo Homes (Dr.), 234
Bethel Cemetery, 23
Bethune, Dr. Norman, 65–6
Bethune Drive, 58, 66
Big Chute marine railway, 49, 50
Big East River, 3, 208, 224
Bigwin family, 14, 183
Bigwin Inn and Island, 181–3
Bildson family, 214
Bird, H. J. and family and woollen mill, 88, 106
Bishop, Col. Billy, 131
Black Lake, 140
Black River, 10, 11, 32–4, 69
Blackwell, Frank and Dick, 188
Board family, 145
Booth, William, 48
Borntraeger, Ruth and Carl, 91
Bowyers Beach Park, 82
Boyd, David, 25
Boyer, Robert J., 78
Brace, P. J., 35–6
Bracebridge, 1, 73, 74–88
Bracebridge Area Parks Board, 70
Bracebridge Centennial Centre, 81
Bracebridge Golf Club, 176
Bracebridge Hall, by Washington Irving, 57, 75
Bracebridge Memorial Community Centre, 80
Bracebridge Memorial Park, 79
Bracebridge Recreation Committee, 79
Bracebridge Resource Management Area, 84
Bradley, William, 52
Brady, Sarah McCulley and William J., 106–8
Brandy Lake, 92
Brass family, 34
Brazier, Bus, 78
Bridgland, J. W., 13–14, 20
Briscoe, Lt. Henry, 10, 184, 187
Britannia Hotel, 191
Broadley family, 138
Brook, Edgar, 222
Brook, Mabel Hart, 220, 222
Brooks, John Henry, 34
Brown family, 215
Brown, Dugald, 57–8
Brown, "Grandma", 200
Brown, W. H., 178, 179
Brown, J. O., 20
Browning, A. H., 54, 75
Browning, Robert Mortimer Glover, 81
Browning Hall, 61
Bruce, Thomas, 177

Brûlé, Etienne, 160
Brunel township, 17, 78, 178, 187
Buck Lake, 54, 227–30
Burgess family, 120, 145, 153
Burns, Robert T., 34, 180
Burton family, 112
Bus (Hammond Transportation), 147
Bush family, 34
Business and Professional Women's Club, 79
Butterfly Lake, 147

CAIN LAKE, 48
Camp Pinecrest, 141
Campbell, John, 52–5, 123
Campbell, Peter and Marjorie, 136
Campfens, Anthony C., 61
Canadian Keswick Conference, 103
Canadian Legion, 64, 79, 94, 124, 131, 195, 204, 205
Canal Road, 39
Cann, William, 209
Cannell, Dr. Douglas E., 98
Canning, John, 21
Canning's Corners, 21
Cardwell township, 11, 17
Carling, John, 24n, 99
Carr family, 34
Carroll, John, 201
Carstairs, Betty, 115
Carthew, John, 11, 34
Catto, Lt.-Col. and Mrs. Douglas E., 97
Cavalcade of Colour, 80, 143, 145, 195, 204
Cavelier, René-Robert (sieur de LaSalle), 8
Centennial Acres, 192
Chaffey township, 209
Champlain, Samuel de, 6, 160
Chaplains Island, 54, 123
Christ Church, Port Sydney, 195–6
Christie family, 25
Christie Lumber Company, 47
Church, Ted, 147
Church, Wayne and Pat, 23
Church of the Good Samaritan (Port Stanton), 47
Church Stitchery (Exhibition of Contemporary Church Stitchery and Banners), 61
Civic Music Association, 65
Clear Lake (Torrance Lake), 139–40
Clearwater Lake, 28
Cleary, Michael H. and Pat, 60, 78
Clements family, 145
Clerk, Rev. Charles Robert, 171–2, 196
Clevelands House, 124
Cliff Bay, 51-4, 64
Clinch, Doris, 170
Clipsham, James Everett, 58, 60
Clipsham, Michael, 45, 58
Clyffe House, 200–1
C.N.I.B., Lake Joseph Centre, 148
Coad, Sam, 35
Coate, Charles and Catherine, 133, 135
Coate, Frederick W., 133
Cockburn, A. P., 49, 54–7, 99, 103, 108, 125, 127, 147

Cockburn, Donald, 99
Cockburn, Isaac, 55
Cockburn, J. D., 57
Cockburn, Prof. J. Roy, 106, 125
Cockburn, P., 55
Cognashene Cottager, 162–3
Cole, Hilary Clark, 60
Cole, Michael, 61
Commandant family, 152, 154, 155, 156
Constance, 118, 121
Conway, Milt and Elizabeth, 48
Cook, Myrna, 208
Cook & Bros. (lumber), 34
Cooper, James, 52, 54, 74
Cooper, Joseph, 74
Cooper, Thomas and Emma, 28–33
Cooper, Tom (grandson) and Doris, 33
Cooper's Falls, 28–33
Cooper's Pond, 84
Corbett's Wildlife Zooette (Gravenhurst), 58
Coulter, Joseph and family, 139–40
Cox, Edward, 119–20
Cox, Enoch, 116, 119–20
Cox, Fanny, 120–1
Cranes (Sandhill), 130
Crompton, William, 236
Crozier, Roger, 80
Currell, Bill, 78
Currie family, 145
Cuthbert, James, 24

DALTON ROAD, 32–3
Davis, Mayme, 21
Davis, Moses, 21
Davis, William (Ont. Premier), 160
Decaire family, 152, 154
Deer Lake, 136
Delafosse, F. M., 225–31
Delawana Inn, 159, 165
Demaine family, 232–6
Dennis, John S., 53, 231
Dennis, Joseph, 53
Denton, Capt. Alfred, 187, 201
Dewasha family, 152
Dickie Lake, 181
Dickie, Mr. and Mrs. Moses J., 181
Dickson, James, 189–90
Dillan, Hugh W., 20, 52
Dinosaur Land, 192
Ditchburn brothers, 135
Ditchburn, Rev. Joseph S., 131, 135
Dodds, Dr. R. J., 76
Donaldson, J. A., 71, 199
Dorset, 182, 185–6
Draper township, 12, 15, 16, 17, 71, 74, 78, 88
Driftwood Ranch 33
Duke family, 92, 95, 108
Dufferin, Lord and Lady, 24, 106
Dunn, Gerry, 142
Durham, Lord, 12
Dwight, 187–90
Dwight, Harvey Prentice, 188–9
Dyer Memorial, 223–4, 232

EAST, MAURICE, 133
Eaton, Lord and Lady, 131, 133
Eaton, Timothy, 112
Echo Lake, 181
Edith May, 102
Eleanor Island, 65
Elgin House, 122-3
Emberson family, 215
Emily May, 52
English Bloods, by Roger Vardon, 225–30
Ennis, Bernard A., 98
Etwell, 236
Evans family, 215
Everbeck, John, 43–5
Everett, Robert, 76
Excelsior, 179

FAIRY FALLS, 176
Fairy Lake, 1, 14, 54, 213, 215, 218
Fall fairs, 19, 81, 108
Fenian raids, 21, 188–9
Ferguson, Donald, 71
Fergusson family, 140
Ferndale Bay and House, 100, 102, 112
Fetterley family, 201, 214
Fife, David, 112
Fitzgerald (Surveyor), 126
Fleming family, 215
Flyer, 102
Foot, William Edward, 148
Foot's Bay, 148, 171, 172
Forest Protection Tower (Cain Lake), 48
Forester, 204
Forge, Francis, 110–2
Forsythe, Samuel, 183
Fowler, Francis, 89
Fox Lake, 54, 228, 231
France, Wilfred and George, 165
Francy family, 215
Franklin township, 187
Franks family, 152, 154
Fraser family, 215
Fraser, W. C. and Isabelle, 88
Fraserburg, 88
Free Grant Gazette, 210
Free Land Grants, 12, 16–7, 57, 71, 128, 138, 180, 198
Free Methodist Camp Ground, 19
Freeman, John Bailey, 172
Freeman township, 160, 172–3
Frère, Gus, 21
Fry, Cyril, 60

GALLA LAKE, 169
Gammage, Bill, 180
Gammage, Daniel, 177
Gartersnake, Lake and River, 25, 36
Geese, Giant Canada, 65
Georgian Bay, 1, 6, 8, 9, 10, 14, 159–66
Georgian Bay Beacon, 169
Georgian Bay Islands National Park, 161
Georgian College, 60, 61, 79, 84, 141, 208
Gibraltar, 24
Gibson, David, 13, 15

Gibson Reserve, 144, 150–6, 158
Gibson Reserve Trailer Park, 156, 166
Gibson River, 166, 167
Gibson township, 152, 160, 172
Glen Home, 123
Glen Orchard, 122, 147
Glen Rose, 47
Gloucester Pool, 50, 166
Go Home Bay, Lake, River, 11, 164, 167
Gouldie, Edmund James and Archie, 188
Govan, John, 185
Grand Falls. *See* Muskoka Falls
Grant, Col. D. M., 82
Grant, James, 25
Gravenhurst, 57–66
Gravenhurst and District Conservation Club, 65
Gravenhurst News, 60
Gravenhurst Recreation Committee, 36
Gray, Sandy, 167-8
Greavette, Thomas, 63
Green family (Bala), 145
Green family (Hillside), 215
Green, Lloyd, 184
Green, Ric, 61
Grierson, William, 164
Grisé family, 89, 123, 165–6
Gull Lake, 58, 65
Gull Lake Park, 65
Gullwing Lake, 140
Guy family, 145

HAMILL FAMILY, 145
Hamilton, W. E., 102
Hammond Transportation, 147
Hanes, Erastus, 55, 168, 198, 210
Hanes, J. F., 211, 214
Hanes, Nehemiah, 55, 198, 210, 234
Hanna Memorial Park, 94
Hanna, Rachel, 70–1
Hanna, Richard, 70
Hanna, William, 70, 92, 94, 121, 188
Hannah, James, 24
Harding, Margaret, 32
Hardy Lake, 140
Harper, James, 54
Hart, Dr. J. W., 212
Harvie, J. T., 58
Haviland, Roberta, 60
Hawk Rock River, 52
Healey Lakes, 88
Heeney Lake, 181
Hekla, 128
Henley, Ruby, 205
Herald-Gazette, 78
Heron, Great Blue, 65
Herring, Rev. A. S., 18, 116
Heyerdahl, Thor, 67
Hidden Valley, 218
High Falls, 83
Hill, Gordon, 219
Hill, Leonard, 215
Hill, Marion, 220
Hill, Rev. Robert Norton, 212, 214–5
Hillside, 212, 215

Historic Sites and Cairns:
  Bala, 143
  Baysville, 180
  Bracebridge, 79
  Dr. Norman Bethune, 66
  Samuel de Champlain, 163
  Explorers, 180
  Madill Church, 203
  Muskoka Falls Pioneers, 70
  Muskoka Road, 25
  Peterson Road, 70
  Port Carling, 97
  Rosseau, 131
  Steamship Docks, 63
  Trains, 58
  Wasdell Falls, 28
Hobby and Craft Show, 94
Hockey Arenas:
  Bala, 143
  MacTier, 169
  Port Carling, 94
Hodgeson family, 215
Hogaboam family, 55, 167–8, 198, 214
Hogue, Capt. A. N., 215–6
Holditch, William, 75
Hollyburn, Camp, 130
Honey Harbour, 165–6
Hoodstown, 187, 201, 230
Horticultural Societies:
  Baysville, 180
  Bracebridge, 76
  Gravenhurst, 60
  Huntsville, 203
Housey, James, 35
Housey's Rapids, 34–5
Huckins, Captain, 179
Huckleberry Rock Cut, 92, 93
Huggett family, 145
Humphry township, 78
Hunt, Capt. George, 203, 207, 209–10, 215
Huntsville, 1, 203-20, 228
Huntsville District Memorial Hospital, 204
Huntsville Memorial Park, 205
Huntsville Recreation Commission, 205
Hurling family, 145
Huronia, 6–8
Hussey, Mr. and Mrs. William, 177, 178

ICELANDERS, 128
Ilfracombe, 230–1
Independent Order of Oddfellows, 60
Indian River, 52, 94, 95, 98
Information centres:
  Bala, 141
  Bracebridge Chamber of Commerce, 79
  Dwight Business Association, 188
  Georgian Bay Islands National Park, Honey
    Harbour, 161
  Gravenhurst Board of Trade, 58
  Huntsville Chamber of Commerce, 203
  Muskoka Tourist Association, 6, 23
  Port Carling Tourist Information, 95
  Port Sydney Resort Association, 195
  Provincial Tourist, Barrie, 148
Iroquois Cranberry Growers, 156, 168

Iroquois II (M.S.), 216
Islander, 121

JACKMAN, HENRY R., 165
Jackson family, 25
Jackson family (Bala), 145
Jackson, James Hankinson and Mary, 20
James, Hugh, 108
Jaspen Park, 143
Jenner family, 200-1
Jennings, Jack and Doreen, 147
Jestin family, 139-41
Johnson, E. Pauline, 130
Johnston, Benjamin Hardcastle, 99
Johnston, Orville, 147, 156
Johnston, W. J., Jr., 98
Joseph (tug), 111
Joseph, Lake, 1, 11, 53, 108, 123, 134, 147-9
Joseph River, 53, 123
Jubilee Park, 80
Judd family, 124–5

KAHSHE LAKE, 25–7
Kampgrounds of America, 67
Karon, Richard, 176
Kawandag, 131-2
Kaye, Mabel and Phyllis, 87
Kelvin Grove Park, 76
Kendall, William and Mary, 155
Kenozha, 121
Kilworthy Road, 25
Kinette Club, Gravenhurst, 60
Kinsmen Beach, 208
Kinsmen Centennial Parkette (Gravenhurst),
  58
Kinsmen Clubs, 79, 85, 208
Kippax, Helen, 180
Kirby's Beach, 85
Kirk, Reginald, 80
Kirkfield lift-lock, 39
Kluey's Bay, 26
Knifton family, 145

LADY FRANKLIN, 47
Lady Muskoka, 63, 108
LaForce, Philip, 152–5
Lake Joseph Community Church, 123
Lake of Bays, 10, 11, 14, 54, 178–84, 188, 216
Lake of Bays Association, 184
Lakefield, 46–7
Lang family, 215
Langford, Alberta, 179
Langford, Henry, 179, 184
Langford, Mark, 176–8, 179
Langford, Thomas, 176–8
Lansdowne, Lord and Lady, 106
LaSalle, sieur de, 8
Lassiter family, 215
Lean, Mary, 26
Leatherby, Lloyd, 48
Lehmann, Adelbert and Kathinka Bruch, 43–5
Leonard Lake, 89
Leslie M. Frost Natural Resources Centre, 185
LeSueur, Dr. W. D., 75
Lewisham, 33–4

Limberlost Lodge, 219
Lions Clubs, 79, 94, 112, 131, 143, 149, 180, 195, 205
Locker, Joseph, 25
Locks:
　Mary River (Brunel), 197, 201-2, 204
　Port Carling, 95–7, 122
　Trent-Severn, 39, 48, 50
Long Family, 34
Long Lake, 141
Longford Lakes (North and South), 33
Longford township, 33–4
Lookout, Gravenhurst, 63
Loppet:
　Muskoka, 195, 206, 218–9, 222
　Skokie, 85
Loshaw family, 34
Lost Channel, 48
Lount, Judge, 70
Love, Lambert, 122-3
Love, Lambert Elgin, 122
Lowe, William and family, 36, 38

McALPHINE, JOHN, 198, 200
Macaulay township, 12, 15, 16, 17, 71, 74, 78, 88
McCabe, Mr. and Mrs. James "Mickey", 51–2, 54–5
MacCallum, Dr. James Metcalfe, 164
McClelland, David, 25
McClure, Dorothy Clarke, 78
McConnell Memorial Foundation, 82
Macdonald, Hiram, 74
Macdonald, J. Sandfield, 116
McDonald family, 215
McDonald River, 166, 167
McFarlane, James, 181
McGee, Thomas D'Arcy, 55
McGibbon, Dr. Peter and Mabel, 76
McKay Lake, 88
Mackenzie, William Lyon, 12
McLean township, 12, 17, 88, 176–80
McLellan family, 24
McMicken, G. (lumber), 34
McMurray, Thomas, 71–3, 79–80, 212, 214
MacTier, 169–72
MacTier, A. D., 171
MacTier Memorial Community Centre, 169
McVittie, John Phillips, 88
Madawaska Club, 164
Madill family, 203, 214
Magnetawan River, 54, 106
Malta, 25
Maps (purchasing of), 6
Margesson, Maurice, 133
Markle, Milan, 55
Marsh, Capt. G. F. and family, 187
Marsh's Falls, 187
Mary Lake, 14, 194–201
Masonic Order, 205
Matthews, Albert, 112
Maude, Col. Francis Cornwallis and Paulina Susanna, 69
May family, 145

Mayflower Lake, 208
Medora, 121
Medora Lake, 147
Medora township, 98, 100, 114, 145, 172
Mentally Retarded (South Muskoka Association), 80
Menzies, Robert, 180
Merkley family, 37
Mesqua Ukie, 14, 78
Mickle, Charles and Emma Rowe, 64
Mickle Memorial Cemetery, 64
Mickle–Dyment (lumber), 58
Midland–Penetang 88, 161
Mildred, 87
Milford Bay, 92
Miller, Frank, 87
Miller, Ross, 87
Miller Hill, 219
Minett family, 115, 124
Ministry of Natural Resources, 80, 83–4
Mink, 121
Miss Canada, 63
Miss White Pines, 204
Mitchell, Dr. John, 8
Mizpah Pioneer Cemetery, 220
Monck township, 11, 78
Monteith House, 127
Montour family, 152
Moon River, 10, 144, 167, 168, 169
Moore, Edward, 170
Moore family, 145
Moose Deer Point Indian Band, 169
Morinus Lakeside Church, 124
Morrison, Angus, 13–5
Morrison Agricultural Society Fair Grounds, 19
Morrison Creek and Lake, 10, 15, 19, 47–8, 141
Morrison township, 11, 15, 16, 19–23, 54, 78
Muldrew Lake, 10, 15, 19, 141
Municipal Government, 3
Murray, Alexander, 14, 184
Murray, Florence B., 204–5
Museums:
　Muskoka Pioneer Village and Museum, Huntsville, 205–7
　Port Carling, 96, 97
　Wood Winds, Barlochan, 136–7
Muskoka Airport, 67
Muskoka Arts and Crafts Exhibition, 80
Muskoka Bay, 63
Muskoka Beach Road, 64
Muskoka Beechgrove Public School, 64
Muskoka Centre (residence), 64
Muskoka Club, 54
Muskoka Concert Association, 60
Muskoka Express (train), 121
Muskoka Falls, 70–2
Muskoka Falls United Church, 70
Muskoka Foundation for the Arts, 60
Muskoka Homecrafts, 95
Muskoka, Lake, 10, 11, 53–7, 87, 89, 92, 94, 95
Muskoka Lakes Association, 89, 97, 108, 114, 125
Muskoka Lakes Golf and Country Club, 114

Muskoka Mills, 162
Muskoka Philatelic Society, 60
Muskoka River, North Branch, 3, 11, 14, 83,
   84, 144, 176
Muskoka River, South Branch, 3, 10, 11, 71, 83,
   144, 176, 178, 180
Muskoka Road, 15, 16, 21, 25
Muskoka Sands Inn, 64
Muskoka Soil and Crop Improvement Associa-
   tion, 81
Muskoka Station, 170
Muskoka Steamship and Historical Society, 63
Muskoka Summer Theatre, 60
Muskoka Tourist Association, 6, 23
Muskoka township, 11, 15, 16, 17, 51, 54, 78,
   88
Muskoka Wharf, 56, 58, 62
Musquedo, 98
Musquosh River, 144, 167
Musquosh Road, 136, 141, 145
Musson, Charles, 47

NAGAYA BEACH, 26
Neilson, Harley, 185
Nelson family, 140
Newminko, 92
News family, 152, 154
Nicholas, Cindy, 112
Nickle, Lawrence, 60, 78
Niederhauser, Ann and Heinz, 194
Nipissing, 101, 103, 104, 106, 108, 113,
   121, 127
Nipissing Road, 126–7
North Falls. *See* Bracebridge
North Portage, 216
Northern, 201
Northern Advocate, 73
Norwegian Air Force, 67, 222

OAKLEY TOWNSHIP, 12, 85
Obogawanung, 98–9
Oliver, R. J., 15–6
122nd Muskoka Battalion, 82
Ontario Road Builders' Association, 63
Opera House, Gravenhurst, 60, 72
Owen, Capt. William Fitzwilliam, 9
Oxbow Lake, 222
Oxtongue River, 3, 10, 186–7

PALMER, FATHER ROLAND, 82
Pamosagay, Chief, 11
Panting, Stephen Bernard, 143
Parlett family, 138
Parry Sound Road, 126–7
Partridge, William, 174
Patterson-Kaye, 87
Peg-a-ma-gah-bo, 123
Peninsula Lake, 14, 54, 214, 215–6, 218
Peninsula Recreation Centre, 124
Penlake Golf Club, 216
Penson, Elizabeth, 103
Penson, Richard George, 100–2
Penson, Seymour R. G., 72, 86, 100–3, 134
Peré, Jean, 8

Perry, R. E., 75
Peterborough lift-lock, 39
Peterson, Joseph S., 69
Peterson Road, 69
Peterson Trail Conservation Association, 69
Pigeon Lake, 136
Pine Lake, 88
Pine Lake, 136
Pittsburgh, 47, 87
Plaskett, John S., 109–11
Plaskett, Josephine, 109–11
Polynesian, 233-4
Port Carling, 52, 92–100, 103, 105, 106, 108
Port Carling Memorial Community Centre, 94
Port Cockburn, 53
Port Cunnington, 186
Port Ideal, 186
Port Sandfield, 53, 116, 118, 120
Port Severn, 50, 160
Port Stanton, 45, 47
Port Sydney, 194–201
Portage Railway, 216–8
Portlock, Lt. Joseph E., 10
Power Squadrons, 81, 149
Pratt, William H., 103, 127
Prebble, Harold, 194
Precambrian shield, 1, 143
Preston, Frank, 23
Prospect House, 116, 120
Prospect Lake, 69
Prowse, Edward, Horace and family, 89, 138
Prussian, 198, 200
Purves, Robert W., 114–5

QUEEN ELIZABETH II, 65, 139
Queen Victoria, 210

RAINBOW RIDGE SKI AREA, 89
Raymond, 194
Reay Road, 67
Reazin, Dr., 219–20
Rebman, Florence (Mrs. Wesley), 35–6
Regional Government, 3
Reid, Gordon, 92
Rennie family, 152, 155–6
Rennie, John, 94–5
Rice, Harmon E., 6
Riley Lake, 34-5
Rivers family, 152
Robinson, Thomas M., 51–4
Robinson's General Store, 185
Roehl family, 45
Rogers, John, 101–2, 120
Roseneath Manor, 92
Rosseau, 131–2
Rosseau (tug), 104, 111
Rosseau Falls, 133–4
Rosseau House, 127, 129
Rosseau Lake, 11, 53, 55, 94, 95, 100, 125,
   127, 128
Rosseau Memorial Community Hall, 131
Rosseau School, 131, 133
Rotary Clubs, 81, 205
Rousseau, Jean-Baptiste, 9

Royal Muskoka Hotel and Island, 125, 132
Royal Ontario Museum, 79, 80
Ruch, Beth and Walt, 124
Rush family, 34
Ruttan family, 25
Ryde township, 33–6, 71, 74

SAGAMO, 62, 63, 106, 118
Sagamo Park, 63
Sahanatien family, 150, 152, 153, 154
St. Paul's Church Emigration Society, 17–8, 116
Salmon, Tom, 188
Sanatoria, 64
Santa's Village, 85, 86
Sargeant, Dr. Lynn, 204
St. Mary's Church, Aspdin, 236
Schell, Bill, 23
Schell, Joyce (Mrs. J. W.), 136, 138
Schell family, 25
Scott, Robert and Gil, 76
Segwun, 62, 63, 106, 131
Senior Citizens:
    Bracebridge Drop-In Centre, 79
    Huntsville Club, 55, 204
    The Pines, 81
Severn Bridge, 1, 19–23, 28, 39
Severn Falls, 48
Severn Lodge, 50
Severn River, 1, 8, 9, 10, 11, 14–5, 39, 47–50
Shadow River, 128–30
Shaw, C. O., 181, 212
Shay family, 210–1
Shea, Bert, 194
Sheil, Eva, 181
Sherwood Inn, 148
Shier family, 25
Shilling, Arthur, 79
Shirreff, Alexander, 10, 184
Shirreff, Charles, 10
Silver Lake, 92, 98, 112
Simcoe, John Graves, 9
Simpson, B. Napier, Jr., 162, 163
Sinclair, Gordon, 76
Sinclair township, 215
Six Mile Lake, 166
Skeleton Lake, 111, 124, 194
Sloan, Gordon, 61
Smith, Alfred, 138
Smith, A. Sydney, 195, 199
Smith, Ernest, 200
Smith, Lily (Mrs. D. R.), 48
Snider, Claude, 60
Snowmobile Clubs and Safaris:
    Milford Bay, 92
    Peninsula, 124
    Port Carling, 95
    Port Sydney, 195
    Windermere, 112
Society of St. John the Evangelist, 82
Solitaire Lake, 219
Sopher, Albert, 25–7
            Jane Fitchett (wife)
            Bertha (sister)

South Falls. *See* Muskoka Falls
South Muskoka Curling and Golf Club, 82
South Muskoka Memorial Hospital, 80, 88, 97
South Portage, 191, 218
Southwood Church of our Lady, 141
Southwood Road, 141
Sparrow, John M., 39
Sparrow, Dr. Malcolm Weethee, 39, 41
Sparrow, William, 41
Sparrow Lake, 20, 21, 39–47
Speicher, Louisa Seehaver, 36
Spencer family, 145
Spring Lake (or Barkway Lake), 36
Springdale Park, 174, 176
Stanton, Thomas and Ellen Franklin, 21, 47
Stein family, 45
Stephenson township, 11, 17, 71, 74, 78, 88, 198
Stewart Lake, 169, 170
Stisted, H. W., 231
Stisted township, 231–8
Stisted Township Hall, 233
Stock family, 152
Stone, Dennis, 6, 222
Stoneleigh Lake, 176
Stoneman, Alma E., 127
Strathcona Golf Club, 218
Strength family, 152, 154
Stromberg family, 140
Stuart & Cruikshank building, 61
Summit House, 108, 120
Sutton, Ephraim Browning, 146
Sutton, F. W., 145–6
Swift Rapids, 46, 48
Symington family, 20, 25

TAMWOOD LODGE, 89
Taylor, Rev. John, 128
Teviotdale, John, 75
Thomas family, 78
Thompson, Charlie and Dorothy, 190–1
Thompson, David, 11, 14, 184
Thompson family, 215
Thompson (Gibson Reserve) family, 152
Three-Mile Lake, 192
Tibbet, Milton, 5
Tobin, James Martin and family, 99–100
Tookey, James, 177, 178
Torpitt, Lodge, 47
Torrance, 139–41
Torrance, William and family, 139–40
Trent-Severn Waterway, 39–50
Trinity United Church, Gravenhurst, 61
Trudeau, Rt. Hon. Pierre Elliott, 63
Turtle Lake, 127
Twelve Mile Bay, 168

ULLSWATER, 194
Utterson, 192, 198, 206, 211

VACATION GUIDE, 203
VanClieaf, Earle, 181
Vancrofter, 162
Vankoughnet, 69

Vankoughnet, Philip, 69
Vaughan, Bryan, 114
Vesle Skaugum, 222
Vernon Lake, 54, 209, 214–5, 231
Victoria Bridge, 33
Victoria Road, 34
Von Alma, Joseph and family, 26–7

WABAMIK, 103, 179
Wadsworth, Vernon B., 131, 231
Wah Wah Taysee (Firefly) Reserve, 168
Waites, Al, 112
Walker, Howard V., 61
Walker family, 215, 219
Walker's Lake, 219
Walkers Point, 136
Wallis, Joseph, 145
Walstrom family, 140
Waome, 138
Wasdell Falls, 28
Washago Mills, 15, 19
Watson, Rev. John, 142
Watt township, 11, 17, 78
Wattie, John, 178
WaWa Hotel, 125, 183
Webber, Frank, 51
Weismiller Lumber Company, 36
Wenonah, 55-7, 75, 100, 103, 110, 138, 139, 145
West Wind Island, 164
Whalen family, 163
White, Aubrey, 83
White family, 152
White, George Harlow, 22, 206–7

Whitefish Lake, 127
Whitton, Donald, 183
Wiancko family, 45
Williams, Dr. James Francis and Gertrude Annie, 85
Williams Memorial Recreation Park, 80, 85
Willison, Olaf, 140
Willson, Rev. Gilman, 70, 75, 84
Wilson, Bruce, 63
Wilson, Harold, 98
Wilson, Woodrow, 114
Wilson (Bala) family, 145
Wilson's Falls, 84
Windermere, 92, 111–3
Windermere United Church, 112
Winter Carnival, 76, 79, 82, 85, 92, 94, 112, 166, 194, 195, 204
Women's Institute:
Bala, 143
Barkway, 34–5
Baysville, 179
Glen Orchard, 147
Port Carling, 94
Port Sydney, 198
Rosseau, 131
Severn Bridge, 19
Wood, Edmund Burk, 139
Wood Lake, 69
Wood township, 114, 138–9, 141, 145
Wright, Harry, 185
Wright, Orville, 163

YARD, Ted and Shirley, 130
Yearley, 237–8
Yellowhead (Chief), 9, 14